Total Skiing

Chris Fellows

Human Kinetics

Library of Congress Cataloging-in-Publication Data

Fellows, Chris, 1959-
  Total skiing / Chris Fellows.
    p. cm.
  Includes bibliographical references and index.
  ISBN-13: 978-0-7360-8365-2 (soft cover)
  ISBN-10: 0-7360-8365-0 (soft cover)
  1. Skis and skiing--Training. 2. Physical fitness. I. Title.
  GV854.85F45 2011
  796.93--dc22

                              2010031232

ISBN-10: 0-7360-8365-0 (print)
ISBN-13: 978-0-7360-8365-2 (print)

Acquisitions Editor: Laurel Plotzke Garcia; **Developmental Editor:** Laura Floch; **Project Consultant:** Darcy Norman; **Assistant Editors:** Elizabeth Evans and Bethany J. Bentley; **Copyeditor:** Joy Wotherspoon; **Indexers:** Robert and Cynthia Swanson; **Permission Manager:** Martha Gullo; **Graphic Designer:** Nancy Rasmus; **Graphic Artist:** Kim McFarland; **Cover Designer:** Keith Blomberg; **Photographer (cover and interior):** Jonathan Selkowitz; **Visual Production Assistant:** Joyce Brumfield; **Photo Production Manager:** Jason Allen; **Art Manager:** Kelly Hendren; **Associate Art Manager:** Alan L. Wilborn; **Printer:** United Graphics

We thank the Center for Health and Sports Performance in Truckee, CA; Sugar Bowl on Donner Summit in Norden, CA; and Squaw Valley USA in Olympic Valley, CA for assistance in providing the locations for the photo shoot for this book.

Selected text in the preface and chapter 1 is adapted, by permission of the Professional Ski Instructors of America Education Foundation, from C. Fellows with N. Norman, 2008, "From the Ground Up: The Psychology of Physiology," *The Professional Skier* (Winter 2008): 12-16.

Human Kinetics books are available at special discounts for bulk purchase. Special editions or book excerpts can also be created to specification. For details, contact the Special Sales Manager at Human Kinetics.

Printed in the United States of America   10 9 8 7 6 5 4 3 2 1

The paper in this book is certified under a sustainable forestry program.

Human Kinetics
Web site: www.HumanKinetics.com

United States: Human Kinetics
P.O. Box 5076
Champaign, IL 61825-5076
800-747-4457
e-mail: humank@hkusa.com

Canada: Human Kinetics
475 Devonshire Road Unit 100
Windsor, ON N8Y 2L5
800-465-7301 (in Canada only)
e-mail: info@hkcanada.com

Europe: Human Kinetics
107 Bradford Road, Stanningley
Leeds LS28 6AT, United Kingdom
+44 (0) 113 255 5665
e-mail: hk@hkeurope.com

Australia: Human Kinetics
57A Price Avenue
Lower Mitcham, South Australia 5062
08 8372 0999
e-mail: info@hkaustralia.com

New Zealand: Human Kinetics
P.O. Box 80
Torrens Park, South Australia 5062
0800 222 062
e-mail: info@hknewzealand.com

To my wife, Jenny: Thank you for the love, support, and strength that you have given me ever since the day we laid out the first plans for the North American Ski Training Center in 1994. Your sense of humor, consistency, and level-headedness have kept us going strong through both good times and challenging times. Your ability to manage a business while raising our three beautiful children and keeping your outdoor passions alive is truly amazing. Thank you.

Contents

Preface

In my developmental years as a ski instructor, I often found myself spouting the dogma of adopting an athletic stance, proper leg steering, functional pole use, early edging, and a variety of other "instructor-speak" catchphrases. Using the latest drills and exercise lines, I had worked with my students ad nauseam trying to ingrain the "proper skiing moves." Eventually the students came to believe that a strict diet of these technique drills would deliver them to greatness. I soon began to question myself, wondering if I was fooling myself and my students by believing their troubles could be cured with technique modification alone. It was hard for me to admit that I might see more success if I approached technique improvement from a different point of view.

Then, in the early 1990s, the legendary ski racing coach Warren Witherell crisscrossed the country introducing ski instructors, ski coaches, ski racing athletes and anyone who desired to ski better to the benefits of balancing boots for optimum ski performance. I remember Witherell swaggering into the Squaw Valley ski school locker room with a roll of duct tape in one hand and an obscure leg-measuring device in the other. He said he could improve our skiing instantly by tipping our boots laterally in the binding, giving us a positive and direct effect on the ski edge. Amazingly, he was right. After measuring, eyeballing, and putting various layers and widths of tape on our ski bindings, he had us ski so we could feel how the edge interacted with the snow. It was unbelievable: the skis actually came around easier and held better on firm snow.

Witherell said he'd done this somewhat crude form of alignment adjustment for World Cup racers with great results. He really knew how to talk to ski instructors.

He also said it might have been the equipment—not the technique or "pilot error"—that had been holding us back. (This gave us another reason to love him.) After much experimentation with different thicknesses and widths of tape on my bindings, I was convinced, and since then I have had my boot soles planed and balanced every season. Witherell's influence has spread throughout the land, and a cottage industry of custom boot fitting has sprung up due to his book, *The Athletic Skier*, as well as to his persistence in getting the ski industry to adopt his methods. But even though many skiers now realize the tremendous benefits of making equipment adjustments of just a few degrees, there are just as many who still aren't taking the time to consider the effects of improper alignment. Before my introduction to Witherell's boot balancing theories, I was one of them.

After I'd been "Witherell-ized," the experience kept nagging at me as I watched student after student fail when trying to make basic movement changes on the ski slope. They all wanted faster results and I wanted to see faster results. So, à la Witherell, I took his alignment approach one step further and measured and tested my students for weakness and asymmetries in their overall physiology. I started by asking students to perform fundamental movements such as a basic squat, a lateral lunge, and balancing on one leg. As I expected, many of them had great difficulty performing these simple tasks on a flat cafeteria floor. To me it was a relief to see students struggling to perform a basic depth squat, because it revealed a limit to what they could physically do. It was absurd to expect deep flexion movements out on the slope from a student who could not flex properly indoors.

The solution was clear as students became aware of their limitations. This awareness was the foundation on which a total program of improvement was built. The students saw improvement in movement, increased performance, and more enjoyment in their skiing.

Acknowledgments

This book represents the collaboration and passion of many. It is impossible to list them all, but here is my feeble attempt. The book wouldn't be half the book it is without the expert photography of Jonathan Selkowitz; thank you, Selko. Thanks to my talented and patient editors, Laura Floch and Laurel Plotzke Garcia. You have taught me much and I owe you a big debt of gratitude. A big shout out to expert reviewers Darcy Norman and Per Lundstam, whose insights in the exercise sections were invaluable. Thanks to Kim Mann, our manager at the North American Ski Training Center (NASTC), who helped on this project. Thanks to Jim Schaffner, Greg Hoffman, Jim Lindsay, and Mark Elling for their helpful reviews and casual chats about the equipment sections. Thanks to Michael Silitch for his two-week intensive on-the-fly interview while climbing and skiing. Jeff Hamilton shared his training insights and continues to show me that pain is lessened when shared with someone else on our weekly rides. Perry Norris is saving the Sierra open space so our kids will have the same wilderness we enjoy. Dave Achey, Ted Pitcher, John Nyhan, and Mike Sodergren (posthumously), thank you for your ongoing insights since the first NASTC course in 1994. Marco Sullivan's support means a lot as he continues to inspire skiing athletes young and old (like me). On the note of skiing inspiration, I wish to thank my past and present PSIA Alpine teammates, whose talents and dedication inspire us all to do our best every day with our students. Very big thanks go out to the skiing models: Mike Hafer, Richie Jamieson, Jenny Fellows, Kim Mann, Trevor Tanhoff, and Heidi Ettlinger. Special thanks to Mike and Heidi for modeling for the gym shots as well. Thanks to Truckee's Center for Health and Sports Performance and Dr. Nina Winans for allowing us to use their facility for the indoor photo shoot and a special thanks to the U.S. Forest Service office in Truckee, California. I wish to thank Mike Iman, Mike Porter, and Victor Gerdin, who are true professionals and mentors. Nick Herrin, Rob Sogard, and Michael Rogan are exceptional leaders in our sport and great sounding boards. Mark Palamaras and Charlie Pendrell offered help and vision from the beginning. Thanks to Howard Shao for his inspiration and loyal support over the years. Thanks to Mike Livak and Tom Murphy at Squaw Valley and to Rob Kautz and John Monson at Sugar Bowl; they all supported the project and hosted our photo shoots. Jason Newell and Jeff Sarlo at Rossignol, Bruce Old and Eric Neuron at Patagonia, Dave Goode at Goode, Dino Dardano at Hestra, Keith D'Entremont and Steve Poulin at Uvex, and Jim Marble at Eurosock, all contributed their resources to this book with their top-notch products. There are so many others who supported this book in spirit. Each of our clients at NASTC and all you skiers out there drive projects like this with your passion. Last but most important, I could not have done this without the loving support of my wife, Jenny, whose shared passion for skiing brings us much joy and adventure together.

1 2 3 4 5 6

PART I

Ski Performance Components

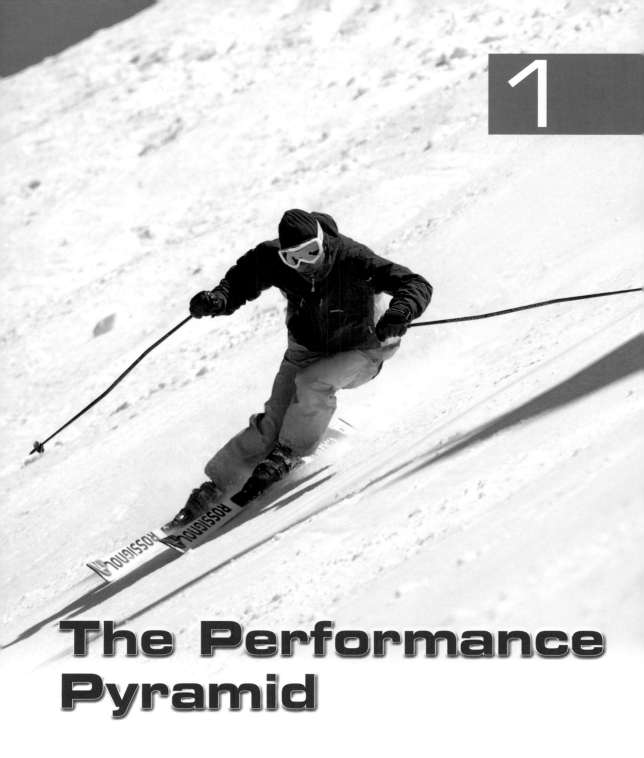

The Performance Pyramid

To say that I love to teach people how to ski would be an understatement. I cannot put into words the feelings that come to me when a student looks me in the eyes and says, "Today ranks in the top 10 days of my life." I have been fortunate to have lived during a time in history in which people have the time and financial resources to come to the mountains in the dead of winter and participate in a sport that stirs the kind of emotions that make even the most stoic and driven folks drop their facades and open themselves to transformation. Learning how to ski requires more than getting into shape and acquiring the ability to turn and stop. It is about learning the ways of the mountain and how to survive by letting go. It's about sliding down a slope and creating a wonderful journey through mountain meadows, pristine forests, and high, snow-blanketed slopes. Once you allow the deep skiing experience to seep into your being, there is no turning back. The skier's obsession is to climb higher, learn more, and experience greater sensations.

This book describes in detail the basic fundamentals of skiing, physical fitness, and technical and tactical concepts. To help you, this chapter draws the map that will guide you through the concepts needed to progress deeper into a sport that has grabbed many of us and shaken our roots, revealing the true importance of our existence. Quality over quantity is the first lesson. Without quality movements, the rest of your efforts will be wasted on compensation and recovery. To experience quality movements, you must have foundational integrity. This is where the performance pyramid begins.

The Performance Pyramid

To assess movement quality, the North American Ski Training Center uses the model of a four-level performance pyramid. Here, the balanced skier's performance is displayed in an isosceles triangle, with a base block of functional movement, a center block of fitness, and two upper blocks of ski techniques and tactics (see figure 1.1). The pyramid's four levels represent an important cause-and-effect dynamic in skiing. The block of functional movement serves as the foundation on which the blocks of fitness, technique, and tactics are built. Although all these components are quite different, they are linked by how well the body moves and reacts under the demands of the performance environment, whether in a gym or on a ski slope. Without the integrity of the

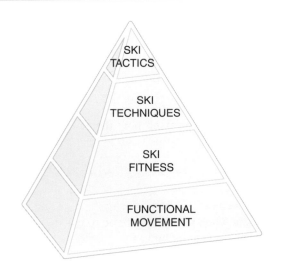

FIGURE 1.1   The performance pyramid.

functional-movement block, the blocks for fitness, techniques, and tactics will soon break down due to fatigue or injury. This pyramid is based on concepts from Gray Cook's *Athletic Body in Balance*, an excellent resource for movement and conditioning.

The bottom level of the pyramid represents patterns of functional movement, or mobility and stability. The next three levels of fitness, technique, and tactics cannot fully develop unless skiers can perform functional movements in a controlled environment. The second level represents fitness, or movement efficiency. These movements enable skiers to produce and absorb power and to generate the endurance and ability to handle challenging snow and terrain. The top two levels represent skiing technique and on-snow tactics. Skiing technique is made up of skill elements that, when solidified, create a launchpad for future maneuvers.

As technique is refined, skiers build confidence and anticipate the approaching terrain and conditions. At that moment, they can visualize tactical solutions to meet the upcoming challenges. As they grow, skiers will revisit the continuum of functional movements, moving through all the blocks and back to functional movement again. The ability to move freely from one block to another shows development. These movements provide the basis of skiing skills.

Evaluating Skill Level With the Pyramid Blocks

Often, skiers fail to improve because they focus on their strengths rather than addressing their weaknesses. Coaches and instructors are just as guilty when it comes to identifying the root cause of a fault, flaw, or error. Most identify the symptom and call it a day. As a ski instructor, I was trained to spend most of my time focusing on my students' skills. Most exams for ski instructor certification focus on developing a skill progression that addresses a skier's symptoms. However, in working with a wide range of abilities throughout my career, I have instead come to realize that optimal skiing performance is the result of a stable performance pyramid, or one in which a skier demonstrates strength and consistency at each level.

Assessing the Pyramid Blocks

In order to identify specific asymmetries or limitations, skiers will be assessed on each block of the performance pyramid in chapters 2 through 5. The assessments essentially provide skiers with a checklist of areas for specific improvement within the parameters of the performance pyramid.

As you age or suffer injury, simple tasks can become difficult, altering your natural movement patterns and causing your body to compensate. Unless you address these compensations before you step on the snow, they will carry over into your skiing, resulting in chronic pain or traumatic injury and affecting your performance. Screening for these asymmetries will give you insight for addressing problematic areas with corrective drills and exercises.

To better understand how the assessments relate to skiing, let's take a look at a specific assessment of functional movement. Begin with the functional movement related to the body mechanics used in everyday tasks, such as squatting down to pick up a heavy object, twisting and turning to open or close a door, running up a flight of stairs, stepping up and over an object in your path, or getting up from the floor after lying on your back. The functional-movement assessments in chapter 2 determine that the most common movement faults in skiing become apparent when performing basic squats, single-leg squats, exercises that demonstrate rotational stability, and lateral lunges.

During these basic exercises, many people struggle to correctly move their hips, legs, core, and upper body because they fail to apply proper compensatory movement to opposing body parts. Instructors see symptoms of these mistakes all the time, particularly with students who can't flex evenly throughout their joints. As a result, they tend to lean forward and flex their ankles or knees too much, causing them to camp out over their skis. Other skiers may not flex the joints enough, causing them to lean backward toward the tails of the skis.

When doing these basic movements, the following tests may identify trouble performing dynamic on-snow tasks. When asked to perform three consecutive squats, do your legs and knees collapse (sharply angle in or out) each time? Do your knees stay aligned while flexing? Do your feet pronate too much, rotating outward? Do you flex your spine? If you have trouble performing a single-leg balance in the lodge, you will have problems with a single-leg drill on the snow.

As Warren Witherell so memorably demonstrated, the center of knee mass must be properly aligned as you flex in your boots so that you can apply direct pressure, transferring energy down to your skis. When isolated from the variables of a ski run, this visual data gleaned from the functional-movement assessment can provide a telling snapshot of your joint movement. If you can perform functional movements smoothly and efficiently, you can incorporate those movements into skiing. On the other hand, if you reveal movement asymmetries in the lodge, you will invariably experience certain limitations on the hill.

Determining Skier Type

You can combine the results of the pyramid-block assessments to determine your skier type. These categories will be discussed further in chapter 6. Placing skiers into one of four types helps us customize drills and exercises that address total performance rather than particular technique.

Once you have determined your skier type, see part III for the full spectrum of training needs based on your unique profile. These chapters address the needs and compensations identified in the performance assessments of the pyramid blocks and provide clear programs for building up areas of weakness and maintaining strengths. In the end, the groundwork laid in this approach clarifies three important concepts for your development.

First, it identifies your skier type and, therefore, your specific needs. For example, are you inflexible, requiring mobility work, or are you weak in your core, requiring strengthening in that area? Are you a combination of both? Although in good general shape, are you a first-time skier or a seasoned pro who needs to get back into shape since raising kids? Gaps in your pyramid are nothing to be ashamed of, but ignoring problem areas will only keep you stuck where you are.

Second, this approach shows that compensating movements can alter the normal reflexive response of muscles needed for proper skiing. The assessments will identify movement patterns affected by poor posture, muscle imbalance, poor mobility, faulty motor programming, and altered nerve responses due to injury or tightness. Finally, you will become aware of how body parts are associated with one another. You will also learn which joints and muscles are most susceptible to injury by identifying problems in related groups. For example, continually injuring your knee indicates a problem with the surrounding joints of the hip and ankle.

Once you have gone through all the assessments and are armed with this valuable information, it's time to ski. Allow sufficient time to relax and enjoy the mountain, but watch how you adapt your movement when faced with challenging terrain. By attempting terrain appropriate for your ability level, you can apply tactics and make the connections between technical movements, both on and off the snow. At the end of the day, the solution to any weaknesses you've identified—along with the next step in your development—should be very clear.

The system described in this book can help you measure the physical barriers that may be blocking you from achieving your potential. It offers complete and concise information for incorporating the drills, exercises, and equipment adjustments into your own training program. This book will give you the knowledge to completely analyze your overall setup so you don't end up overlooking the most important piece of equipment of all, your body.

Focusing on Functional Movement

From the time I met Warren Witherell in 1990 to the time I was introduced to Gray Cook's work in 2005, I spent countless hours watching skiers repeat the same patterns of limited movement that failed to advance their proficiency. As a prudent coach, I tried to prescribe exercises that would address their missing skills and to make equipment suggestions that would improve their balance and efficiency, but it was not until I began to include assessments for functional movement and performance solutions that I began to see lasting and dramatic changes.

To assess a skier's ability in functional movement, I use an adaptation of the functional-movement screen (FMS), which is described in www.functionalmovement.com, a Web site developed by exercise and movement physiologists Gray Cook and Lee Burton. This adaptation of the FMS consists of tests for the overhead-depth squat, single-leg squat, rotational stability, and lateral lunge. Essentially, this assessment of the functional-movement block of the performance pyramid measures the body's ability to perform basic movement patterns on stable ground without sensory challenges, such as steep slopes, variable snow conditions, and flat light. This assessment determines how well a person moves in a variety of different planes. A parallel can be drawn between any movement problems or left- or right-side asymmetries and difficulties on the ski hill. The invaluable information gained helps establish a baseline for how skiers are set up for the long haul in this dynamic sport. This snapshot of their personal geometry reveals chinks in their physical armor, as well as areas of strength and durability.

This chapter tests your abilities for functional movement in order to determine weaknesses or limitations, to increase your body awareness, and to help you modify your movements in order to eliminate errors and misalignment. As you establish a solid foundation for continuous improvement you will also increase your strength and endurance for skiing.

Injuries can sideline you from skiing and extend into other aspects of your life. Negative side effects include loss of income from missed work, academic challenges for students, emotional depression from this setback in your training and from inactivity, and loss of fitness during the recovery process. Preparative conditioning will not eliminate all risks, but it will help you build strength. It also plays a key role in recovery if you do experience an injury.

Concepts of Functional Movement

As chapter 1 illustrates, the bottom level of the pyramid is functional movement. Here, the focus is on coordinating muscle groups that create the movement patterns needed for successful skiing. It can be further broken down into the categories of stability and mobility. These elements are often confused with strength and flexibility. Although they are both important, they do not provide the total picture. Dynamic balance plays the role of consolidator in the world of functional movement. Once you begin skiing down a slope, dynamic balance helps you coordinate your movements by making continuous and efficient adjustments and by precisely executing skills.

Stability

Stability is the body's ability to remain unchanged (aligned) in the presence of external changes or outside forces. Remember the last time you skied in uneven terrain or in heavy snow? You probably felt the push and pull of the snow and the bumpy terrain working together to knock you off balance. In extreme cases, you might feel like a dingy caught in a hurricane. A balanced stability component helps you retaliate against the maelstrom.

Stability combines balance, strength, and muscular endurance. In archery, keeping the bow stable as you pull the string back requires the three elements of stability, and the same principle is involved in the mechanics of good skiing. The ability to keep one part of your body secure while stretching and contracting adjacent segments lets you manage your speed and maintain consistent posture throughout skiing turns. This is true body stability!

Mobility

Mobility, on the other hand, combines normal range of motion in the joints and proper muscular flexibility. It is crucial for executing proper mechanics, preventing injury, and skiing well. Mobility lets you move in all planes of motion, thus allowing you to perform any motion without sacrificing stability. It also allows your body to stretch while maintaining enough functional tension to control and guide your energy in any direction. Mobility is created when muscles, joints, and tendons work together to coordinate your action. As one set of muscles contracts, another extends, and a third supports. Developing mobility engages these complementary groups and alerts your body that it's show time.

Without mobility in your muscles and joints, your range of motion is limited, resulting in movements that are as resilient as a flat basketball. For example, many skiers love to cycle in the off-season. As the first flakes of snow signal the end of biking season, they rush to the gym to power up their underdeveloped upper bodies and to stretch their hamstrings and hip flexors, which are as tight as guitar strings. I speak from experience—it's next to impossible to get me off my mountain bike and into the gym in the summer. Still, I have learned some specific workouts that smooth out imbalances and are necessary for avoiding injury and for skiing athletically in tough terrain. Be aware that your off-season sports could derail your skiing athleticism.

Linking good mobility and core stability is not enough for refining athletic skiing movements. The challenge of a sliding sport like skiing is that you must balance on a slippery surface while simultaneously twisting your legs, planting your poles, and edging your skis. Your dynamic balance depends on your base of support. If you are correctly centered, you will be able to change positions and blend movements at will. For some, this matrix of movement is a bit overwhelming. If you add body imbalances to the mix, you may wonder why you are even trying. It's not that difficult if you make the process a journey instead of a trudge! Shifting your perspective helps you learn quickly and experience the joyful benefits of exploring new territory and expanding awareness in your skiing.

Most of us can remember the learning curve of riding a bicycle. At the beginning, we struggled to balance while barely moving. Once we got up the courage to roll the bike a little faster, it became easier to balance. This is balance in motion, or dynamic balance, in its purest form. This element, also called movement in motion by the Canadian Ski Instructor's Alliance, is the cornerstone to their teaching methodology. The basic premise is that, unlike sports in which speed is generated by internal muscular force, skiing relies on gravity for forward motion that generates speed. Therefore, an expert's success is based on skiing a predetermined track as efficiently as possible. This interplay between external (gravity) and internal (muscular) forces illustrates effective technique (CSIA 2006).

Sensitivity for moving or stabilizing a body part during skiing is the foundation for future skill development, so don't skimp! Skimming over the basic movement patterns inherent in good mechanics and relying on default body compensations weakens your foundation. Very few skiers have faultless technique; nearly everyone compensates with something. However, the more efficient your mechanics are, the more seamless your improvement will be.

Functional-Movement Assessments

The following assessment sections test your stability and mobility. These dryland tests of functional movement will act as a mirror to help you see weakness and strengths in your skiing technique, providing a clear picture of how you move in relationship to the demands of skiing.

These assessments evaluate strengths and weaknesses for the functional-movement block of the performance pyramid. They are made up of four basic tests: the overhead-depth squat, the single-leg squat, rotational stability, and the lateral lunge. They will rule out any special physical needs, establish a baseline for further evaluations, determine a general level of mobility and stability, and point out asymmetries of the body.

Each assessment should be executed three times. Use your best score of the three. Be honest with your score, since the results will pinpoint the areas of compensation you need to work on. As you accumulate scores, you will begin to see areas of weakness. These will become your main training focus, since it is hard to improve by concentrating on your strengths.

If you score a total of 12 or an average of 3 on each of the four tests, you have good mobility and stability for skiing. You should retest every four to six weeks just to make sure you stay functionally fit. If you score a total of 8 and an average of 2 on all four tests, you still need to work on functional movement, but you are doing well in some tests. If you score a total of 4 or lower, you must specifically focus your workouts in this area until you have sufficiently strengthened the functional-movement block of the pyramid.

When performing these assessments, your results will fall into one of the following four categories:

- *Score of 3.* You have the movement patterns needed to physically manage pressure and terrain changes in skiing. Your flexion movements come from the lower body. You do not create asymmetries in your body or bend at the waist to absorb pressure.

- *Score of 2.* You may exhibit limited mobility in the lower body, including poor ankle flexion and tight ankle tendons. You may also have trouble flexing the hips properly. You may be unaware of tightness in the shoulders. However, after repeatedly practicing the movement in front of a mirror, you will easily be able to score a 3.

FIGURE 2.1　Functional-Movement Assessment Summary Sheet

Functional-movement test	Score	Solution exercises	Assessment notes
Overhead-depth squat test	❑ 3 ❑ 2 ❑ 1	**Stability** **Mobility**	
Single-leg squat test	❑ 3 ❑ 2 ❑ 1	**Stability** **Mobility**	
Rotational-stability test	❑ 3 ❑ 2 ❑ 1	**Stability** **Mobility**	
Lateral-lunge test	❑ 3 ❑ 2 ❑ 1	**Stability** **Mobility**	

From C. Fellows, 2011, *Total Skiing* (Champaign, IL: Human Kinetics).

- *Score of 1.* You continue to display poor form and to make repeated compensations during the movement.
- *Score of 0.* You associate pain with any portion of the test. See a medical professional for a thorough evaluation of the painful area. This evaluation will identify your movement limitations as well as improper alignment that could cause pain.

Next, as you perform the assessments, use the summary sheet for functional movement (see figure 2.1) to guide you toward the areas that need attention. Use this reference sheet in conjunction with the functional-movement test, recording your results as you perform each assessment. As you fill in your summary sheet, you will begin to see patterns of your strengths and weaknesses. You can easily track any changes in your scores over time. This summary sheet will become your road map to improvement, helping you accurately prescribe solutions for any barriers to functional movement.

The simplicity of the assessments in this block of the pyramid makes it easy to revisit the fundamental concepts of mobility and stability. Once you have performed the assessments and have gathered your results, you can easily establish a program of correctional exercises that addresses any weaknesses and asymmetries. By isolating the weak links, you will move toward identifying the root causes of your inability to perform functional movements, learning how the movement connects to your performance, and how to properly perform a specific technique. Many excited skiers rush right into these techniques on the slopes without noting key compensations and performance faults that can be determined from a functional-movement assessment.

These assessments should not take a great deal of time or space. It is best to perform them in basic workout attire, such as shorts and a T-shirt, rather than in ski clothing. Be sure to move normally. Do this test in front of a full-length mirror. Before you begin, review the description and photos for proper execution. If you are unsure of how to move as the instructions describe, try the movement out a couple of times to get the proper feeling.

Overhead-Depth Squat
`TEST`

The overhead-depth squat is used to assess bilateral, symmetrical, and functional mobility and stability of the hips, knees, ankles, and spine. To accomplish the task, you need full range of motion in all your joints and the stability to coordinate all the moving pieces. This test is difficult because your lower body flexes from the hips down and your upper body extends from the hips up. This requires a great deal of neuromuscular coordination even if you have a good range of motion. People tend to either flex everything, which does not allow them to keep their arms overhead, or to extend everything, preventing them from doing a complete squat even if they have the necessary range of motion.

Your range of motion in the overhead-depth squat is related to the force you can absorb and manage on your skis. Consider a spring with a big range of motion. When released, it has more elasticity than a spring with a smaller range of motion. In this exercise, you hold a dowel overhead while performing a squat to assess bilateral and symmetrical mobility of the shoulders as well as mobility of the thoracic spine. This information is vital for assessing the movement patterns you will bring to the snow. You will soon see that the limitations detected in this test can become barriers to free movement while skiing.

To perform the overhead-depth squat, stand with your feet hip-width apart, hold a dowel, and extend your arms over your head, as shown in figure 2.2. Slowly lower yourself to a low squatting position, using your ankles, knees, and hips. Keep your torso and tibia at the same angle as you move your femur at or past the horizontal position at the bottom of the squat. Keep your knees aligned over your feet and avoid tracking outward or inward. Extend back up to a standing position. Repeat the motion two more times. If you notice that you are making compensations, such as lifting your heels off the ground, place a block under your heels and repeat the squat.

Proper performance of the overhead-depth squat demonstrates fluid flexion of the ankles, knees, and hips, as well as extension of the upper spine and shoulders. These movements match the patterns needed for dynamic flexion and extension over the tops of your skis, such as when you move over a mogul or a roller. If you notice compensation movements in this test, you will also notice similar faults while skiing as you try to absorb terrain or avoid an obstacle. An example of a related fault is breaking at the waist to absorb bumpy terrain or choppy snow conditions.

a   b

FIGURE 2.2   Overhead-depth squat test.

TABLE 2.1   Scoring and Functional-Movement Solution Exercises for the Overhead-Depth Squat Test

Score	Functional-movement solution exercises
SCORE OF 3 Give yourself a 3 if the following apply: • You easily glide down to your haunches, keeping the dowel over the vertical plane of your feet and your knees tracking over your feet • Mobility in your hips is visible and stability can be witnessed, since your torso is parallel to your shins	To maintain a score of 3, no corrective functional-movement exercises are needed. However, a retest in 4-6 weeks is recommended.
SCORE OF 2 Give yourself a 2 if the following apply: • Your upper torso is parallel with your tibia • Your femur is at or below a horizontal position • Your knees are aligned over your feet • The dowel is aligned over your feet or toes • You have made corrective adjustments with a 2 in. (5 cm) lift under each heel.	To improve a score of 2, practice these exercises 3 or 4 times per week: **Stability** • Depth-squat progression, page 94 • Dumbbell-assisted squat, page 95 • Depth squat with lowered heel, page 95 **Mobility** • Toe-touch progression, page 96 • Hurdle step, page 96 • Butterfly wall sit, page 97 • Depth-squat stretch, page 97 • Stretch for quads and hip flexors, page 97
SCORE OF 1 Give yourself a 1 if you are standing on a 2 in. heel lift and the following apply: • Your tibia and upper torso are not parallel • Your femur is not below the horizontal position • Your knees are not aligned over your feet • You note lumbar flexion • Your feet are splayed out or in	To improve a score of 1, practice these exercises 4 or 5 times per week: **Stability** • Miniband walking routine, page 95 **Mobility** • Toe-touch progression, page 96 • Stretch for quads and hip flexors, page 97 • Thoracic 90-degree stretch, page 98 • Reach, roll, and lift on stability ball, page 98

If your lower body is incapable of flexion movements, the flex pattern to absorb inconsistencies often takes place somewhere else. Since some movement faults are not as obvious, they take longer to pinpoint. Hunching your shoulders while skiing is a common mistake that can be related to poor mobility in the lower body and limited range of motion in the knees. You can quickly see that some of these reactions on the snow may be the symptom, not the cause, of the problem. For this reason, feedback such as "Don't hunch your shoulders" does nothing to address the real problem of poor mobility in the lower extremities. See table 2.1 for information on scoring and solution exercises related to functional movement for the overhead-depth squat test.

Single-Leg Squat   `TEST`

The single-leg squat assesses the stability of the knee and the mobility of the hips when full body weight is applied. This is an important screen because at high speeds, elite skiers can bear up to three times their body weight on the outside ski alone, especially while turning. If skiers are off balance, affecting alignment even by a few inches, their ability to deal with the forces of abrupt terrain or the momentum of the turn will be compromised. If you are standing off balance and someone nudges you, you will easily topple over; however, if you are standing in a stable and aligned position, it takes much more force to knock you over. The ability to perform the single-leg squat parallels that required for the depth squat. During the test, look for disparity between your left and right sides. An imbalance could lead to injury and could affect your dynamic balance as you transition between turns on the hill.

To perform the single-leg squat, as shown in figure 2.3, stand with your feet hip-width apart and center your weight over one leg (you may use a board to lift your heel). Balance on that leg, and then slowly lower yourself into a squatting position, bringing your thigh parallel to the floor. Move back up to a standing position and repeat the movement three times. If you notice that you are making compensations, place a block under your heel and repeat the movement.

FIGURE 2.3   Single-leg squat test.

You should be able to move fluidly through your hips and to explode off one leg as all your joints synchronize and provide maximum alignment for takeoff. You should land softly on your opposite foot, retaining balance and preparing to recoil and spring into the next single-leg lunge. This movement is identical to recoiling out of one ski turn and into the next. If your mobility and stability are good, you can properly manage the lateral pressure and terrain changes inherent in Alpine skiing. Your joint mobility and core stability will help you master new movements more easily. Single-leg drills on the snow also strengthen and increase your range of motion.

If you are unable to balance on a single leg in the gym, you will not be able to do it on the ski slope either. Single-leg balance is a basic skill requirement for Alpine skiing because the connections among the ankle, knee, hip, and core transfer energy to the ski. As you complete the single-leg squat, watch for slight compensations, such as angling your knee inward or outward. In skiing, these movements compromise the alignment between your hip and ski, resulting in problems transferring energy. Common symptoms include dropping one shoulder or bending at the waist. Any stability and mobility compensations made indoors will follow you out onto the snow unless you address them with the prescribed solution exercises. See table 2.2 for information on scoring and solution exercises related to functional movement for the single-leg squat test.

TABLE 2.2   Scoring and Functional-Movement Solution Exercises for the Single-Leg Squat Test

Score	Functional-movement solution exercises
SCORE OF 3 Give yourself a 3 if the following apply: • You can isolate the muscles in one leg • Your upper torso is parallel with your tibia • Your shoulders are level with the floor • Your knee is aligned over your foot • Your back is straight and your stomach muscles are engaged as you lower into the squat	To maintain a score of 3, no corrective functional-movement exercises are needed. However, a retest in 4-6 weeks is recommended.
SCORE OF 2 Give yourself a 2 if the following apply: • Your upper torso is parallel with your tibia or placed slightly forward • Your shoulders are level with the floor • Your knee is aligned over your foot or toes • Your back moves forward or arches backward • You have limited mobility in your lower extremities, including inability to articulate your ankle • You make compensations due to tight shoulders or lack of awareness of how to flex your hips properly • You have made corrective adjustments with a block	To improve a score of 2, practice these exercises 3 or 4 times per week: **Stability** • Single-leg squat progression, page 99 • Single-leg squat with medicine ball, page 99 • Single-leg squat with miniband, page 100 • Single-leg balance, page 100 **Mobility** • Single-leg bridge for glutes, page 102 • Leg drops (with resistance band), page 103
SCORE OF 1 Give yourself a 1 if the following apply: • Your upper torso is not parallel with your tibia • Your shoulders are not level • Your knee is not aligned over your foot or toes • You flex one or both hips poorly	To improve a score of 1, practice these exercises 4 or 5 times per week: **Stability** • Indoor stork, page 100 • Knee-and-ankle grab, page 101 • Single-leg balance, page 100 • Standing split squat, page 101 • Single-leg squat with opposite-hand reach, page 101 • Single-leg squat with assistance line, page 102 **Mobility** • Leg drops, page 103 • Backward stretch for quads and hip flexors, page 104 • Stretch for frontal range, page 104 • Standing split squat with dumbbells, page 103

Rotational-Stability

Many functional activities in sports require trunk stabilizers to transfer force asymmetrically from the lower extremities to the upper extremities and vice versa. An example of this type of energy transfer is exploding out of a tight turn, quickly exchanging edges and redirecting the skis. The rotational-stability test requires proper coordination and core stability. Skiing requires similar movement coordination and energy transfer when balancing over the outside ski while maintaining pillarlike strength. Leg turns depend on rotational stability as you work to face the fall line with your upper body. This test clearly shows your torso's stability (or lack thereof) as you move the upper and lower extremities. Strong core stability is the foundation for enhancing hip mobility and bilateral movements between the upper and lower body.

To perform the rotational-stability test, as shown in figure 2.4, position your shoulders and hips at a 90-degree angle and knees and hands about 6 to 8 inches apart. Lift both your right arm and leg off the ground, pointing your arm forward and your leg backward. Next, touch your right elbow to your right knee while balancing. Again, return to the extended position. Perform this movement, keeping your back as flat as possible, and then return to the starting position.

FIGURE 2.4   Rotational-stability test.

TABLE 2.3   Scoring and Functional-Movement Solution Exercises for the Rotational-Stability Test

Score	Functional-movement solution exercises
SCORE OF 3 Give yourself a 3 if the following apply: • You can steer your leg while maintaining core strength • You perform one unilateral repetition correctly, keeping your spine parallel to the floor • Your knee and elbow are aligned as they touch each other	To maintain a score of 3, no corrective functional-movement exercises are needed. However, a retest in 4-6 weeks is recommended.
SCORE OF 2 Give yourself a 2 if the following apply: • You perform one diagonal repetition correctly, keeping your spine parallel to the floor • Your knee and elbow are aligned as they touch each other, but you compensate slightly or feel unstable at times	To improve a score of 2, practice these exercises 3 or 4 times per week: • Forward plank with alternating arm lift, page 105 • Plank progression, page 105 • Lunge chops, page 106
SCORE OF 1 Give yourself a 1 if the following apply: • You cannot perform diagonal repetitions • Your torso twists and you lose balance • You lift your knee or repeatedly touch the floor with your elbow	To improve a score of 1, practice these exercises 4 or 5 times per week: • Half-kneeling dowel twist, page 106 • Hip crossover, page 107 • Circus pony, page 107 • Knee plank, page 108 • Stability-ball twist, page 108 • Seated rotation, page 108

Repeat on the left side. If necessary, you can modify this test by touching your right elbow to your left knee. Repeat the diagonal pattern with your left arm and right leg.

If you lose energy because of weak trunk stabilizers, you will have a tendency to overrotate because you won't be able to resist rotational forces in the turn. You may also fail to complete full turns, resulting in uncontrolled speed and loss of ability to change direction. The transition between the end of one turn and the start of the next is a critical point in which the legs turn against the stable upper body. Weak core muscles will not provide support as you attempt to steer the skis across the hill. Your only tool may be total-body rotation in the direction of the new turn, which is very inefficient. This habit sets up a series of rotations initiated by the upper body.

In addition, if you cannot stabilize your core at the end of each turn, using the turn to generate power will be difficult. Spinning on a bar stool by simultaneously countering the movement of your upper and lower body exemplifies the power mechanics in a short-radius turn. As you twist your shoulders to the left and swing the stool with your hips to the right, countering the two halves of your body, you will feel a stretch and will use your core muscles to rebound. When the motion slows or stops, swing and twist back in the opposite direction. See table 2.3 for information on scoring and solution exercises related to functional movement for the rotational-stability test.

TEST Lateral-Lunge

The lateral-lunge test simulates the full range of lateral flexibility and core strength required for demanding edging and carving movements. In addition to testing lateral range of motion in the hips, this screen also tests your ability to keep your torso upright as you extend your outside leg and flex your inside leg. Skiers often extend the outside leg and counter their upper-body position to edge the skis for a tighter radius and higher speed turns. Flexing the inside leg allows the hips to lower closer to the ground, resulting in a higher edge angle and a tighter turn radius. Many skiers have a limited lateral range of motion, which directly affects their intensity and velocity during turns.

The lateral lunge combines the best of the single-leg squat and the depth squat as you squat with one leg and lunge with the other. Examples of this movement on the snow include the long outside leg and flexed inside leg required in a high-speed giant slalom turn. To resist the forces pulling you outside the turn, you must extend and align your outside leg. Once you step on the snow, the variable environment of the ski run will up the ante of any movement.

To perform the lateral lunge, as shown in figure 2.5, step out to the side. Centering your weight over one foot, flex back into your hip, knee, and ankle and slowly lower into a squat. Keep your opposite leg extended and your foot flat on the floor. Flex as low as you can or until your thigh is parallel with the floor. Plant both feet on the floor and point them straight ahead. Keep your chest up and facing forward. Perform this movement three times on each side.

Transferring power to the ski and absorbing power from it requires a sequence of movements that originate in the core and travel through the lower body. The upper body's role is to create consistency with balance and a stable counterweight. Imagine that you are trying to push a kitchen table. If you push at an angle that is slightly off, your force is dissipated because a direct line of pressure is not formed from

FIGURE 2.5 Lateral lunge.

your chest muscles, through your arm and hand, and then to the table. If you align your arm with your shoulder before pushing the table, you will have much more power. The same is true for the lateral alignment of your ankle, knee, and hip in the middle of a ski turn. If you align too far inside or outside the middle of the ski, your direct power is muted. It would be more effective if you positioned yourself in the middle of the ski. See table 2.4 for information on scoring and solution exercises related to functional movement for the lateral lunge test.

TABLE 2.4   Scoring and Functional-Movement Solution Exercises for the Lateral-Lunge Test

Score	Functional-movement solution exercises
SCORE OF 3 Give yourself a 3 if the following apply: • You feel an even stretch on the inside of your thigh and your weight is concentrated on the ankle of your flexed leg • You can move fluidly without coaching or external adjustments • Your thigh is parallel with the floor • Your knee does not move in front of your foot • Your feet remain pointed forward • You can fully extend your straight leg	To maintain a score of 3, no corrective functional movement exercises are needed. However, a retest in 4-6 weeks is recommended.
SCORE OF 2 Give yourself a 2 if the following apply: • You begin to feel lateral extension, but your range of motion is somewhat limited • Your thigh is parallel with the floor • Your knee does not move in front of your foot or toes • Your knee is aligned over your foot • Your feet remain pointed forward • You can keep your straight leg fully extended • You must place a block under your flexed leg to help with alignment	To improve a score of 2, practice these exercises 3 or 4 times per week: **Stability** • Backward lunge with arm raise, page 109 • Straight-arm lateral lunge with dumbbells, page 109 **Mobility** • Drop lunge, page 111 • Stretch for adductors and abductors with resistance band, page 112
SCORE OF 1 Give yourself a 1 if the following apply: • Your lateral range of motion is limited • Your thigh is not parallel with the floor • Your knee moves in front of your foot • Your knee is not aligned over your foot • You cannot keep your trail leg extended • You must place a block under the flexed leg to help with alignment	To improve a score of 1, practice these exercises 4 or 5 times per week: **Stability** • Resistance-band rotation, page 110 • Hip stretch with resistance band, page 110 • Lateral lunge on stability ball, page 110 • Lateral lunge with arm reach, page 111 **Mobility** • Inchworm, page 112 • Ankle stretch, page 113 • Stretch for quads, page 113 • Lateral hip adduction with resistance band, page 113

Three-Dimensional Skiing

Since skiing movements are done in three dimensions, it is important to understand the three planes of motion that pass through the body. Although the body works in all three planes at once during skiing, for the sake of simplicity, the following section breaks each plane down to basics.

Frontal Plane

The frontal plane, as shown in figure 2.6a, is a vertical line that divides the body into anterior and posterior (front and back) halves. Stepping sideways up the slope highlights movement in the frontal plane as you engage your edges, bend your leg, and gradually apply weight to your uphill ski. As your technique develops, you will redistribute weight in a similar manner, progressively and subtly moving from the right ski to the left. This choreographed set of movements results in the flow and rhythm at high speeds exhibited by expert skiers.

Sagittal Plane

The sagittal plane, as shown in figure 2.6b, is the vertical line that divides the body into right and left halves. You operate in this plane if you move either side of your body. Every skiing movement that involves flexing up and down or forward and backward happens in this plane.

For beginners, a simple straight run over small rollers clearly illustrates these movements, since you must flex and extend your legs in order to maintain ski contact through terrain changes. Advanced skiers can try an aggressive bump line to observe movements in this plane, since you must use your full range of movement to control the forces generated by speed in variable terrain.

Transverse Plane

The transverse plane, as shown in figure 2.6c, is a horizontal line that divides the body into upper and lower halves. The skiing movements that usually dominate in the transverse plane involve rotation, adduction and abduction of the legs, and countering with the upper body. Imagine turning your legs without moving your upper body. As you turn your legs, your pelvis remains stationary, maintaining functional stability in your core and providing a solid foundation for your legs to turn against. This movement, called *counter*, aids with edging and balance over your outside ski. The more acute the turn is, the more counter you will feel in the pelvic area.

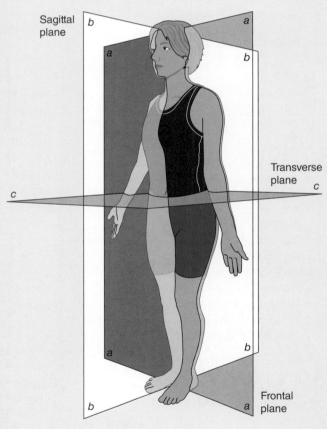

FIGURE 2.6 Planes of movement: *(a)* frontal, *(b)* sagittal, and *(c)* transverse.

Body Awareness

Developing good body awareness while skiing can be like imagining what the back of your head looks like. You can do it, but you have to stop and think about it for a second. Skiers with open minds and keen body awareness can often change their movement patterns on the fly, but many depend on trusted coaches for corrective feedback and kinesthetic cues. In either case, being in touch with the way you move and the feeling of quality movement is essential for peak performance and an injury-free skiing life. Cultivating your body awareness will make it easier to apply the functional movements you learned in the gym to skills on the slope.

The following body-awareness exercises, which are performed on the snow, provide clear and concise sensations of how the body feels when successfully dealing with the forces encountered in skiing. By tuning in to these sensations, you will become more able to adjust your performance movements. The most effective way to use these exercises is to practice them minutes before your ski run in order to keep the feelings fresh. The combination of functional-movement assessments and body-awareness exercises is crucial for pinpointing any weaknesses or limitations and for guiding your training program.

TEST ## Vertical Movement   **TEST**

This sensitivity exercise makes you more aware of how your body stabilizes the alignment of your ankles, knees, hips, and spine under external force. Stand rigid, feeling functional tension in your joints. Have a partner stand behind you and apply quick bursts of pressure to your shoulders (see figure 2.7). Your awareness comes as the pressure from your partner forces your loosest joints to bend or collapse. Some people fold under pressure, resulting in an eye-opening experience. This is a coachable moment, since you are now open to receiving cues that will improve your stance and posture for maximum stability.

FIGURE 2.7   Vertical-movement exercise.

If you are aligned and balanced, you will withstand downward pressure and flex slightly in the ankles, knees, and hips, maintaining a solid stance and feel over the skis. If excessive folding in the joints occurs or if you are pushed completely off balance, it is obvious that a weak spot exists in your overall alignment and stability. This awareness of stance stability and joint mobility will carry over to challenges on the snow. See figure 2.8 for an example of good athletic stance in a turn.

Some common stance faults result from skiing with limited pillar strength in relation to vertical movement (sagittal plane). Table 2.5 lists these faults, their causes, and their corrections.

FIGURE 2.8   Skier in a good athletic stance during a turn.

TABLE 2.5   Vertical-Movement Faults

Fault	Cause	Correction
Stance appears as a low crouch with over-flexed joints.	Overflexing the joints is caused by trying to move closer to the ground for perceived stability or contracting muscles to guard against perceived risk.	Think of any sport that requires quick movements and split-second responses. The proper stance for any of these is the classic ready position. Flex all joints evenly to prepare for movement either up or down.
Stance appears too high. Joints are over-extended or hyperex-tended.	Extending to the top of the range of motion is caused by overcom-pensating during the rising move-ment on skis. An overly-tall stance compromises your balance by moving your center too far from your base of support.	Maintain a midrange stance that allows you to efficiently rotate or move up, down, or sideways.
Swayback or hunch-back stance	If your hips are stiff and your vertical movement is limited, you may arch your back, giving you a swayback appearance. If your core is weak, you may round and firm up your shoulders (hunch-back) to secure a weak torso.	Keep your chest up by angling your spine to a position perpendicular to the pitch. Match the angles of your spine and lower leg to the amount of flexion. Too much flexion moves you too far forward and too little moves you to the back seat.

TEST ▶ Fore and Aft Movement

In skiing, you must be able to adjust forward, backward, up, and down in response to forces. Assuming a ridged stance, using stiff equipment, or freezing your joints limit your options for recovery or for proactive movements. Developing awareness of your best balance point in relation to this plane of movement puts you in a secure and functional place. The following exercise provides insight for recruiting key muscle groups for stance stability. Begin by facing a partner without skis. Both you and your partner should stand in a solid skiing stance. Each of you should hold your hands in front of your chests and then attempt to knock each other off balance by hitting the other's hands (see figure 2.9). Keep your hands up and continue to face your partner. As soon as your feet move out of place, the exercise is over.

This exercise brings sensitivity to the anterior and posterior muscle groups. Your muscles will stabilize your stance to resist or block the blows from your partner. This is a coachable moment, since you are now more open to the sensations inherent in variable snow conditions, including speed and mixed terrain. The fore and aft forces in skiing are constant, but vary in intensity. You make powerfully coordinated fore-aft muscle movements to maintain balance when slowly gliding down a gradual slope, to maintain your stance

FIGURE 2.9   Fore-aft movement exercise.

in the middle of the ski, to attack big moguls, or to ski in deep powder that pitches you forward and backward. As in the partner exercise, you must make fore-aft adjustments as you encounter terrain and conditions that slow your skis down or speed them up. The difference is that you will feel the force in your feet first, not in your hands. See figure 2.10 for an example of a skier remaining dynamic in rough conditions.

Some common stance faults result from skiing with limited pillar strength in relation to fore-aft movement (frontal plane). Table 2.6 lists these faults, their causes, and their corrections.

FIGURE 2.10   Dynamic skiing in rough conditions.

TABLE 2.6   Fore and Aft Faults

Fault	Cause	Correction
Overflexing joints in the lower body while keeping the upper body too erect, giving the appearance of a stick running straight up your back	An inefficient starting point with unequal flexing through the kinetic chain causes misalignment and strain on the knee joints and calf muscles.	Hop two times before taking off! Land softly on flat terrain and feel your joints align to absorb your landing equally. This is a great pretakeoff ritual.
Lurching forward in your stance, giving the appearance that you are hanging over your boot cuffs	This is caused by moving too far forward to find a comfortable, but aggressive stance.	Find a comfortable position in the boot in which you feel equal pressure from all sides of the cuff. Make sure your power strap is tight enough so that the cuff wraps around your ankle. From this home base, you have the range to move forward and back.
Inability to make anticipatory stance adjustments	This is caused by fear, which can mess up the best technique and can force you to react instead of execute. Your weight is shifted back and you feel the back of the boot on your calf.	Move toward, not away, from the next turn, bump, rollover, or trail edge. Lower-leg adjustments will keep your movements efficient and restrained. Know what you want to do and do it with conviction.

TEST ▶ Lateral Movement

Centrifugal force allows you to move your center beyond the base of support provided by your skis. As your speed increases, you can move further outside of this base. This exercise gives you the feeling of leaning outside of your base of support with a little help from your friends. Stand in a narrow stance between two partners, remaining aligned and functionally tense. You must trust your partners as they push you to the left and right (see figure 2.11). You should feel like a metronome tipping back and forth. Resist the temptation to step in the direction of the push, and check your body for broken alignment. This is a coachable moment, since arching or breaking at the waist is a cue that lateral movements in dynamic skiing generate forces that challenge your stance and alignment. See figure 2.12 for an example of a skier at the top of a turn. The skier exhibits lateral movement by tipping over the skis with the entire body, similar to leaning on a bike.

FIGURE 2.11   **Lateral-movement exercise.**

Some common stance faults result from skiing with limited pillar strength in the lateral, or sagittal, plane. Table 2.7 lists these faults, their causes, and their corrections.

FIGURE 2.12   **Skier at the top of a turn with inclination.**

TABLE 2.7   Lateral-Movement Faults

Fault	Cause	Correction
You cannot move your center outside of your base of support when stemming the ski to initiate a turn.	You are afraid to commit across the skis and to allow your body to cross over to initiate the turn.	Practice crossing your skis on flat terrain without moving. Like riding a bike, it is easier to cross over your skis when centrifugal forces are at work, adding helpful speed to your turn. In skiing, you can experience the same sensation that you do on a bike if you get the courage to go a little faster.
You are afraid of the fall line and are unable to commit to the downhill ski.	A lack of commitment to the downhill ski often makes you lean on the uphill ski.	Balance on the downhill ski. Practice balancing on one ski to ingrain a base for the necessary skills for lateral balance.
You lack positive-edge engagement.	Your skis are too flat, preventing you from feeling an edge.	Practice engaging your edge and reengaging from ski to ski by tipping your legs into the hill and releasing them back away from the hill.
Your hands are too low or are placed back, or your shoulders and hips are twisted uphill. Each postural affectation interrupts stance mechanics in the lateral plane.	Fear of the fall line causes the body to lean too far inside, resulting in poor alignment and ineffective preparation for the next turn.	Practice the basic engaged stance to ingrain proper lateral alignment and to prepare for the new turn.

Rotational Movement

`TEST`

The upper body can be a powerful mechanism for turning. As you rotate the greater mass of your upper body against the smaller mass of your lower body, a reaction of rotational movement is transferred to your legs as soon as you begin to slow or stop your upper body. Many beginners turn this way because it is easier to use big muscles to initiate a turn. Although this approach is powerful, it is inefficient and will disrupt your balance

a   b

FIGURE 2.13   Rotational-movement exercise 1.

at the end of the turn. Turn initiation is most effective when you stabilize your core and turn your legs with your adductors and abductors. Two exercises work well for practicing rotational movement.

To perform the first exercise, stand erect, holding your poles across your body and out in front of you. Have a partner twist and pull your ski poles as you resist the force in the rotational plane (see figure 2.13). The coachable moment is to observe whether your pillar strength breaks down and if your upper body can resist your partner's twisting movements. As your partner twists the poles, your core muscles will tighten and your ability to withstand the twisting will increase.

For the second exercise, assume the skiing stance, using your poles for balance (see figure 2.14). To feel the mobility needed for leg rotation, stand on a platform with a raised middle, such as the toe piece of your bindings. Twist your legs first all the way to the right and then all the way to the left. Maintain stable hips as you twist your legs from side to side as far as your range of motion will allow. This exercise can be used for much more than just rotational movement, as you will see in chapter 9. It has also been included there to practice

FIGURE 2.14   Rotational-movement exercise 2.

leg turning (see Leg Turn with Feet on Bindings drill on page 148). When done together, these exercises are powerful because they couple the feelings of stability in the core and mobility in the hip and pelvis.

Some common stance faults result from skiing with limited pillar strength in relation to rotational movement, or the transverse plane. Table 2.8 lists these faults, their causes, and their corrections.

TABLE 2.8   Rotational-Movement Faults

Fault	Cause	Correction
Your chest and upper body rotate into the turn before your legs do.	You use your upper body to initiate the turn because gross-muscle movement is easier than finite-muscle movement in the legs.	Learn to initiate the turn with your legs and skis by stabilizing your core and by turning and tipping with your legs.
Your arms rotate across your body to start the turn.	You are winding up your upper body by swinging your downhill arm away from the turn.	Stabilize your arms and torso as you initiate the turn and steer your legs into it.
Your upper and lower body face the same direction at all times.	You cannot separate your upper and lower body. This skill is needed for advanced and high-speed skiing.	Work on stabilizing your core. This helps your lower body actively turn, regardless of where your upper body is facing.

Understanding the results of the functional-movement screen and gauging your ability from the body-awareness exercises will give you a huge advantage when preparing a ski-conditioning program. Finding your weakest link can help you target asymmetries and movement limitations for better performance and enhanced long-term body durability.

If the assessments and prescribed solution exercises for your score do nothing more than increase your awareness of your movement, they have helped you take the first step toward better performance. In most cases, they will help you identify imbalances, limitations in range of motion linked to performance issues, and skill enhancement limitations due to poor balance. Establishing a program that meets your individual needs depends on how thoroughly you evaluate and integrate the results. Once you have addressed these issues, you can initiate the next block of the performance pyramid, skiing fitness. After the two blocks of the base are in place, you can move on to the technique and tactics blocks.

Targeting Ski Fitness

This chapter shifts the focus from the fitness program itself to individualizing workouts for your specific needs. Many well-intentioned skiers prepare for the season with a generic dryland program that could come from any fitness magazine or skiing Web site. Of course, using such a program is better than doing nothing, but it is not nearly as effective as using a routine tailored to your cardiorespiratory and muscular weaknesses and gaps in terms of power and agility. Once you are armed with the information from these tests, you can adopt a streamlined approach to get fit faster.

The fitness block of the performance pyramid contains power and gross athletic movements. Imagine skiing for two to five hours over varied terrain and conditions, making short, quick turns down steep terrain and long, wide turns through flat terrain, jumping over obstacles, and bending and flexing your joints as you absorb bumpy terrain. Your muscles are activated in a chorus of contractions and cocontractions that keep you balanced over your skis and provide power and elasticity in your movements. Depending on the demands of that particular slope, your pulse could be at 70 to 90 percent of your maximum heart rate after each run. The assessments in this chapter test the basic foundations of your gross athletic abilities and provide solutions for the areas that need improvement. As in chapter 2, the integrity of the pyramid's fitness block is essential to the program as a whole. Eliminating it increases risk of injury and imposes a ceiling on your performance.

The fitness block sets the gears in motion by tailoring exercises to meet your specific needs. Once you have filled in the gaps in your fitness profile, you will move seamlessly toward higher education in technique and tactics. To assess your fitness needs, you will look for areas of improvement in four training areas.

Begin with the old adage "quality over quantity" when building a fitness program—your fundamental movement must be sound! Building a fitness program on a shaky platform will only incorporate compensations and inefficient movement patterns. Solidifying the functional-movement block of the pyramid is an important prerequisite that lays the groundwork for the fitness block. Establishing a good foundation builds endurance, strength, power, and agility. With a solid grasp of your functional-movement needs, you are now ready to take a closer look at the fitness block of the pyramid.

Concepts of Skiing Fitness

Endurance, strength, power, and agility make up the fitness block of the pyramid. Endurance and strength act as the motor and fuel of your body, supplying the infrastructure that makes it go. Your level of fitness also determines your long-term durability and susceptibility to chronic injury. Power and agility are like the fuel injection, providing the turbo action that gives your body the initial kick and final power-gear overdrive.

Most ski injuries happen during the last run of the day. When you tire, you begin to lean back, inside, on a pole, or on anything that will support and prop you up for the last few turns. Without knowing it, you begin to rely on your connective tissues to support your body weight through a turn. Suddenly, you get knocked back. You make one last effort to pull forward again and you hear and feel a loud pop! Injuries of the knee and hip joints are becoming a regular ailment for skiers. Most can be related to fatigue and reliance on improper positioning. Endurance, strength, power, and agility will be your safety net for avoiding injuries or recovering from them when hitting the slopes for the last few runs.

Cardiorespiratory Fitness

Cardiorespiratory fitness, or endurance, allows you to repeat ballistic movements for the length of a ski run 8 to 10 times, resting only for the duration of a ride on the chair lift. The demands of Alpine skiing require specific endurance in order to go hard for several days in a row and sustain long runs of more than 10 turns in a row. A strong aerobic base gives you a bigger fuel tank for recovery and a reliable energy source when hiking to a favorite powder stash or keeping up with your skiing pals. You must have a reserve in your tank for getting out of those difficult situations when you need to "throw the hammer down," such as getting thrown off balance by an unexpected change in terrain or snow density.

The cardiorespiratory system is broken down into three areas: the aerobic system and the two parts of the anaerobic system, the lactic system and the alactic system. In the aerobic state, your lungs send oxygen to your muscles as fuel to prolong your activity. After a certain period of intense work, your lungs can no longer deliver enough oxygen. You surpass the lactate threshold and move into the shorter but more powerful *anaerobic* state, which means without oxygen. You can feel the transition into anaerobic threshold when skiing a long, sustained run. Halfway down, your breathing becomes labored and your legs begin to burn. Anaerobic power comes into play when you are gassed beyond what you think you can do, but you kick in for the last 3 to 20 seconds. This push can help you hop over an obstacle, cut an abrupt turn, or recover from a near-disastrous fall. Luckily, since ski runs are connected by chair lifts, you can easily recover during a 7-minute lift ride. The fitter and more efficient you become, the easier it will be to stay in an aerobic state. Beginning skiers often experience the anaerobic state quickly due to the intensity of their work output.

You build your endurance by doing a sport you enjoy, such as hiking with ski poles, trail running, mountain biking, and road cycling. These activities are best because they can be regulated to include days of high, moderate, and low intensity. Although most of us train in the middle range of our heart rate, this variety of intensities is needed for maximum cardiorespiratory improvement. A sound program for cardiorespiratory base training includes anaerobic-interval workouts that range from 20 seconds to 5 minutes and aerobic training of lower intensity for 30 minutes or more. Perform your aerobic sessions at an intensity that allows you to carry on a conversation with your partner. Since anaerobic activity is more strenuous, you will only be able to maintain casual conversation of a few words. This activity level is reached on a steep bike ride uphill or on a high-paced run. When targeting anaerobic threshold, maintain moderate intensity for 2 to 5 minutes at a time. Anaerobic power is sharpened during high-intensity bouts that range from 20 seconds to 2 minutes. At this intensity, you will not be able to talk, working instead to suck in all oxygen molecules in the vicinity.

Muscular Fitness

Strength training for skiers relates to the amount of work that you can do at any point. Strength endurance focuses on the length of time for which you can do the work. Because of the immense forces inherent in skiing, strength training plays a big role in preseason conditioning. World-class skiing athletes look like linebackers from the NFL for good reason! Skiers need power and strength to perform and to stay healthy. For most people, bulking up to NFL standards is overkill; however, strong leg, core, and back muscles provide the stability needed for active movements in quick turns and for terrain management. Fit skiers perform at their highest levels for longer periods, thus ingraining good movement patterns and placing less strain on their connective tissue. In this case, success does breed success. As your body gets stronger, you gain the ability to ski longer and harder with better technique.

Muscle strength for skiing is different from strength training for general fitness. Many contemporary strength programs focus on a particular exercise or group of drills. Although these programs may make you look better or help you get strong in one plane of movement, skiing requires a different type of strength. Muscle strength for skiing is about balance, powerful movements in a wide range of motion, increased joint stability, and muscle coordination in three planes.

Skiing is also a balance sport—the more balanced you are, the less you will rely on pure muscle strength to hold you upright. However, even the most balanced athletes need strength to repeat turning and terrain-absorbing movements over the course of the entire day. To combine the balance and strength components in your ski-specific workouts, challenge your balance while working on a muscle group. For example, do push-ups on a balance ball or squats on a foam roller.

Since strength exercises like biceps curls are one-dimensional, they are not as effective for skiing fitness as exercises that require stability, coordination, and strength in several planes at the same time. Adding a balance ball and resistance bands to your exercises can transform one-dimensional strength exercises into three-dimensional ones. The added component of balancing on the roller requires support from muscle groups in the torso and hips, as well as from the primary movers needed for the lift. Ski-specific strength exercises must combine stabilizing muscle groups with the major movers. Too much strength work with weight machines is not recommended because it takes away from the stabilizing muscle component.

Think of a beginner hill as one-dimensional. It is an easy, constant slope with a consistent fall line and terrain. A black diamond run is three-dimensional; it requires you to handle a variety of terrain and conditions at different intervals against increasing and decreasing forces. Weight machines and one-dimensional exercises are fine for beginners because that type of training reflects the type of demands they face on the slope. As you progress and begin to explore different slopes around the mountain, use multidimensional exercises, such as ones that use free weights or move your body weight in a variety of directions. These give you skills that carry over for skiing expert terrain. Practice controlling the external forces of the weights as you will control the external forces of the hill. The ability to react to a wide range of variables while making athletic movements comes from strengthening your core muscles and stabilizing muscles in multiple planes.

These exercises not only build strength, but also set your balance sensors on alert. Skiing requires constant response to changes in surface consistency, slope angle, and speed. Confusing your muscles by varying intensity, weight, and reps is a strength-training technique that can be helpful in sports like skiing because it reproduces the mixed signals your nerve endings receive from the varied terrain and conditions on the mountain.

As the repeated demands of terrain and conditions hammer away at your energy stores, strength endurance comes into play, determining how long you can work a muscle to its full capacity. An example is doing 50 hop turns down a narrow chute. This differs from pure muscle strength, such as doing a leg press with as much weight as you can possibly lift. Muscle strength, endurance, and the stabilizing strength you built through the functional-movement exercises in chapter 2 are all required for proper skiing.

Power and Agility

In skiing, power and agility involve explosiveness and quick bursts of energy. However, without the prerequisites of endurance and strength, power is as hard to find as the Holy Grail. This ingredient adds force behind your strength; without it, your strength stays in a state of limbo, never reaching full potential. Adding power with plyometric exercises, quick stop-start activities, and fast-twitch strength moves will enhance your reaction times and your ability to recover when knocked off balance. Most of us have jumped rope and are familiar with the bounce needed to successfully clear the rope on each swing. This act is the most basic form of quick-response muscle action. Examples of ski-specific exercises include quick-foot activities with an agility ladder, box jumps in different planes of motion, and quick-foot running drills. Chapter 8 covers this type of exercise in more detail, explaining its importance in the fitness block and for your skiing.

Power and agility increase your precision, your foot speed, and your ability to make fast adjustments in several planes. Dynamic ski turns are a result of synchronized muscle groups extending, flexing, and articulating, all working to maintain your balance and the interaction of your feet and skis with the snow. If power and agility are missing from the fitness package, your movements become sluggish. Precision turning is replaced with heavy pushes and misguided slides.

Assessments for Skiing Fitness

Practice makes perfect! You can maximize your valuable time on the snow if you prepare functionally and become fit. Learning bad habits because of holes in the functional-movement and fitness blocks damages your skiing technique and makes you prone to injury. The screening process identifies weaknesses before you become comfortable with making these compensations. Rushing through the screens only produces gaps that can tear apart your technique and tactics later. Skiing is fun for those who experience success, but it can be a struggle for those who are missing the building blocks of development. Resolve to build a solid skill base so you can have limitless fun on the slopes.

You can perform the following fitness assessments in a gym or outside, depending on your preferences or setup. Their goal is to identify the strengths and weaknesses in your cardiorespiratory, muscular, power, and agility output. Precise assessments will pinpoint the areas that you need to spend the most time on.

The ultimate goal of the analysis is to generate an effective series of exercises that will build the physical components best related to your skiing needs. As in the functional-movement assessments in chapter 2, you will begin to see regular patterns in your abilities, such as consistently running out of energy during the endurance test or lack of leg strength in the quick stop-start drills. As you chart your progress, you will learn valuable information that will lead to specific performance programs. The assessment will also pinpoint any asymmetries in muscular strength, which can lead to injury since we often create adaptations that are not conducive to expert skiing or functional joint movements. However, your results can vary depending on your level of recovery from a recent workout or your current nutritional levels. Rest and replenish your energy the day before the test for the best results.

The cardiorespiratory-fitness tests will highlight your different training levels and will help you feel confident working in all intensities. The strength test identifies imbalances in muscle development and strength. The test for power and agility shows you how to utilize your strength in several planes at different speeds and intensities. When performing these assessments, your screen results will fall in one of three categories: level 3, level 2, or level 1.

- *Score of 3.* This score in the cardiorespiratory tests indicates a solid aerobic and anaerobic base. You are comfortable working at higher output levels and you know how to vary your workouts for optimal improvement. This score in the strength test shows that you have a solid foundation needed to handle the forces that build up in skiing. Your core strength allows your legs to work independently and freely for precise turns. A score of 3 in power and agility means you can use your strength in a wide range of intensity levels and can adjust the speed of your muscular output. In most cases, a score of 3 in the fitness block means you are physically well balanced and are ready to do on-hill work in technique and tactics.

- *Score of 2.* This score in the cardiorespiratory tests indicates that you are meeting many of the assessment benchmarks, but your performance is slightly less than optimal. Your workouts do not vary in terms of speed, intensity, and duration. The results of your strength test correlate to the holes in the cardiorespiratory tests, since endurance is closely tied to your strength. You may often run out of gas after an intense set. You have favorite exercises and exercises you hate. This leads to asymmetries in your muscularity, causing compensations and weak spots. Power and agility are hit and miss; in one moment, you are on, and in the next, you are as wobbly as a newborn fawn. You struggle with consistency when you are tired.

- *Score of 1.* This score indicates that you need work to progress safely into the subsequent blocks of technique and tactics. You score consistently below the benchmarks of 3 and 2. You are often gassed when skiing or trying to meet the demands of the test. Your muscles feel like jelly and your balance is compromised due to lack of core strength. Your power and agility are limited to short durations and are muted, resulting in a low-level output.

- *Score of 0.* Record a score of 0 if you experience pain during any portion of the test. Ask a medical professional to perform a thorough evaluation of the painful area. This evaluation identifies movement limitations and improper alignment that could cause pain.

As you perform the assessments, use the summary sheet for fitness assessment (see figure 3.1) to highlight the areas that need attention. Use this sheet as a reference in conjunction with the fitness tests. As you perform each assessment and record your results, you will begin to see patterns in your strengths and weaknesses. Keep the sheet for future reference. As you record higher or

FIGURE 3.1   Fitness Assessment Summary Sheet

Skiing fitness test	Score	Solution exercises	Assessment notes
CARDIOVASCULAR FITNESS			
Aerobic	❏ 3 ❏ 2 ❏ 1		
Anaerobic threshold	❏ 3 ❏ 2 ❏ 1		
Anaerobic power	❏ 3 ❏ 2 ❏ 1		
MUSCULAR FITNESS			
Upper-body strength (push-ups)	❏ 3 ❏ 2 ❏ 1		
Core strength (sit-ups)	❏ 3 ❏ 2 ❏ 1		
Lower-body strength (squats)	❏ 3 ❏ 2 ❏ 1		
POWER AND AGILITY FITNESS			
Power (box-jump test)	❏ 3 ❏ 2 ❏ 1		
Agility (hexagon test)	❏ 3 ❏ 2 ❏ 1		

From C. Fellows, 2011, *Total Skiing* (Champaign, IL: Human Kinetics).

lower scores over time, use the summary sheet for easy tracking. It will become your road map for improvement and will help you accurately prescribe solutions to any future barriers in your fitness.

Cardiorespiratory Assessments

Cardiorespiratory testing evaluates your heart's ability to meet the demands of skiing. It also measures how well your muscular system gets rid of the by-products of intense activity. Cardio-respiratory testing is the easiest to track because your heart rate and breathing constantly measure your performance, signaling the muscles' need for oxygen and nutrients as your activity increases. Once you stop or slow down, you recover a normal heartbeat and breath. Take note of your recovery time. The faster you return to normal levels, the more aerobically fit you are. The longer you are able to maintain higher workloads at lower heart rates and levels of perceived exertion, the higher your anaerobic capacity is. The following tests provide results related to your cardiorespiratory fitness and areas for improvement.

Aerobic Assessment

If your cardiorespiratory system is strong, you have a big motor that will get the job done. If your aerobic capacity is lacking, you will always feel like you are one click behind, gasping and struggling to keep up. A well-developed endurance base provides energy stores that meet your body's demands for fuel. Your thinking and ability to make decisions will be altered by operating with limited oxygen. Poor judgment in skiing is dangerous and can lead to dire results. Efficient movement and a big fuel tank lead to better performance and resistance to injury.

To assess your cardiorespiratory fitness, find your specific heart-rate zones. The common formula for determining maximum heart rate (HRmax) of 220 minus your age is only correct for 50 percent of the population. HRmax can vary greatly, depending on your age, training level, and training history. For greater accuracy, use a formula with one extra calculation. First, take your resting heart rate (RHR) when you first wake up in the morning by determining your beats per minute (bpm). Count the number of heartbeats in 15 seconds and then multiply that number by 4. Once you have found your RHR, put it into the following calculation: ((220 − age) − RHR × 60 to 70 percent) + RHR = 60 to 70 percent of the training zone. For a 40-year-old with an RHR of 60 bpm, the formula to determine 60 percent looks like this: ((220 − 40) − 60) × .60) + 60 = 132 bpm. The number for 70 percent is 144. Therefore, the easy-training zone for this athlete is 132 to 144 bpm. You can see the difference between this calculation and the first formula. In other zones, the difference is not as dramatic.

Another way to make sure you are working in the right zones is to use a scale that measures rating of perceived exertion (RPE) on a scale of 1 to 10. For the easy zone, you should work at a 5 or 6. For the medium zone, you should work at a level around 7 or 8, and for the high-intensity (hard) zone, you should work at a level of 9 or 10. When working out, you can always check your numbers. If you are in your medium zone, but your RPE is only 5 out of 10, adjust your numbers by 5 percent until you feel that your RPE matches the zone you are in. Once you have the cardiorespiratory fitness to challenge your hard zone, keep track of your highest HR number. Perhaps you start your training with a calculated HRmax of 180. As you get stronger and more fit, you might achieve a training HR of 186. If so, recalculate your zones based on your new HRmax.

Once you have determined your zones, look at the sample activities in table 3.1 to evaluate your level of aerobic fitness. If you can stay in zone 1 for the duration of the activity as shown in the table, you will have a basic idea of your level of aerobic fitness. As previously mentioned, if you are unable or barely able to maintain an activity within a zone, you receive the score that corresponds to the zone number. For example, if you can run 30 minutes or less in zone 1, you get a score of 1. In order to score a 2, you must be able to run for 30 to 60 minutes in your zone 1. To get a score of 3, you would have to run for at least 60 minutes in your zone 1. Once you complete

TABLE 3.1   Aerobic Scoring and Prescription for Continuous Activity in Zone 1

Activity	AEROBIC PRESCRIPTION		
	Score of 1	Score of 2	Score of 3
Running	3 or 4 times per week for 30 min. or less, increasing time by 5 percent each week	2 or 3 times per week for 30 to 60 min., increasing time by 10 percent each week	For maintenance, run 1 or 2 times per week for more than 60 min.
Road cycling	3 or 4 times per week for 60 min. or less, increasing time by 5 to 10 percent each week	2 or 3 times per week for 60 to 90 min., increasing time by 10 to 20 percent each week	For maintenance, cycle 1 or 2 times per week for more than 90 min.
Mountain cycling	3 or 4 times per week for 40 min. or less, increasing time by 5 to 10 percent each week	2 or 3 times per week for 40 to 60 min., increasing time by 10 to 20 percent each week	For maintenance, cycle 1 or 2 times per week for more than 60 min.

each test, see how long it takes for your HR to recover 40 beats directly after you stop your activity. Your goal is for your heart rate to drop 40 beats in 1 minute, indicating a good aerobic base. This will give you an idea of your anaerobic capacity and will help you determine how many intervals you can do in the second portion of the test.

TEST ▶ Anaerobic Assessment

Once you have determined your level of aerobic fitness, move on to testing your anaerobic capacity. If you scored 1 in the first test, train with the prescribed program for two to three weeks before attempting the second portion of the test.

Since this test uses the second zone as previously determined, be sure to have those heart rates on hand. Begin by warming up for 5 to 10 minutes in your first zone, performing any stretches that you like, since this test will challenge your capacity for work. Once you have warmed up, complete repetitions of 3-minute work intervals. Try to get your HR into zone 2 as quickly as possible and keep it there for the remainder of the time. Once 3 minutes have passed, reduce your intensity to an easy walking or cycling effort and monitor your HR for 2 minutes to see how many beats it drops. Your goal is for your HR to drop to zone 1 within 2 minutes. If it takes longer than 2 minutes to drop, your test is complete. Wait at least 48 hours before doing this program again.

If your HR drops to zone 1 within the two minutes, repeat another three-minute interval, raising your HR back to zone 2. The more you progress in your workout, the less effort you will need to get your HR to zone 2. The exception is if you are very fit. The fitter you are, the more effort you must exert to get your HR into zone 2 in the same amount of time. When you are fit, your HR drops quickly during active-rest periods, and thus must climb farther to get back to zone 2. A less-fit person may only recover to the top end of zone 1. Remember, your goal is to quickly return to zone 2 in order to keep your HR in zone 2 for as much of the interval as possible. This may require more effort early in the workout if you are very fit. As the workout progresses though, every athlete will struggle to recover to zone 1 in time. Therefore, the more intervals you are able to perform and recover from, the more fit you are.

Keep repeating this cycle of three-minute intervals of work followed by two minutes of active rest, monitoring your RHR until it no longer recovers to zone 1 within the rest period. If your HR does not recover after two minutes, gently cool down for another three minutes to finish your test. Next, count the intervals you were able to complete and use this number to determine your score for the anaerobic-threshold test in table 3.2.

If you're like most people, your brain and heart are willing to push to get your heart rate up, but your body just can't muster the energy to run faster, climb a steeper incline, or peddle harder. If this is the case, your muscular system is incapable of challenging your cardiorespiratory system any longer. Remember that it is much easier to get your numbers in a ground-based activity, such as hiking, running, or stair stepping, when working against the consistent force of gravity. It is much harder to get your heart rate up on a bike because cycling is an inertia-based sport and is not greatly affected by gravity. Keep the intervals for every activity to three minutes since your heart does not know what you are doing. It just knows that it needs to supply blood to the system during your activity. Although there are exceptions to the rule, skiing runs tend to max out around three minutes.

If you scored a 2 or higher in the anaerobic-threshold test, you might be ready to challenge your anaerobic power (see table 3.3). A score of 2 or higher in the previous test is a prerequisite for this test. You should have also been training in zone 2 for at least two weeks. This test takes you into zone 3 and requires everything you have, so make sure you are mentally and physically prepared for performing at a high level in fatigued conditions. With a little work, you will have the reserves and capacity to pull it off.

TABLE 3.2   Scoring and Prescriptions for Anaerobic Threshold Based on the Three-Minute Interval Test in Zone 2

Score	Prescription for anaerobic threshold
SCORE OF 3 Give yourself a 3 if you can do 6 or more 3-min. intervals with 2 min. of active recovery in zone 1.*	To further improve or to maintain a score of 3, do 2 workouts** per week at 3- to 5-min. intervals.
SCORE OF 2 Give yourself a 2 if you can do 4 or more 3-min. intervals with 2 min. of active recovery in zone 1.*	To improve a score of 2, do 2 workouts** per week at 3- to 4-min. intervals.
SCORE OF 1 Give yourself a 1 if you can do 3 or fewer 3-min. intervals with 2 min. of active recovery in zone 1.*	To improve a score of 1, do 2 workouts** per week at 2- to 3-min. intervals.

*Your HR must return to zone 1 by the end of the two-minute period of active recovery or the interval portion of the workout. If not, recover for another three minutes.
**See chapter 8 for more information.

TABLE 3.3   Scoring and Prescriptions for Anaerobic Power Based on 30-Second Intervals in Zone 3

Score	Prescription for anaerobic power
SCORE OF 3 Give yourself a 3 if you can do 8 or more 30-sec. intervals with 1.5 min. of active recovery in zone 1.*	To further improve or to maintain a score of 3, do 2 workouts** per week at 30- to 120-sec. intervals.
SCORE OF 2 Give yourself a 2 if you can do 5 to 7 30-sec. intervals with 1.5 min. of active recovery in zone 1.*	To improve a score of 2, do 2 workouts** per week at 30- to 60-sec. intervals.
SCORE OF 1 Give yourself a 1 if you can do 4 or fewer 30-sec. intervals with 1.5 min. of active recovery in zone 1.*	To improve a score of 1, do 2 workouts** per week at 20- to 30-sec. intervals.

*Your HR must return to zone 1 by the end of the two-minute period of active recovery or the interval portion of the workout. If not, recover for another three minutes.
**See chapter 8 for more information.

Your warm-up should include at least 5 minutes of the activity you are testing with. Once you have warmed up, perform a hard, 30-second interval of short, high-intensity, aerobic activity that brings you close to capacity such as running, cycling (mountain or road), stair stepping, or elliptical work. Actively rest for 1.5 minutes and repeat the interval. You must be able to recover to your zone 1 within the rest period. If you are unable to resume work or if you feel uncomfortable, stop the intervals and cool down for a total of 5 minutes.

Although you should be able to reach zone 3 by the third interval, it might be very difficult to get your HR up to your high zone in the first and second intervals, since your muscular system will be the first to be challenged. You may be suffering from muscular fatigue, which limits your ability to challenge your cardiorespiratory fitness to its fullest. As previously mentioned, the body systems interact constantly, and the function of one system depends on the function of the other. By taking a step-by-step approach, you start to realize your limits. To score a 1 in the anaerobic-power test, you must be able to perform up to four intervals; for a score of 2, you have to complete up to seven intervals; and for a score of 3, you need to complete eight or more intervals.

As you become more fit, your tolerance for higher workloads and your ability to operate at higher heart rates improve. You can then start to combine the zones by working two or three of them into the same workout, making your training more efficient. You can mix cardio zones if you score a 2 or better in all three of the cardiorespiratory-fitness assessments (aerobic, anaerobic threshold, and anaerobic power). Chapter 8 provides samples of mixed-cardio workouts beginning on page 121. Note that whenever the routine asks you to go into zone 3, the cardiorespiratory workout is considered difficult. This helps you get out of sticky situations while completing a hard run to the bottom without stopping. For example, work really hard for 30 seconds in zone 3, reduce your intensity to zone 2 for 3 minutes, and then repeat the interval. This teaches your body to buffer the lactic acid it accumulates from the workload and reuse it as fuel for the 3-minute interval.

Assessments for Muscular Fitness

The following tests measure your muscular fitness and ability to meet the demands of skiing, both in terms of strength and muscular endurance. These demands are placed on the full body. Although working on the legs alone results in imbalances, many skiers only think of leg strength during preseason training. Instead, focus on a full range of strength movements, including core strength for stabilizing posture and adjusting balance, upper-body strength for separating the upper and lower body, countermovements, pole planting, and lower-body strength for suspension and leg turning. Good, overall muscular balance is essential for avoiding injury and attaining peak performance. You must be able to repeat a muscular effort while balancing on a moving platform. Muscular endurance gives you the energy to ski longer, sustained runs without melting halfway down.

The short, all-out effort described in the following assessments best illustrates the demands of Alpine skiing. To get an honest reading here, push through the discomfort of the final reps. Go back later and reassess your performance to track your progress. The push-up test provides a snapshot of your upper-body muscular endurance. The sit-up test gives you a similar view of the core as you try to maintain effort without stopping or losing rhythm. The squat test for the lower body highlights muscular output and endurance. Repeat the squats with good form until you fatigue and lose your balance.

Assessment for Upper-Body Strength   TEST

The objective of this test is to do as many push-ups in a row as possible in one effort. You will need an object, such as a ball or a pillow, approximately 3 to 4 inches (8-10 cm) high. This serves as a guide for how far you should lower yourself with each rep. To test your upper-body strength, assume a push-up position and decide where your chest will touch the floor. Place the object underneath your chest. Starting with your arms, extend your body in a straight line from your shoulders to your ankles and begin your push-ups. To complete a rep, you must lower yourself, touch your chest to the object, and then push back up. Complete as many push-ups as you can without pausing or stopping. See table 3.4 for information on scoring and solution exercises related to ski fitness and upper-body strength.

TABLE 3.4   Scoring and Solution Exercises for Upper-Body Strength Based on Push-Ups Completed

Score	Solution exercises for upper-body strength
SCORE OF 3 Give yourself a 3 if the following apply: • You are male and can complete 45 push-ups or more • You are female and can complete 20 push-ups or more	To further improve or to maintain a score of 3, practice these exercises 2 times per week: • Push-up, page 124 • Push-up on stability ball, page 124 • Bench press with dumbbells (alternating arms), page 125 • Supine row with feet elevated (stability ball), page 125 • Kneeling single-arm row (both legs), page 126
SCORE OF 2 Give yourself a 2 if the following apply: • You are male and can complete 21 to 44 push-ups • You are female and can complete 10 to 19 push-ups	To improve a score of 2, practice these exercises 2 or 3 times per week: • Push-up (feet on a step), page 124 • Bench press with dumbbells (both arms), page 125 • Supine row with feet elevated (step), page 125 • Kneeling single-arm row (one leg), page 126
SCORE OF 1 Give yourself a 1 if the following apply: • You are male and can complete 20 or fewer push-ups • You are female and can complete 9 or fewer push-ups	To improve a score of 1, practice these exercises 3 or 4 times per week: • Push-up (hands on a step), page 124 • Chest press, page 126 • Horizontal row, page 127 • Lat pull-down, page 127

Core-Strength Assessment   TEST

After completing your upper-body assessment, test your core strength. Compensations due to a weak core include bobbing the head in rough terrain, bending at the waist to support the core against the thighs, and leaning inside the turn. These symptoms result from holding on with the passive, connecting structures of the body rather than activating the core. Compressing or hanging on structures that were not designed to withstand those forces can result in breakdown or failure. In terms of the body's structure, this leads to pain. Skiers who exhibit these compensations often resemble rag dolls, since they cannot seem to coordinate their lower and upper body in short turns. Their balance is easily challenged by changes in snow conditions or terrain.

Watch any professional athlete at the moment of impact with another object, whether the sport is baseball, golf, tennis, soccer, cycling, skiing, or horse riding. The athlete's core is wound up, stabilized, and ready to explode. A good example of this loaded relationship between two body parts is the finger snap. Try to snap your fingers without generating any torque between your thumb and middle finger. The result doesn't generate much noise. Now, snap with purpose, creating resistance between your thumb and middle finger. As the torque builds against your stable thumb, the tendons in your middle finger tense and prepare for an explosive release. In skiing, your explosive power comes from loading the hips throughout the arc of the turn, preparing them to release, snapping out of that turn, and moving into the next. The following core-strength test assesses the elastic muscle tone that allows you to load your core and release your legs at the right moment. Just like the snap, the functional tension of the core leads to a dynamic release of the legs, feet, and skis.

To perform the core-strength assessment, lie flat on your back and bend your knees to 90 degrees, keeping your heels in contact with the floor. Place your arms across your chest and point your toes inward with your heels flared out. If you have a metronome at home or on your computer or phone, set it to 55 beats per minute. Perform your sit-ups to the beat, maintaining a constant rhythm either up or down with each stroke. When you fall out of rhythm, conclude the test and count your reps. See table 3.5 for information on scoring and solution exercises related to ski fitness and core strength.

TABLE 3.5   Scoring and Solution Exercises for Core Strength Based on Sit-Ups Completed

Score	Solution exercises for core strength
SCORE OF 3 Give yourself a 3 if you can do 40 or more sit-ups.	To further improve or to maintain a score of 3, practice these exercises 2 times per week: • Medicine-ball toss (chest pass) with sit-ups, page 128 • Medicine-ball side toss, page 128 • Hanging-leg hip raise, page 129 • Stand-up paddle board, page 129
SCORE OF 2 Give yourself a 2 if you can do 20 to 39 sit-ups.	To improve a score of 2, practice these exercises 2 or 3 times per week: • Medicine-ball toss (overhead pass) with sit-ups, page 128 • Medicine-ball side toss, page 128 • Supine leg-ups (with weight), page 129 • Stand-up paddle board, page 129
SCORE OF 1 Give yourself a 1 if you can do 19 or fewer sit-ups.	To improve a score of 1, practice these exercises 3 or 4 times per week: • Sit-ups, page 130 • Supine leg-ups (without weight), page 129 • Stand-up paddle board, page 129

TEST Assessment for Lower-Body Strength

Before beginning this assessment, check chapter 2 to ensure that your technique is correct. You must be able to move correctly in a basic squat and score a 3 for the overhead-depth and single-leg squats in the functional-movement assessment (see pages 11-14).

To perform the assessment for lower-body strength, stand in front of a chair as if you are going to sit down. Place your feet hip-width apart. Keeping your back straight, squat and touch the chair lightly with your buttocks, then stand back up immediately. Continue these squats as quickly as you can with good form until you are fatigued. Keep track of the number of squats you perform to establish a baseline and to indicate your lower-leg strength. See table 3.6 for information on scoring and solution exercises related to ski fitness and lower-body strength.

TABLE 3.6   Scoring and Solution Exercises for Lower-Body Strength Based on Squats Completed

Score	Solution exercises for lower-body strength
SCORE OF 3 Give yourself a 3 if you can do 25 or more squats.	To further improve or to maintain a score of 3, practice these exercises 2 times per week: • Split squat (with weight and rear foot elevated), page 131 • Lateral lunge (weight and shoulder press), page 131 • Bridge on stability ball (one leg with hamstring curl), page 132 • Romanian deadlift (one leg elevated with weight), page 132
SCORE OF 2 Give yourself a 2 if you can do 10 to 24 squats.	To improve a score of 2, practice these exercises 2 or 3 times per week: • Split squat (hands behind head and rear foot elevated), page 131 • Lateral lunge (weight, without shoulder press), page 131 • Bridge on stability ball (two legs with hamstring curl), page 132 • Romanian deadlift (with weight), page 132
SCORE OF 1 Give yourself a 1 if you can do 9 or fewer squats.	To improve a score of 1, practice these exercises 3 or 4 times per week: • Split squat (without weight and no foot elevation), page 131 • Lateral lunge (without weight), page 131 • Bridge on stability ball, page 132 • Romanian deadlift (with dowel), page 132

Assessments for Power and Agility

The final round of tests consists of the repetitive box-jump test and the hexagon test. The box-jump test examines your gross power and the power endurance of your lower body as you repeat jumps during a certain amount of time. The hexagon test shows how quickly you can move in a predetermined area. It measures your ability to maintain a good stance and to control your body in multiple planes. It also shows any right-left imbalances and identifies your dominant side.

Having fast feet and feeling comfortable moving in any direction at a moment's notice for long durations results in optimal performance in a variety of terrain and conditions. The adaptability gained from agility exercises like the hexagon and box-jump tests is the key to moving your skis in the direction you want instead of where the terrain or snow want to take them.

Power Assessment (Box-Jump Test)   TEST

The box jump is more difficult than the other tests, combining muscular strength, strength endurance, power, and power endurance. When these components are balanced, you move closer to skiing-specific power. Heavy loads for a few reps build pure muscle strength and power. Lighter weight for many reps builds muscular endurance. Skiing demands both types of power and strength. The box jump also tests anaerobic-lactate endurance, which is part of the cardiorespiratory system. If your anaerobic lactate is out of balance, you will not be able to move enough blood to the muscles for multiple repetitions. This test also involves the bigger muscles in the body, which create burning sensations and slower reactions when fatigued.

Determine if your gross power is ready for this test with some full-body squats. You must be able to do 15 reps without any problems, maintaining good form with your thighs parallel. If you are unable to do the exercise as described on page 11 of chapter 2, do not attempt this test. Attempt one rep to determine your gross power, but if you cannot complete it, call it a day or take a rest. Gross power is about linking up multiple turns or jumps to complete a run. You need to transform the power of jumping once into power endurance for jumping multiple times consecutively. This comes from good form and endurance strength in the lower body.

To determine your result, you will need boxes of a variety of heights. Beginners will need a box 6 inches (15 cm) high and a platform on which they can stand comfortably with feet shoulder-width apart. If this is too easy for you, choose a box that is 12 inches (30 cm) high. If you are very advanced, choose a box that is 16 inches (40 cm) high. Your aim is to complete as many jumps on and off the box as possible in the allotted time. Both feet must take off and land at the same time. Do not count any efforts where only one foot touches or lands. Start by standing on top of the box. When the clock starts, jump down to the floor and then jump back on the box immediately to complete one repetition.

If you have never done a test like this before, start with level 1. If you are able to complete it, move on to level 2. Going for the highest level right out of the gate can be too challenging. Since the challenge of this test is relative to body type, it is gender neutral. Award yourself a score of 1 even if you can't complete one repetition. Also give yourself a score of 1 if you can complete the first level but cannot reach the second level. If you can complete the test for a score of 2 but cannot complete the test for a score of 3, give yourself a 2. If you can complete the test for a score of 3, award yourself a 3. Keep track of your repetitions for 90 seconds.

The exercises prescribed for improving your score are consistent to help you learn the movement and progressively get stronger within a known parameter. Continually changing exercises engages your proprioceptors for adaptability training, but progressing with a known quantity measures your progress and aids your motivation. See table 3.7 for information on scoring and solution exercises related to ski fitness and muscular power.

TABLE 3.7 Power Scoring and Solution Exercises Based on Box Jumps Completed

Score	Solution exercises for muscular power
SCORE OF 3 Give yourself a 3 if you can do 70 or more box jumps on a 16 in. box in less than 90 sec.	To further improve or to maintain a score of 3, practice these exercises 2 times per week: • Lateral box blast (page 133): 6 sets of 20 with 1 min. of rest in between • Tuck jump (page 134): 4 to 6 sets of 10 with 1 min. of rest in between • Reactive step-up (page 133): 4 to 6 sets of 6 with 1 min. of rest in between • Lateral hurdle jump (page 134): 3 consecutive sets of 8 using 12 in. hurdles • Uphill running or downhill hiking (page 135): Take 6 steps as quickly as possible.
SCORE OF 2 Give yourself a 2 if you can do 30 to 69 box jumps on a 12 in. box in less than 60 sec.	To improve a score of 2, practice these exercises 2 or 3 times per week: • Lateral box blast (page 133): 4 to 5 sets of 20 with 3 min. of rest in between • Tuck jump (page 134): 1 to 3 sets of 5 to 10 reps with 3 min. of rest in between • Reactive step-up (page 133): 1 to 3 sets of 6 with 3 min. of rest in between • Lateral hurdle jump (page 134): 3 sets of 4 using 12 in. hurdles • Uphill running or downhill hiking (page 135): Take 12 steps as quickly as possible.
SCORE OF 1 Give yourself a 1 if you can do 0 to 29 box jumps on a 6 in. box in less than 30 sec.	To improve a score of 1, practice these exercises 3 or 4 times per week: • Lateral box blast (page 133): 1 to 3 sets of 20 with 5 min. of rest in between • Tuck jump (page 134): 1 to 3 sets of 20 with 1 min. of rest in between • Reactive step-up (page 133): 1 to 3 sets of 20 with 1 min. of rest in between • Lateral hurdle jump (page 134): 3 sets of 6 using 12 in. hurdles • Uphill running or downhill hiking (page 135): Take 24 steps as quickly as possible.

Agility Assessment (Hexagon Test)

For the agility assessment, use the hexagon test, which measures your ability to move quickly while maintaining balance. This is a key feature for getting yourself out of sticky situations. The test is easy to set up. You need a stopwatch and a hard floor or surface where you can outline the pattern of the hexagon (six-sided shape) with sidewalk chalk or athletic tape. Each side of the hexagon should be 24 inches (60.5 cm) long, and each angle should be 120 degrees. To begin the test, stand in the middle of the hexagon with both feet together and face the front line. When you start the stopwatch, jump across the line, and then return to the middle of the hexagon, jumping backward over the same line. Continuing to face forward with your feet together, jump over the line that forms the next side of the hexagon and then back again. Moving clockwise around the shape, continue this pattern for three full revolutions. Perform the test again, moving counterclockwise for three full revolutions. Be sure to mark your starting line to easily track each revolution. Your score is the time needed to complete three full revolutions in each direction.

Record your best score from two trials. Compare the clockwise and counterclockwise results to see if you have any movement imbalances between your left and right sides. Give yourself a score for each side. Note any movement imbalances with asterisks. A favorite leg or side of the body or a dominant eye are all asymmetries that can be identified with a different test. This test shows muscular dominance during dynamic motion.

Most technical skiing demands explosive power and an equal amount of finesse. Combining these moves adds necessary speed to your skiing. The best way to replicate the short-term power output found in a typical run is to focus on ballistic agility drills. Muscular-endurance exercises that are specific to skiing train your muscles to repeat an effort at high intensity over a period of time. These movements are necessary for skiing moguls or making quick, short turns on steep terrain. The following exercises build muscular endurance and aid repetitive movements like those you will experience on the snow. See table 3.8 for information on scoring and solution exercises related to ski fitness and agility.

TABLE 3.8 Agility Scoring and Solution Exercises Based on the Hexagon Test

Score	Solution exercises for agility
SCORE OF 3 Give yourself a 3 if the following apply: • You are male and can perform 3 reps in 11 sec. or less. • You are female and can perform 3 reps in 15 sec. or less.	To further improve or to maintain a score of 3, practice these exercises 2 times per week: • Jumping rope, page 136: 3 to 6 sets of 30 sec. • Agility ladder (crossover zigzag), page 136: 3 times through the ladder
SCORE OF 2 Give yourself a 2 if the following apply: • You are male and can perform 3 reps in 12 to 15 sec. • You are female and can perform 3 reps in 16 to 18 sec.	To improve a score of 2, practice these exercises 2 or 3 times per week: • Jumping rope, page 136: 3 to 6 sets of 30 sec. • Agility ladder (Ickey shuffle), page 136: 3 times through the ladder
SCORE OF 1 Give yourself a 1 if the following apply: • You are male and can perform at least 3 reps in 16 sec. or more • You are female and you can perform at least 3 reps in 19 sec. or more	To improve a score of 1, practice these exercises 3 or 4 times per week: • Jumping rope, page 136: 3 to 6 sets of 15 sec. • Agility ladder (in-in-out-out), page 135: 3 times through the ladder

By identifying and resolving your weak areas with these tests, you will shore up one of the two blocks of the pyramid's base, providing a foundation for developing your future skills. Endurance, strength, power, and agility will give you the motor and overdrive to conquer any challenge on the snow. The ski fitness tests in this chapter are designed to address the specific needs of the modern skier. The skiing landscape has not changed, but skiers' desires and expectations have. To jump off a cornice, to ski nonstop in powder for 1200 vertical feet, to navigate tight chutes, and to carve flawless turns are realistic goals for all skiers with the right fitness levels and ingrained technique. We live in a time where half the U.S. population is over 50 years old. Like never before, skiers are improving and maintaining their skills well into their sixties and seventies. By identifying strengths and weaknesses, it is possible to design a complete ski fitness program that will meet individual needs and prepare anyone at any age for the unique demands of the sport. Younger skiers can also benefit from these tests by identifying specific fitness needs early, thus providing long-term performance opportunities and continued body durability.

Mastering Essential Technique

Great skiers all have one thing in common—a foundation of solid essential movements. Once you have assessed your abilities in the areas of functional movement and performance and have located solutions for your particular weaknesses, you will be ready to thoroughly examine your skiing technique. Assessing your technique is more challenging and slightly more subjective than using indoor assessments. The ski slope has many more variables than a gym, and the conditions can change from day to day and hour to hour. The good news is that the body alignment and movement patterns described in these technique assessments are derived from fundamental mechanics of ski turns that can be measured via basic relationships between body parts, your body position and the skis, your body position and the slope, and among movement sequencing, speed, and intensity.

Concepts of Skiing Technique

Progressing from the basic stance to precise, carved turns is a process that builds from one core-skill competency to the next. If you skip a component, you may overlook a skill, causing affectations and abnormalities that compromise your technique. However, even if you are on the path already, it's never too late to revisit the fundamentals. In fact, skill revision is recommended.

The fundamental aspects of the neutral and engaged stances form the foundation for the rest of the technical components. No shortcut exists for mastering a good stance that provides a base of support for all skiing movements. The mechanics for turning depend on the reliability of your stance alignment and your confidence in your base. Once you learn how to turn properly, your progress takes a quantum leap, due to the increase in mileage and opportunities for exploring terrain.

Faults at this stage may take years to address. The ability to turn the legs while maintaining stability in the upper body during advanced turn technique, called dissociation or upper- and lower-body separation, is a major breakthrough. When trying to synchronize the movement of body parts while gliding on snow, this separation of the different halves of the body is a true accomplishment. Once turning with your legs has become a natural part of your skill set, you can easily learn to refine edge engagement and disengagement, pressure control, and recovery movements. As you reach the milestones of carving and managing variable snow conditions, you will experience new control and confidence that will open up a vast array of options for terrain and snow quality.

The basic goal of skiing technique is to control your descent down the mountain. Efficient technique is made up of the simple skills of edging, rotation, pressure, and balance. Your body movements affect these elements either positively or negatively depending on how precisely you apply the skills. Standing in an unbalanced position on your skis results in poor technique because you must compensate in order to apply the skills of rotation, edging, and pressure. When your stance is balanced, you can access and execute these skills more easily. These concepts are discussed in more detail as follows.

Balance

Balance is essential to all skills, playing a key role in how effectively you can apply your technique. Balance that is specific to skiing can be improved with exercises and mileage. Without balance, you cannot access other technical skills. Once you are comfortable balancing on moving skis, you can expand your skill base and can continue to challenge yourself as you move up the rungs of skiing proficiency.

Rotation

This skill involves body mechanics that result in rotational action of the skis. As you improve, you isolate rotation to your lower body, keeping your upper body stable and quiet. The most effective rotation also involves pressure and edging, resulting in the ability to steer the skis through turns.

Edging

Edging can be as simple as standing in an engaged stance with your skis embedded in the snow or as complex as applying a carved turn on an icy racecourse. In both cases, you gain an awareness of the holding power of an edged ski. As you develop the skill of edging, you learn how to balance on skis while moving through an arc, both with and without skidding. Efficient skiers use the ski as an edging tool and utilize the design characteristics for precise speed and directional control.

Pressure

As your skis interact with the terrain, you can directly affect how they react by making pressure adjustments. With too much pressure, skis can buck, skid out, or scoot away. However, the right blend of pressure movements allows skis to caress the snow, creating a smooth and even ride. Standing on one ski is a basic pressure move that can benefit performance tremendously at the beginning stages. As you balance and pressure the outside ski, it reacts and bends, providing stored energy that you can use to transition into the next turn. Honing and practicing the skill of applying pressure helps you effectively absorb transitions in terrain and naturally flex and extend your joints.

Blending these concepts makes technique precise and effective. As you develop your skills further, you will focus more on the whole than on the different parts of skiing. You will eventually experience a comingling of all the skills that provides a technical foundation on which you can build tactics. Of course, technique and tactics are closely tied, and you will move freely between the two areas as you move around the mountain. However, proper technique makes tactical choices easier and tactical applications more effective.

Assessments for Skiing Technique

These fundamental assessments cover the skills needed to perform the basic technical building blocks of good skiing. The screen identifies strengths or weaknesses in alignment, joint flexion, and hand positioning in the neutral and engaged stances. It also examines turning with your legs, focusing on alignment, flexion movements, edging movements, and turning impetus. It identifies details of parallel turns, including turn initiation, basic stance, edging movements, flexion movements, pole use, and continuous parallel skiing. Finally, it covers carved turns, highlighting alignment through angulation, edge-to-edge initiations, lateral flexion, and clean, arc-shaped tracks.

The biggest challenge I have faced in my career as an instructor is the subjective nature of quantifying skiing movements. However, my experience has led me to believe that if you understand the fundamental ski movements and develop an eye for recognizing good form, you can begin to assess yourself and make the changes that allow you to progress. With a little practice, you can judge movements and even score skiing maneuvers based on the sensations you experience, the appearance of your skiing track, the sound of your skis, and your results. These assessments provide a standard to shoot for as you progress. They also serve as a checklist that you can revisit after you have achieved higher levels. The integrity of this block, as in the blocks of functional movement and fitness previously mentioned, sets the parameters for what you can attain in the tactics section. When performing these assessments, your screen results will fall into level 3, level 2, or level 1.

- *Score of 3.* You nailed the task. You executed all the components listed in the assessment, held the alignment necessary for dynamic balance, and carried out multiple turn sequences, adjusting your mechanics as needed for pitch, speed, and direction.

- *Score of 2.* You displayed most of the components listed in the assessment, with a few exceptions. You were able to maintain proper alignment most of the time, but you showed weakness in basic skills as the terrain got steeper or the conditions got trickier.

- *Score of 1.* You were unable to maintain your alignment for more than a few minutes and wobbled as you executed turns. You couldn't own the movements or perform them as described in the assessment.

As you perform the assessments, use the summary sheet for assessing skiing technique (see figure 4.1) as a guide for the areas that need your attention. As you fill it in, you will begin to see patterns highlighting strengths and weaknesses. This summary sheet will become your road map for improving technique and accurately prescribing solutions for barriers to your progress.

FIGURE 4.1 **Ski Technique Assessment Summary Sheet**

Ski technique test	Score	Solution exercises	Assessment notes
Neutral stance	❏ 3 ❏ 2 ❏ 1		
Engaged stance	❏ 3 ❏ 2 ❏ 1		
Leg turn	❏ 3 ❏ 2 ❏ 1		
Parallel turn	❏ 3 ❏ 2 ❏ 1		
Carved turn	❏ 3 ❏ 2 ❏ 1		

From C. Fellows, 2011, *Total Skiing* (Champaign, IL: Human Kinetics).

Before moving on to assessments, note that these screens should not take a great deal of time. Use them to establish a baseline for further development. It is beneficial to perform these assessments as soon as you hit the snow so that the tasks set you up for good mechanics throughout the rest of the skiing day. You should understand what the end product looks like and what its components are. As you begin to identify the aspects of good skiing, the path to mastery becomes clear. Before beginning on-snow assessments, review these key points:

- When choosing terrain for these assessments, pick a groomed, empty slope with a consistent pitch. Icy conditions, bumpy slopes, and recent snowfall can affect the outcome of the task (see chapter 5 for all-mountain skiing tests).
- Check your equipment to ensure that your boots are buckled and that the top power strap is secure. Your skis should be waxed so they can glide freely. Their edges should be sharp to properly hold on firm snow (see chapter 6 for more information on equipment).
- If you are using a partner, ski past the observer to provide a front, side, and back view of your performance. If you are using a video, instruct the observer to keep your image as large as possible in the frame for easy viewing later.

Neutral Stance

A good skiing stance sets you up for efficient movements as you begin gliding downhill and turning your skis. In a good stance, the feet, knees, hips, shoulders, and hands are parallel in the lateral plane and the shin and spine are aligned in the fore-aft (frontal) plane. Keep your body supple, yet functionally alert, to allow for adjustments on the snow. See figure 4.2 for an example of a skier in the neutral stance.

Skiing posture is established in the early stages of development and determines your durability and performance level for the rest of your career. Most recreational skiers never address basic posture until they have a problem. Even then, they look to other events that may have caused their woes. In most situations, they never learned the proper stance. If they did, they rarely revisited it for continued success. Expert skiers, excited to get to their favorite cliff huck, take the first chair to the top and launch off a rock into a back bowl. This type of warm-up, referred to as stretching on impact, is not recommended. So much for a gradual warm-up and basic posture cues! Avid beginners are also guilty of missing key stance fundamentals when pursuing the next rung of the development ladder. Paying close attention to the details that make up functional skiing posture establishes a home base for all your movements and serves as a regular check point for optimal performance and long-term durability.

FIGURE 4.2   Skier in the neutral stance.

To perform the neutral-stance assessment, choose a gentle slope, such as a green-circle run for beginners. Push off and glide on flat skis, maintaining a solid, athletic stance throughout the entire straight run. If your skis begin to swim back and forth, feel square, or get caught on edges, you may want to check your boot alignment (see page 82 of chapter 6 for more information). Many skiers dismiss this test as too basic or a waste of time, but this is a huge mistake. This stance serves as both the starting point for all skiing and the framework on which all subsequent skills are built. See table 4.1 for information on scoring and technique drills related to the neutral stance.

TABLE 4.1   Scoring and Technique Drills for Neutral Stance

Scoring	Technique drills
SCORE OF 3 Give yourself a 3 if the following apply: • The angles of your shin and spine match • The center of your knee aligns over the midline of your boot • Your shoulder line, hip line, knee line, and foot line are parallel • Your joints flex evenly • Your hands and arms are held in a ready position	To maintain a score of 3, practice these drills: **On-snow drills** • Lateral-step drill, page 140 • Hop drill, page 141 **Dryland drills** • Lateral lunge, page 131 • Lateral box blast, page 133 • Tuck jump, page 134 • Reactive step-up, page 133

> *continued*

TABLE 4.1 *continued*

Scoring	Technique drills
SCORE OF 2 Give yourself a 2 if the following apply: • The angles of your shin and spine match after equipment adjustments • The center of your knee is slightly inside or outside the midline of your boot • Your shoulder line, hip line, knee line, and foot line are roughly parallel • Your hands are either slightly low or high	To improve a score of 2, practice these drills: **On-snow drills** • Shuffle drill, page 141 **Dryland drills** • Plank progression, page 105 • Single-leg squat progression, page 99 • Toe-touch progression, page 96
SCORE OF 1 Give yourself a 1 if the following apply: • Your shin and spine lines do not match • Your knee aligns grossly (3-6 degrees) inside or outside the midline of your boot • Your shoulder line, hip line, knee line, and foot line are not parallel • Your joint flexion is fragmented • Your hands are too low or too high	To improve a score of 1, practice these drills: **On-snow drills** • Marching drill, page 142 • Pole-spin drill, page 143 • High-low drill, page 142 **Dryland drills** • Indoor stork, page 100 • Circus pony, page 107 • Lateral lunge with arm reach, page 111 • Single-leg squat with opposite-hand reach, page 101 • Single-leg squat with assistance line, page 102

TEST Engaged Stance

Since you spend most of your time on your edges when Alpine skiing, an engaged stance and lateral alignment are very important. The amount of time during turns in which you stand on flat skis and assume an athletic, neutral stance is minimal; however, this baseline position supports all other movements. The alignment established in the neutral stance makes the engaged stance possible, allowing for lateral balance and effective edging and steering movements. Lateral balance, which differentiates the engaged stance from the neutral stance, is needed for all turning applications. Proper balance over tipped edges is achieved when all joints align in a lateral relationship, regardless of the skier's body type (see figure 4.3). As the pitch or speed increases, the angle between body parts becomes more acute.

FIGURE 4.3 **Every body type presents a unique silhouette in the engaged stance; however, the components of the stance are consistent for all skiers.**

When learning the engaged stance, you must also learn the basics of the traverse. In this position, you move forward across the hill in the engaged stance. The traverse position has been around since the beginning of organized skiing instruction. It is a common tactic for skirting steep and icy slopes and serves as the basis for good mechanics. Today it is an important milestone for correct posture on edged skis. In the traverse position, you tip both skis onto their edges, distributing your weight equally. As you move across the hill, keep your hips aligned with your feet for maximum balance and edge grip. Balancing against tipped skis takes practice, but once you ingrain the moves needed to glide on two edges, you will have mastered the fundamental ingredient for lateral alignment during carved turns. It's rewarding to look back and see two trenches etched in the snow.

Once you begin to balance on your edges, as opposed to flat skis, you progress from two-dimensional skiing to three-dimensional skiing, or moving in multiple planes at the same time. The basic premise for skiing is that, unlike sports in which speed is generated by internal muscular force, it relies on gravity for forward motion and speed. The success of experts is based on skiing a predetermined track as efficiently as possible so that the interplay between external (gravity) and internal (muscular) forces creates effective technique (CSIA 2000). Dynamic balance in the lateral plane requires standing on ski edges that are embedded in the snow

FIGURE 4.4   Dynamic skiing is possible with the foundation of good stance and alignment.

and traveling along a specific path. This takes some agility and muscular strength in order to stay upright. If your posture is twisted or misaligned, you will soon fall inside the turn and will find it difficult to balance on tipped skis. Dissociation of body parts is critical here; without it, your entire body will lean to one side, resulting in inefficient position on the skis. For correct execution of the engaged stance, you must counterbalance your upper body over your lower body as it tips (see figure 4.4). Lateral balance is another necessary milestone for effective skiing.

The Side Slip

The side slip is a variation of the basic engaged stance, which involves flattening the skis with control (figure 4.5). The side slip is a good way to regulate the speed of a pure, engaged traverse, to build feeling, and to gain control of the edges. It will direct you across and down the hill in equal increments. To perform the side slip, begin with an engaged stance and roll your knees downhill. This results in less edge bite and a smeared track in the snow. Practice moderating the amount of edge angle until you can slide sideways with ease, controlling the lateral and forward drift

The side slip serves not only as a speed moderator but also as a gradual direction-change move and an intermediate-checking move that you can

FIGURE 4.5   Side slip.

use before reestablishing your next line. Use of the side slip will help you gradually ease into the next turn as your speed slows and you scout out your next line or passage. Side slips are often used to redirect your skis to accurately enter your next descent line. A few extra seconds to look at your entry point is never a bad thing!

The framework established in the engaged stance serves as a home base for the edging movements needed for precision turns. If you make mistakes here, rest assured that those glitches will derail your attempts to ski without affectations. Don't skimp on these fundamental movements!

To perform the engaged-stance assessment, stand on a gentle slope with your skis across the fall line, digging your edges in to hold yourself in place. Your uphill tip should be slightly ahead of your downhill tip. This offset relationship between ski tips is the baseline for the lateral alignment of your major joints and hands. This line should match four parallel lines going through your knees, hips, shoulders, and hands, which can be seen as you stand on the slope and place a pole across both knees (see figure 4.6).

See table 4.2 for information on scoring and technique drills related to the engaged stance.

FIGURE 4.6 Basic alignment is the foundation for optimal performance.

TABLE 4.2 Scoring and Technique Drills for the Engaged Stance

Scoring	Technique drills
SCORE OF 3 Give yourself a 3 if the following apply: • The lines of your shoulders, hips, knees, and feet are parallel • Your joints flex evenly • Your hands and arms are in ready position • Your skis leave two clean edge tracks in the snow • Your ski tracks are etched and curved, leading back uphill	To maintain a score of 3, practice these drills: **On-snow drills** • Engaged stance at higher speeds, page 144 • Traverse drill on steeper terrain, page 144 • Traverse drill, page 145 **Dryland drills** • Plank progression, page 105 • Lateral lunge, page 131 • Indoor stork, page 100 • Stability-ball twist, page 108
SCORE OF 2 Give yourself a 2 if the following apply: • Your shoulder line, hip line, knee line, and foot line are roughly parallel • Your hands are slightly low or slightly high • Your skis sometimes leave two clean tracks in the snow • Your ski tracks trend uphill more often than downhill	To improve a score of 2, practice these drills: **On-snow drills** • Traverse and reverse traverse drill, page 145 • Traverse drill on steeper terrain, page 144 **Dryland drills** • Hip crossover, page 107 • Stability-ball twist, page 108 • Backward lunge with arm raise, page 109 • Plank progression, page 105
SCORE OF 1 Give yourself a 1 if the following apply: • Your shoulder line, hip line, knee line, and foot line are not parallel • Your knee moves in and out of alignment • Your hands move in and out of position, or are placed too low or too high • Your ski track is washed out or intermittent • Your ski track is straight or veers downhill	To improve a score of 1, practice these drills: **On-snow drills** • Engaged stance with low-edge angle, page 146 • Engaged stance on one ski, page 146 **Dryland drills** • Indoor stork, page 100 • Circus pony, page 107 • Knee-and-ankle grab, page 101

Leg Turn

Releasing your edges takes a leap of faith, but it is the easiest way to start a turn. It flattens the skis and decreases resistance against the edges. Once you have initiated the turn, a blend of turning the legs and tipping the skis to a higher edge leads you into a basic parallel turn (see the following section for more information). The most efficient way to turn your skis is to stabilize your core and turn with your feet and legs. Of course, applying leg turns correctly depends on many weather and terrain variables that dictate the turn's amount, speed, intensity, and rhythm.

Turning with the legs also facilitates balance on the outside ski because it allows the upper body to counterbalance over the turning skis. As you turn your legs, angle your torso over your outside ski to maintain balance. Initiating a turn with the upper body is not as effective as turning with the legs. The wedge position is an intermediate step before the parallel turn that lets you turn your legs at slower speeds, using a wider base of support. This position shares mechanics with the parallel turn, but differs in terms of base of support and dynamics produced by speed. (See figures 4.7 and figure 4.8 to compare the two techniques.) At slower speeds, you can practice proper movements in a comfortable environment and can progress at your own rate. Once you are comfortable, increase your speed. This makes it easier to balance on the outside ski, which is narrower but more effective. The outside ski will become the base of support at higher speeds.

Lack of torso mobility causes many skiers, both beginners and experts, to struggle with leg-turning movements. Any leg turn requires maintaining core stability while freeing up the hip flexors to work with the glutes, hamstrings, and quads to rotate the femurs. Beginners commonly rotate the entire body, resulting in poor speed control due to lack of edging. Skiers skilled in proper leg-turning movements have learned to dissociate the legs from the torso. When skiing down the fall line, if you're using correct technique, the zipper of your jacket faces downhill as your legs turn freely and independently.

Separating the two halves of your body during dynamic motion is difficult in any sport. In skiing, adjusting upper-body balance while turning the lower body may feel strange or even impossible. However, once you get used to it, dissociation becomes as natural as the countermovements in the gait of your walk. By focusing on the ball-and-socket joint in your hip, you will learn what it feels like to keep your upper body and your lower body active. Adduction and abduction of the inner- and outer-leg muscles also facilitate leg turning.

FIGURE 4.7   The wedge position.

As you sit reading this page, stick your legs out and rotate them both completely to the left and then completely to the right. This movement illustrates basic leg turning. Remember the simplicity of this act when you are out on the slopes. Don't overcomplicate or overanalyze this fundamental movement.

To perform the leg-turning assessment, choose a groomed pitch that is flat or moderately steep and is wide enough for medium-sized leg rotations. Face down the slope, then stabilize your torso and tighten your glutes and abs. Next, rotate your femurs as you move progressively across the slope. If your rotation is too fast, your skis will skid out of control and you will lose the natural sequence of the turn. If your movements are too slow, your skis will lag and move away from you, causing you to do the splits. Align yourself over the outside ski by increasing the pressure. Next, turn your foot, ankle, and leg through a progressive arc. Gradually shift your weight to the other ski, which is now on the outside, and repeat the sequence. See table 4.3 for information on scoring and technique drills related to leg turning.

TABLE 4.3   Scoring and Technique Drills for Leg Turning

Scoring	Technique drills
SCORE OF 3 Give yourself a 3 if the following apply: • A basic stance is present • Your legs progressively initiate the turn independent of the torso • Your joints flex evenly and in a timely manner • Your upper- and lower-body alignment facilitates balance and control over the outside ski • Your hands and arms are in a ready position; the line bisecting the hands is parallel with the angle of the traversing slope	To maintain a score of 3, practice these drills: **On-snow drills** • Leg turn on one ski, page 147 • Clock-face drill, page 148 **Dryland drills** • Hip crossover, page 107 • Drop lunge, page 111 • Seated rotation, page 108
SCORE OF 2 Give yourself a 2 if the following apply: • A basic stance is present • Your legs initiate the turn most of the time; your upper body rotates at the end of the turn • Joint flexion is present but is sometimes fragmented • Your hands are slightly low or high, but the line bisecting the hands is still parallel to the slope angle when moving across the hill	To improve a score of 2, practice these drills: **On-snow drills** • Leg turn with feet on bindings, page 148 • Hands-on-hips, page 149 **Dryland drills** • Knee-and-ankle grab, page 101 • Hip crossover, page 107 • Stability-ball twist, page 108 • Circus pony, page 107
SCORE OF 1 Give yourself a 1 if the following apply: • You notice poor basic stance • The turn is initiated by your pelvis or upper body, not your legs • Your joint flexion is uneven or nonexistent • Poor alignment results in loss of control of the outside ski and poor speed control • Your hands are too low or too high, not parallel with the slope angle	To improve a score of 1, practice these drills: **On-snow drills** • Wedge leg turn, page 149 • Cross-hill leg turns, page 150 **Dryland drills** • Plank progression, page 105 • Hip stretch with resistance band, page 110 • Resistance-band rotation, page 110

Parallel Turn

The parallel turn in skiing is the equivalent of the basic swing in golf, groundstrokes in tennis, or the proper gait for running. It provides the fundamental movements on which good skiing mechanics are built. Combined with proper stance, balancing in a traverse, and turning with your legs, the parallel turn takes you into the dynamic world of balance in motion.

The parallel turn consolidates basic positioning, leg turning, and dynamic balance into a choreographed turn sequence. Turning with your legs helps you transfer energy from your body to the skis and helps you control and generate speed and direction. Mastering the parallel turn lets you explore a variety of terrain and conditions, which exponentially builds both your all-mountain skill set and your confidence. It consists of a sequence of movement patterns that begin with a neutral stance, progressively flow into the initiation, blend into the shaping phase of the turn, conclude with the end of the turn, and then return to a neutral stance (see figure 4.8).

A symphony of directional movements along the length of the ski keep the kinetic chain aligned and ready for continuous turning. As you ski, changes in the snow and the pitch can knock you off balance, compromising your ability to access the functional movements needed to turn your legs, flex, extend, and counter with your upper body. Fore and aft movements along the length of the ski are driven by your glutes and hamstrings as you extend your legs from a flexed position, staying centered over the ski. Staying back in a flexed position prevents you from recentering and beginning the next turn with athletic movements. The synergy of turning and flexing the legs to guide the skis through an arc is the true cornerstone of Alpine skiing. Tactics, or adapting the blend of skills in the parallel turn to meet challenges on the snow, is the next step in your development.

To perform the basic parallel-turn assessment, choose a moderate, groomed pitch that is wide enough to allow for progressive turning. Perform at a speed that promotes parallel turns. If you move too slow, you will have to stem the ski to begin the turn; if you move too fast, you will lose all progressive movement. Time your pole action with the end and beginning of each turn. Maintain a stable core and balance over the outside ski for precise interaction between ski and snow. See table 4.4 for information on scoring and technique drills related to the parallel turn.

FIGURE 4.8 Like a basic golf swing, tennis stroke, running stride, or peddle stroke, the parallel turn exemplifies fundamental mechanics of a skiing turn.

a

b

c

d

TABLE 4.4   Scoring and Technique Drills for the Basic Parallel Turn

Scoring	Technique drills
SCORE OF 3 Give yourself a 3 if the following apply: • A basic stance is present • Both legs move simultaneously to initiate the parallel turn • Joint flexion and extension movements are progressive and rhythmic, matching the timing and duration of the turn • Both skis flatten between turns and balance is maintained on parallel edges throughout the rest of the turn • Pole plants complement the flattening of the skis and initiation of the next turn	To maintain a score of 3, practice these drills: **On-snow drills** • Stepping through the turn, page 151 • Pole plant and release, page 152 **Dryland drills** • Single-leg balance (with closed eyes), page 100 • Leg drops, page 103 • Forward plank with alternating arm lift, page 105 • Push-up on stability ball, page 124
SCORE OF 2 Give yourself a 2 if the following apply: • A basic stance is present • Both legs move simultaneously to initiate the parallel turn • Joint-flexion movements are present • Your skis flatten between turns and gradually progress to parallel edging • Pole plants are sometimes present and match the flattening of the skis	To improve a score of 2, practice these drills: **On-snow drills** • One-leg pivot, page 152 • Two skis to one ski, page 153 **Dryland drills** • Indoor stork, page 100 • Plank progression (side plank), page 105 • Backward lunge with arm raise, page 109 • Lateral lunge on stability ball, page 110
SCORE OF 1 Give yourself a 1 if the following apply: • You notice poor basic stance • Your legs move sequentially to initiate the turn, beginning with the outside leg • Joint flexion is fragmented or absent • Your skis remain flat throughout the entire turn or your edges are intermittently engaged or flattened • Pole plant is not visible or is present on the opposite side	To improve a score of 1, practice these drills: **On-snow drills** • Simultaneous edge change, page 154 • Hand on hip and hand in the air, page 156 • Parallel-turn garland, page 155 **Dryland drills** • Seated rotation, page 108 • Plank progression, page 105 • Knee-and-ankle grab, page 101 • Single-leg squat with medicine ball, page 99

TEST Carved Turn

Carving the skis through a clean arc is one of the milestones of expert skiing. Imagine leaving two parallel tracks from slicing your edged skis into the snow. When you balance on top of your skis with the edges tipped up, you feel as though you are riding an arcing track that generates speed and precise directional change. The art of carving becomes possible when you become comfortable immediately moving from one set of tipped-up edges to the other. This fast edge exchange requires you to balance on the outside ski as you move through an arc. This is difficult, but if you have refined the early skills of stance, traversing, leg turning, and parallel turning, you will be prepared to take on this next challenge.

Stability in carved turns comes from creating a wide base of support (assuming a wider stance) and balancing the weight over the center of the outside ski. Alignment over the outside ski helps the ankle, knee, hip, and spine work together to apply maximal force at the right moment in the turn, generating velocity as the arc is carved. Creating lateral angles with your knees, hips, and spine facilitates edge hold by permitting an efficient anatomical solution for precise interaction between ski and snow. If your alignment is compromised, you cannot handle the higher speeds and forces created by precision turning.

The carved turn requires a strong connection between the ski edge and the snow. If your ski is washing out or chattering through the arc, you may be overpivoting. This makes it difficult to carve a clean turn. After you have practiced the basic movements, move on to a carved turn that is more precise. Experimenting with higher and lower edge angles will lead you to adjust the shape of your turns by tipping higher or flattening the skis.

The dynamic balance in a carved turn is the result of committing to early edging and applying pressure to the outside ski. Shifting your weight to a ski that is ready to take you through a clean and precise arc is like a highwire balancing act in the snow. Once you are comfortable carving at higher speeds, you will begin to generate more g-force. The ride will start to feel magical as the seamless interplay between body, equipment, and snow elicits feelings of excitement and exhilaration and your edges scribe pencil-line trenches in the snow. See figure 4.9 for an example of the carved turn.

To perform the basic carved-turn assessment, start on a cat track or an easy green run to get accustomed to the arcing action of the skis. Balance over both skis and tip your edges up. Once you have simultaneously engaged both skis and gained some speed, fight the urge to twist or pivot. Instead, let the design characteristics of the ski take you through the predetermined arc. Trusting that the ski will turn and staying balanced on the edges without twisting the legs are the crucial concepts of this turn. See table 4.5 for information on scoring and technique drills related to the carved turn.

FIGURE 4.9 Tipping the ski to tighten the carved turn.

TABLE 4.5 Scoring and Technique Drills for the Basic Carved Turn

Scoring	Technique drills
SCORE OF 3 Give yourself a 3 if the following apply: • Basic mechanics of parallel turns are present • Faster speeds that facilitate carving action with both edges are consistently present • Balanced, angulated position over tipped-up edges is supple, but stable • Minimized skidding action of the skis, leaving a narrow swath in the snow • Precision edging leaves a precise track in the snow • Pole action is timed with the edge release	To maintain a score of 3, practice these drills: **On-snow drills** • Short-turn pole touch, page 157 • Carved turn with hands on knees, page 158 **Dryland drills** • Straight-arm lateral lunge with dumbbells, page 109 • Single-leg squat progression, page 99 • Miniband walking routine, page 95
SCORE OF 2 Give yourself a 2 if the following apply: • Basic mechanics of parallel turns are present • Moderate speed facilitates a slight carving action from both skis • A balanced and slightly-angulated position is often seen • Skis leave a swath in the snow that is sometimes feathered, not etched, at the initiation of the turn • Pole action is present most of the time	To improve a score of 2, practice these drills: **On-snow drills** • Long leg, short leg, page 158 • Advanced railroad track, page 159 **Dryland drills** • Backward lunge with arm raise, page 109 • Straight-arm lateral lunge with dumbbells, page 109 • Hip crossover (on stability ball), page 107 • In-in-out-out agility ladder, page 135
SCORE OF 1 Give yourself a 1 if the following apply: • Basic mechanics of parallel turns are not present • Slower speed inhibits carving action of the skis • Total body position is inclined toward the hill, sometimes resulting in a loss of balance and grip of the outside ski • Skis skid through parallel turns, leaving a wide swath in the snow • Pole action interrupts the flow down the hill	To improve a score of 1, practice these drills: **On-snow drills** • Traverse edge change, page 160 • Outside pole drag, page 161 • Tuck turn, page 162 **Dryland drills** • Lateral hurdle jumps, page 134 • Ickey shuffle agility ladder, page 136 • Seated rotation, page 108 • Drop lunge, page 111 • Single-leg squat with medicine ball, page 99 • Tuck jump, page 134

Technique is the framework that adds integrity and reliability to your skiing and gives you the movements you need to efficiently ski with control and confidence. From the beginning, you will master fundamental movements on which more complex movements can be added for continued improvement. This process is never a steady climb of continuous progress; expect setbacks and frustration. However, with perseverance, you will improve and make unexpected breakthroughs.

Adjusting Tactics for All-Mountain Skiing

Imagine finding a toolbox of tactics that will help you assess situations and apply a game plan to any obstacle on the mountain. All-mountain skiing requires both good technique and the ability to access diverse strategies for meeting the challenges of varied landscape. These tactics are not limited to finding the fastest line down a slope; they also involve perceiving the situation mentally and visually, adjusting the intensity and shape of turns, managing speed, and making line choices. All this culminates in the ability to intuitively adapt to whatever the environment has to offer.

Ski Tactics and Assessments

The core competencies built in this chapter are based on earlier work in functional movement, fitness, and technique. The chasm between these essentials and the competencies of skiing tactics is not as wide as it may initially seem. The first step is to look beyond your personal space bubble. You must shift your mindset from just moving your body to the challenges that are coming toward you, quickly setting a plan in motion for realistically solving the task. Looking at the situation is different than seeing both the situation and the solution. Reading terrain is the first concept in tactics. Turn shape comes next, providing the options for directional control needed for tight, wide, slow, and fast turns. Speed management follows, which involves the descent skills that provide a three-phase dial for speed control. These phases help you control your intensity, speed, and energy down the slope. Although they all come from the same tactical family, each level of ability has different skill competencies. Finally, line choice comes into play, since it relates to your level of commitment and skill. As you progress, your creativity and inspiration will grow, opening up new challenges and possibilities not yet seen.

The starting point for developing a tactical toolbox is identifying strengths and weaknesses in your skill set. The assessments for reading the terrain, applying turn shapes, managing speed, and choosing your line provide the glue that bonds the other pyramid blocks together. Surveying the fundamentals needed to negotiate various terrain and conditions and reading the tactical abilities described for each creates a total picture of your skiing type.

Although scoring for tactics is even more subjective than for techniques, some key points will help you quantify each score. Certain abilities or faults will increase or lower your score. For example, if you cannot control your speed or lose control quickly, you will lose points in speed management. If you can only perform one type of turn, you will score lower in turn shape. Interpret the scores loosely based on the mountain you are skiing and the difficulty of the conditions on that day. The assessments merely serve as a guide to help you identify your tactical baseline. Use them as a starting point for future development. If you never get off the beaten track, you limit yourself to one stage of the skiing experience. When assessing your tactical ability, you will fall in one of three scoring categories:

- *Score of 3.* You have a wide range of experiences off groomed snow already. You can apply appropriate technique to situations as they arise.
- *Score of 2.* You have some experience off groomed terrain, but you don't necessarily own the tactics needed for upper-level terrain challenges.
- *Score of 1.* You are beginning to venture out into tougher conditions and terrain. You are also developing basic knowledge of how to adapt your technique to all-terrain skiing.

Reading the Terrain

Groomed and even slopes with a single fall line are the basic playing field in the sport of skiing. If you add in the challenges inherent in off the groomed terrain, you enter the realm of three-dimensional skiing. Ungroomed runs can be slightly uneven with a smattering of small moguls and pitch changes or they can be gauntlets of tight bumps, steep rollovers, narrow passages, double fall lines, and variable conditions. Reading terrain takes practice. A good place to start is by scanning the complete slope from two perspectives:

1. *Soft focus.* Look at the total parameters of the slope, including the length, width, pitch, and overall condition. These observations will give you a sense of which overall game plan might work best.
2. *Hard focus.* Look for details, such as spacing between obstacles like bumps, rocks, trees, ridges, and spines. The detailed view provides hints about specific tactics.

If you cannot identify the features of a run that will hurt or help you, your chances of success are less than average. Planning your moves in various conditions and terrain will help your run. Charging into a piece of terrain without noting subtleties hidden in the natural underworld is dangerous and cocky. Taking the time to scope out your descent provides a road map of the tactics needed for a successful run, resulting in a magnificent skiing experience.

Skiers who don't visualize their runs often start off on the wrong foot, jumping into a run without a second thought. They ski in reaction mode until the speed, terrain, or conditions overwhelm them and they fall or are forced to stop. Skiers who visualize know what they want to do and how to accomplish it. Good visual skills differ from good eyesight. They require the ability to scan the terrain before you, observe it, and process valuable cues to create a plan of attack.

Take a few seconds to scan your run and visualize how you will attack it. Begin your first turns with controlled excitement, and then establish a rhythm you can sustain for the complete run. Finally, finish with strength and balance. As you stand at the top of your chosen run, visualize with detail how a successful run will feel, sound, look, and even smell. This practice run in your mind's eye prepares you for the real thing.

Applying Turn Shape

One of the first tactical choices after reading the terrain and the contours of the slope is the type, sequence, and shape of turn you will make for a successful and controlled run. Each mountain situation presents its own array of terrain configurations that must be approached like moves in a chess game. Like players with only one game strategy, beginning skiers always turn with the same intensity, speed, shape, and line. Although they feel at home in this arena, it limits their on-mountain experience. As you progress in skill, begin to venture outside the parameters of the basic turn to apply multiple shapes, sizes, speeds, and lines while maintaining proper mechanics. Experienced skiers have a solid command of the various turns. They can utilize their honed skills to create a unique signature on the mountain and to interpret good tactics.

S-Shaped Turns

Varied terrain requires active turning with both legs that is rhythmic and consistent. The most efficient way to accomplish this is by practicing a turn shape that can be repeated, built on, and adapted to a pitch. To seamlessly enter and exit each turn, feather the top of the turn and progressively tip your edges into the snow, beginning a carve. Too much edge will make you pick up speed like a kid on a garbage bag. If you have too much skid, you will never achieve rhythm. The right blend of edge and skid results in a round, S-shaped turn that maintains rhythm and manages speed (see figure 5.1).

FIGURE 5.1 S-shaped turn.

J- and Z-Shaped Turns

The J-shaped turn is best described as the path surfers take as they shoot down the face of the wave, fishhook, and pivot the board at the bottom of the wave. This turn looks like the letter *J*. The fall line is straight and the finish hooks sharply (see figure 5.2). If you apply this tactic in a carve, you will experience a buildup of force at the end of the turn that makes balancing over the outside ski difficult. A steered turn that blends carving and pivoting mutes the forces and facilitates balance in the transition. This ski tactic is important because it elongates the fall line, generating the speed and power needed in variable conditions on steeps. The finish of the J-shaped turn quickly redirects the energy, which is critical for linking the turns together. It is used to navigate tight or narrow lines through obstacles, to lighten the load over dips or bumps, to increase speed in deeper snow, and to avoid bogging out due to twisting the skis across the hill too soon.

The Z-shaped turn, as shown in figure 5.3, is for quickly pivoting across the slope, usually on steep or narrow trails. This turn is overused by beginners, who often overcorrect, twisting the legs or the upper body to move the skis around quickly. On the other hand, if the terrain requires a quick pivot, the Z-shaped turn is a useful tool.

FIGURE 5.2   J-shaped turn.

FIGURE 5.3   Z-shaped turn.

C-Shaped Turns

The C-shaped turn is a fundamental, all-mountain shape that enlists your best leg-steering skills as you guide the skis from the beginning to the end of the turn, controlling speed and direction through a continuous, round contour. Focus on rounding the turn into the shape of the letter *C* (see figure 5.4 for an example of a C-shaped turn). Practicing this turn shape enhances precision and control and establishes a good foundation for turning tactics. You can easily modify it for several other shapes as your skill level increases.

FIGURE 5.4   C-shaped turn.

Each turning shape has its own characteristics that produce different results on the mountain. In the beginning stages, you will feel more comfortable with minimal environmental variables and simple turns that produce a consistent and reliable feeling. As you progress, a wider range of turns will unlock the path to freedom on the mountain.

Speed Management

You must be able to control three speed phases before mastering all-mountain tactics. You can't perform at any skiing level unless you are in motion. The speed of that motion will determine your level of expertise. Mastering the following three phases establishes the basis for your tactics package.

Managing speed is like using gears in a car. The first gear is for starting and is used for slow movement. When driving, you shift to low gear to add power, and then progress through the higher gears to increase speed and momentum. Some skiers get stuck at this gear, or phase 1, slowly hunting and pecking through varied terrain. If you want to reach peak performance, use this speed sparingly. Signs that you are using this level of speed too often are lowering your head and focusing somewhere 3 feet (1 m) in front of you. This is not a good way to look for opportunities!

Phase 2 is more proactive, since you spend more time anticipating terrain and preparing for your next series of turns. This approach builds confidence and creates rhythm as you link several turns in succession. This phase is like the middle gears of a car. You cruise along without reaching top speed. However, phase 2 can become a ceiling if you never push into your highest zone of speed and energy. In phase 3, you begin to visualize lanes down a steep face with good snow for easy turning, terrain features that facilitate a good rhythm, and continuous turning opportunities. Skiers in phase 3 can bounce from one turn to the next with energy and precision.

The true sign that you have mastered speed management is the ability to move through all speeds on demand. Having three speeds that you can access at will opens up many terrain options and gives you confidence on the hardest runs. The following sections take a closer look at each of the three phases.

Phase 3

Expert run skiers rarely put on the brakes to check their speed, but they also don't usually floor the gas from the top of the run to the bottom. They use a combination of intensities that can be regulated to maintain maximum momentum in all sections of the run. You can do the same by using a combination of each of the speed phases.

Phase 3 is your personal speed limit. Listen to your body to determine your top end and play with 70 to 90 percent of that speed. Spending more time in that higher realm builds poise and composure, resulting in movements that are proactive rather than reactive. Keeping your motor revving for longer durations is the best way to gain self-confidence at your top speed. See figure 5.5 for an example of a skier moving in phase 3.

FIGURE 5.5 Skiing at your top speed requires physical and mental commitment to the run.

Phase 2

Skiing with moderate speed increases your energy but keeps things in control. To progress into moderate speeds on steeps, try to quickly ski a slow line. Skiing a nonthreatening pitch faster than you normally would helps you build confidence when terrain and obstacles crop up quickly. Use this cruising phase to meet moderate terrain with a balanced, heads-up attitude and a controlled rate of speed. Soon you will start looking for steeper terrain, beginning the process again.

Phase 2 is your cruising gear for gradually building momentum and progressively turning (see figure 5.6). You will move at 50 to 70 percent of your maximum speed. This gives you time to scope out the best line while keeping your wheels rolling along.

FIGURE 5.6   Your cruising gear should flow like water.

Phase 1

Slowly skiing a fast line is the basic task of speed control for intermediates. This practice encourages slower precision movements on progressively steeper terrain. Whether the line is fast due to pitch, width of slope, firmness of snow, or tightly arranged obstacles, you can ski it at a pace that is right for you. A low first phase allows you to grind it out as you piece one turn into another to navigate through the perceived challenge. These controlled turns will soon be replaced by flowing, connected ones as your confidence builds and your vision stretches down the hill.

Phase 1 is your "low and slow" speed (see figure 5.7). Use it to shut down

FIGURE 5.7   Skiing at low gear makes you feel powerful and in control.

your thrusters to avoid obstacles and prepare for challenging terrain. Ski at 10 to 40 percent of your maximum speed for a rate that can be used either as a breaking tool or a caution mode for anticipating upcoming challenges.

Playing with the speed continuum is closely tied to practicing turn shape in that they both depend on what you do with the skis. Moving the skis around quickly with a heavy edge set bleeds your speed, quickly scattering those high-speed demons just as keeping the skis in the fall line increases your speed and adrenaline levels. Practicing a wide spectrum of speed options on steep slopes provides needed experience in and out of your comfort zone. We all have a speed that works for us and a range that helps us feel in control.

Line Choice

Lines that match intensity and tempo to the pitch of the slope will greatly determine your success. The more direct the line down the slope is, the more speed and energy it will create. Lines that meander or round provide a slower descent and mute the energy coming back from the terrain. The four most common choices down a bump run are the zipper, trough, shoulder, and basic lines. They all require a short to medium radius turn that is fundamentally sound. Using a big turn in the bumps is an advanced tactic that you can develop with short and medium turn practice. These common bump lines are often blended together in a single run where knowledge and experience in all four tactics becomes essential.

Knowing where, when, how fast, and how much to turn in the chosen line is the foundation for good tactics. Aggressive lines involve minimal turning and extreme absorption with the ankles, knees, and hips. Forgiving lines follow a rounder path at a slower speed that lets you anticipate the next turn and maintain balance. As your skill progresses, choose straighter and faster lines to ramp up the excitement. All great skiers have progressed from using basic lines that control their descent to steeper, straighter lines that increase dynamics.

Whether the terrain is a big, steep face, a ribbon of snow through a gully, or a channel in the bumps, you must make clear judgments based on your current skill set and the objective and subjective hazards. When making your choice, ask which line is right for you. The only way to truly assess which choice is best is to understand what you are getting into. Objective hazards include snow inconsistency, rocks, stumps, avalanches, runnels, sloughs, and crevasses. They exist whether or not you are there. Subjective hazards are those you personally bring to the situation, including insufficient levels of skill or fitness, mismatched equipment, bad mental approach, or poor judgment. When choosing lines, take all these variables into account and make the best decision you can.

Applying Tactics to Specific Terrain

Once you're in the right frame of mind, you can master strategies for your chosen terrain and conditions. Envisioning an outcome before it happens is the advantage that makes fair skiers good and good skiers great. Here are some common conditions and terrain that you will encounter on the snow.

Steeps

Since steep terrain, as shown in figure 5.8, has an inherent intimidation factor, driving most skiers to easier slopes, the best snow often goes untouched. Steep terrain has a way of forcing you to live in the moment, as losing focus can result in unfavorable consequences. Without confidence on steeps, you are caught in a state of uncertainty, bringing your performance level down by at least half. With a proactive attitude, your technique stays intact and you control your movements in a succession of crisp turns down the intended line.

FIGURE 5.8 Mental focus is developed by skiing with a purpose on steep terrain.

Lines for Steeps

The most common lines in steeps are face, finger, and wind-lip lines.

Face Line

Face lines are uniquely located on open, unobstructed slopes. They have a sustained and consistent pitch. You can gain speed quickly on the face because the pull of gravity is so great. Your result will vary depending on your desired outcome, fitness level, skill level, and equipment setup. The direct, open face lines performed by pros are fast, with straighter, open turns that can reach 50 to 70 mph (80-110 kmph). A medium-radius face line keeps turns within a boundary to protect against objective hazards like crevasses, cliff bands, or rocks. Short-turn face lines keep speed low and controlled during the descent.

Finger Line

Off-piste slopes can be divided into parallel lanes by obstacles, such as vertical rock bands, tree islands, or fluted ridges. They look like the fingers of a hand. Skiing these lines is like going through a chute or gully, since you stay within the parameters set by the fingers.

Wind-Lip Line

The wind-lip lines created by crosswinds load steep slopes with snow. The deposits create vertical lines called wind ridges. They can also be formed by snow that is carried from the windward side of a slope to the leeward side.

Good tactics for steeps come from precise execution of the parallel turn, the ability to read terrain, turn-shape application, and trajectory control down the fall line. Speed management builds your tolerance for high energy coming from the ski, develops poise, and helps you make quick decisions when adrenaline is surging through your body. The following section lists qualities for each level when skiing steeps.

Score of 3 for Steeps

With this score, you have a solid foundation of speed management, line choice, and effective turn shape that lets you move around the mountain with confidence and vision. You are ready to train in a professional or competitive venue. Choices include ski racing, free-ride competitions, or professional instructor certification. Retesting is recommended every four to six weeks.

Score of 2 for Steeps

You must learn to ski proactively, with a plan in mind. Your skiing skills are solid enough to let you focus more on where you are going and what turn you will make rather than how you are moving your body. Reading simple changes in terrain, such as a run with a series of rolls or a slope that changes from groomed to powder, can be great practice for the tactical skills needed on steeps. Successfully anticipating changes in terrain enhances the flow of your descent on sustained, steep slopes. You will also build confidence for challenging terrain.

Score of 1 for Steeps

You may feel a bit frazzled due to the emotional intensity and sheer, precipitous nature of the slope. Your objective at this level is gaining the confidence, flow, and natural rhythm that come from a good foundation of skills in turn shaping and speed management. You must learn to choose a turn shape that matches your desired outcome. Shaping a turn that is gradual and complete is your first hurdle. Once you have mastered complete J- and C-shaped turns, you can practice skiing fast in a slow line, which results in seamless transitions on steeper, faster slopes.

At this level, you also need to visualize runs and then apply appropriate turn shapes for challenging sections. Competitive racers and free-skiers memorize all the turn combinations, terrain changes, tricky sections, and blind rollovers of particular runs.

See table 5.1 for information on scoring and tactics drills for steeps.

TABLE 5.1   Scoring and Tactics Drills for Steeps

Scoring	Related tactics drills
SCORE OF 3 Give yourself a 3 if the following apply: • Strong carving mechanics are present at faster speeds with coordinated suspension movements, edging movements, and pole plants. • You can change the shape and tempo of the turn at will by tightening or lengthening its arc. These movements result in immediate speed and directional control on steeps. • You can switch tactics as needed by reading terrain and adapting to cues. • You can improvise as terrain and conditions change. • You can ski at 75 to 90 percent of your top speed on steeps.	• Redirecting focus, page 164 • Creating symmetrical patterns in turns, page 165 • Pushing the envelope of speed and tempo, page 171
SCORE OF 2 Give yourself a 2 if the following apply: • Consistent parallel mechanics with some carving are present at faster speeds. Legs are used to absorb terrain and pole plant is present. • You can reduce or increase speed by changing rhythm, amount of skidding, and intensity of leg turning. • You know when and where to turn for a smooth, continuous ride in the steeps. • You ski proactively, maintaining rhythm down a moderately steep pitch and skiing directly in the fall line. • You manage turn shape for speed control. • You visualize and verbalize positive affirmations with confidence. • You can ski a fast line slowly and a slow line quickly.	• Unlocking freeze frame, page 164 • Maintaining a strong finishing turn, page 166 • Checking your speed, page 171 • Regulating pressure and edge on turns, page 166
SCORE OF 1 Give yourself a 1 if the following apply: • Basic parallel-turn mechanics are present at faster speeds. • You can maintain consistent speed and rhythm on moderate to slightly steep terrain. • You react to changes in terrain and conditions but stop to look at the line. • You understand basic tactics for steeps but are unsure how to best apply them at the intermediate and advanced levels. • You can only turn in J- or Z- shapes, resulting in a stop-start rhythm. • You can ski a fast line slowly.	• Having a plan B, page 165 • Ingraining the C-curve, page 167 • Getting into gear, page 171 • Using pole plants to maintain your line, page 173 • Anticipating terrain changes, page 164 • Maintaining three points of contact, page 171

Bumps

The rhythm and symmetry of a perfect bump line can only be found when you mingle with nature to create a distinctive, primal sensation. Your stomach quickly rises and falls, creating the same funny feeling as when you go over a bump in the car. Let go and enjoy the ride! If you want to become a better all-mountain skier, you must be comfortable skiing bumps, as shown in figure 5.9. The simultaneous execution of quick response, athletic movement, and line preparation can be used in most ungroomed situations. Skiing bumps helps you create your own destiny, see your path, mentally prepare for a challenge, and execute it. This is a good lesson for life!

FIGURE 5.9   A wide range of movement in bumps will allow for consistent and uninterrupted technique.

In this terrain, lack of suspension in your lower body will send you rolling down the bump line. Suspension abilities begin with your ankles and work up the kinetic chain through your spine, requiring functional mobility in the joints and reactive elasticity in the muscles. Any weak or stiff points in this chain compromise your flexion and extension. Inflexibility and bad body alignment are the two biggest culprits for stunting development in bump skiing.

Developing true consistency in the bumps also requires attention to outside factors, such as slope pitch, bump spacing and height, and the condition of snow in your line. To become proficient, you must practice on varied terrain and in different conditions. Moving from the two-dimensional, level, manicured slope and into three-dimensional skiing is always challenging. Expect to be bucked and tossed by bullying bumps during the learning process. However, line choice softens

Lines for Bumps

The most common lines in the bumps are the zipper, trough, shoulder, and basic lines.

Zipper Line

The aggressive zipper line is straight and direct, demanding rigorous flexion and lightning-quick leg turning. It looks like a zipper running straight down the slope, with teeth formed by bumps that alternate left and right. Expert skiers choose this line for its speed, energy, and big air potential. Besides the intimidation factor, common difficulties include losing balance due to firm conditions and runs that are too steep. You must have a full range of flexion and a strong core. The zipper line is often avoided by skiers who prefer control and continuous balance. However, anyone who wants to experience higher bump mastery can learn to navigate this line.

Trough Line

The trough line is rounder than the zipper line and is slightly faster and more direct than the basic and shoulder lines in the next sections, since it follows a deep path through the valley between moguls. Speed control is a factor that can be managed by steering the skis aggressively and bleeding speed at the end of each turn. You can also slow down by adjusting to a line higher on the rut wall. Staying low in the bottom of the rut requires quick turning reflexes and responsive flexion movements. This line becomes more demanding as the snow hardens and the line deepens from heavy use. It is appropriate for skiers who are comfortable with speed in the bumps and can sustain shoulder lines at a consistent speed and pitch.

Shoulder Line

The shoulder line takes a round path that follows the upper outskirts of the trough and leads to the side of the flanking bump. Staying outside the fast trough line provides turns that are slower, rounder, and more forgiving. As you end the turn and your tips begin to climb the next bump, flatten the skis and change edges. You will now be on the new bump, with your skis pointing toward the shoulder of the flanking bump. As you roll over the bump, place your feet in the line early for maximum turning space. The speed of this line depends on the spacing of the bumps, pitch of the slope, and amount of snow on the ground. This line is appropriate for intermediate bump skiers who have progressed from the basic line and can link turns with confidence.

Basic Line

Confidence in the moguls comes from the ability to link consecutive turns at a comfortable speed. The basic line is achieved by choosing widely-spaced bumps that have a flat trough and soft sides. Follow a path that goes from a turn on one bump, then skid down the back and turn onto the bump directly downhill. As seen from overhead, this line takes a zigzag path over bumps that are spaced vertically down the fall line. The basic line is appropriate for skiers who can perform a solid short turn with a good pole plant and who have good rhythm, pole timing, and turning mechanics.

the transition from groomed snow to bumps, making the process more enjoyable. The following section lists the qualities of each level when skiing bumps.

Score of 3 for Bumps

This score means you have a solid foundation of speed management, line choice, and turn shape that allows you to move around the mountain with confidence and vision. You are ready to progress to competitive venues, such as freestyle, ski racing and free-ride competitions. You might also consider professional certification as a ski instructor or guide. Retesting is recommended every four to six weeks.

Score of 2 for Bumps

You can successfully navigate various lines in the bumps, maintaining continuous rhythm and movements down the slope. Success at this level varies depending on the conditions and depth of the ruts on a certain day. You are aware of line opportunities and have the skills to take advantage of them. You see options and can experiment with a wide range of formulas, which is important for building a knowledge base for bump tactics.

Score of 1 for Bumps

You will choose more forgiving lines that allow for some mistakes. The occasional bobble or missed pole plant may not throw you out of the line. However, keep working on the fundamental mechanics from chapter 4 to stay on the track.

See table 5.2 for information on scoring and tactics drills for bumps.

TABLE 5.2   Scoring and Tactics Drills for Bumps

Scoring	Related tactics drills
SCORE OF 3 Give yourself a 3 if the following apply: • Strong parallel-turn mechanics are present at faster speeds, along with coordinated suspension movements and well-timed, continuous pole plants. • You can change your line and the speed of leg turning on the fly. • You have a good command of suspension adjustments needed for bump lines that are more demanding and committed. • You can improvise if the conditions, pitch, or bump line change. • You ski the basic, shoulder, and trough lines with confidence and speed.	• Redirecting focus, page 164 • Pushing the envelope of speed and tempo, page 171 • Matching turn shape with conditions, page 165
SCORE OF 2 Give yourself a 2 if the following apply: • Consistent parallel-turn mechanics are present at faster speeds. Legs are used to absorb terrain. Pole plant is present. • You can reduce and increase the speed by changing rhythm and leg-turning intensity. • You know when and where to turn in the basic, shoulder, and trough lines. • You can see and inspect the width and depth of the trough or the height and length of the basic or shoulder and make proper tactical adjustments. • You ski proactively down the trough, basic, and shoulder lines.	• Unlocking freeze frame, page 164 • Establishing turn shape with ski placement, page 166 • Fishhook ending in a J-shape, page 165 • Choosing the correct tempo, page 171 • Getting out of a rut, page 173 • Checking your speed, page 171
SCORE OF 1 Give yourself a 1 if the following apply: • Basic parallel-turn mechanics are present at faster speeds on groomed slopes. Suspension is limited by the range of motion available. • You maintain a consistent speed and rhythm on moderate to small bump runs. • You can react to changes in terrain and conditions, but may stop to look at the line. • You understand basic bump tactics and can apply them if the line is gentle and requires gradual leg turning alone.	• Anticipating terrain changes, page 164 • Having a plan B, page 165 • Maintaining three points of contact, page 171 • Using pole plants to maintain your line, page 173

Chutes and Gullies

Skiing chutes and gullies, as shown in figure 5.10, is as mental as it is physical. If you lack the confidence and the ability to see the path through the narrows in your mind's eye, you are doomed. Associating positive mental pictures with tight situations will help you relax enough to seek passage through tight spots. Any terrain that is flanked by rock, trees, rolls, or fences can be seen as a chute or gully. When a predetermined corridor limits your usable terrain, you need tactics for chutes and gullies.

Blasting down the barrel of a chute while throwing caution to the wind is a good way to end up tomahawking several hundred feet, leaving your equipment back where you started. Although many skiers never look at the topography of the chute or gully, you can glean valuable insight if you take a few seconds to plan before you attack. When assessing topography of the chute, keep these questions in

FIGURE 5.10 Setting up for success with a solid entry is the first step in effective chute and gully skiing.

mind. Where do I enter? How do I enter? What line do I ski? What are the objective hazards? The following terms are used to explain chute-and-gully topography (see figure 5.11 for an example):

Lines for Chutes and Gullies

The most common lines in chutes or gullies are the center punch, the straight line, and the safety line.

Center-Punch Line

Taking the center-punch line means skiing down the middle of the chute without stopping. This line requires focus, a rhythmic turn sequence, and continuous pole plants.

Straight Line

The straight line was made famous by free-ride skiers who ski straight down a chute without turning and bleeding the speed at the end with a huge smear. You must build up to this advanced tactic. When executed correctly, this can be an exhilarating ride.

Safety Line

The safety line is any line that provides a passage through the least-exposed section of the chute. You can minimize your risk in tight spots by choosing a line with the best snow and reduced exposure to hazards. Look for a line that keeps speed to a minimum. Maintain a calculated distance from the sides of the chute so a bobble or missed turn doesn't make you collide with a wall or a tree. Plan your descent line ahead of time and make adjustments to avoid obstacles.

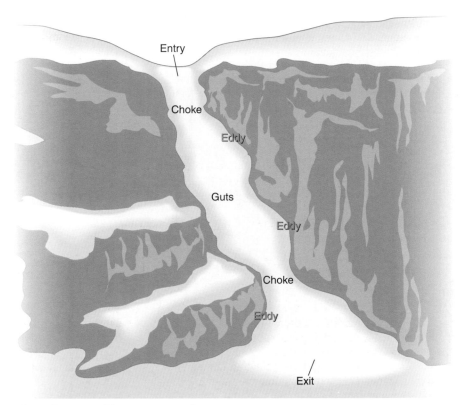

FIGURE 5.11   Chute topography.

- *Entry.* The entry is the top of a chute or gully that can include a cornice, the "in," the first-turn mark, and points for air-in, slip-in, and hop-in takeoffs.
- *Guts.* The guts of the chute or gully include the turn lines, snags, the fall line, the runnel line, and the control zone.
- *Choke.* The choke includes the setup turn, the narrows, the crux line, and the eddy (a protected area behind a rock outcropping).
- *Exit.* The exit includes the finish zone, exit-turn direction, and the stopping area.

Explosive leg power and core stability can be muted or rendered ineffective when skiing chutes and gullies if a weak core or an ineffective range of power prevents you from loading your body's springs. Core stability gives the extremities something solid to work against. If your core is wobbly, your legs can't find an anchor to push off from.

Skiing down the narrow swath of chutes and gullies can all but paralyze you if you let fear take over. Having a plan of attack will dissipate the feeling of intimidation. The tactics of a successful run include entering a chute properly, managing your descent, adjusting the line of attack, and controlling loose snow challenges. These all demand precise movements and cognitive focus. The prerequisites are dependable short-radius parallel turns, a repeatable pole plant, and a mental desire to explore challenging terrain. Therefore, the scoring for ski tactics in chutes and gullies is closely tied to understanding the terrain and properly executing a game plan within the terrain parameters. The following section lists the qualities of each level when skiing chutes and gullies.

Score of 3 for Chutes and Gullies
You have a solid foundation of speed management, line choice, and turn shape. You can ski chutes and gullies with complex turn sequences and can avoid natural obstacles. You may also be ready

to train in a professional or competitive venue. Options include ski races and free-ride competitions or professional certification as a ski instructor or guide. Retesting is recommended every four to six weeks.

Score of 2 for Chutes and Gullies

You command your descent due to sound fundamentals, terrain-assessment skills, tight-turn mastery, and good entry tactics. You have the skills to deal with surprises like snow sloughs or spring runnels.

Score of 1 for Chutes and Gullies

Although you may have a basic understanding of chute-and-gully skiing, you have not logged the miles needed to ski more difficult lines. A solid and consistent short turn is required for narrow passages. Once you have perfected your short turn, log mileage in tight corridors. Pole plants will also help you time your turn transitions in tighter situations.

See table 5.3 for information on scoring and tactics drills for chutes and gullies.

TABLE 5.3   Scoring and Tactics Drills for Chutes and Gullies

Scoring	Related tactics drills
SCORE OF 3 Give yourself a 3 if the following apply: • Strong carving mechanics are present with a focus on leg rotation and refined edging that results in short-radius turns. A trusted pole plant is present. • You can control speed by tightening the turn radius with edging and pressure while simultaneously alternating between staccato tempo and even-paced tempos. • You can quickly switch your line of descent as the path tightens or widens. • You can enter a chute with a slip-in, side-hop, and air-in approach. • You have mastered skills for runnel management. • You can improvise in narrow, tight terrain.	• Redirecting focus, page 164 • Creating symmetrical patterns in turns, page 165 • Pushing the envelope of speed and tempo, page 171 • Managing runnels, page 172
SCORE OF 2 Give yourself a 2 if the following apply: • Consistent parallel-turn mechanics are present with good short-radius turns and pole plants. • You can reduce and increase your speed by changing rhythm, turn shape, and intensity. • You know when and where to turn in chutes, controlling speed and direction. • You know how to manage sloughs. • You can ski proactively into a chute with a slip-in.	• Unlocking freeze frame, page 164 • Choosing the correct tempo, page 171 • Avoiding gridlock, page 173 • Checking your speed, page 171
SCORE OF 1 Give yourself a 1 if the following apply: • Basic parallel-turn mechanics are present. You touch poles on both sides. • You can maintain a consistent speed and rhythm on moderately steep gullies. • You can react to changes in terrain and conditions, but stop to look at the line. • You understand chute tactics but are unsure how to best apply them. • You can enter into a chute with a slip-in. • You can stop after a fall.	• Using pole plants to maintain your line, page 173 • Having a plan B, page 165 • Anticipating terrain changes, page 164 • Getting into gear, page 171 • Facing the line, page 173

Back Bowls

Front-side skiing usually conjures pictures of groomed terrain and intermediate runs for cruising and carving. On the other hand, back-bowl skiing lies on the wild side of any resort. It is loaded with multiple terrain configurations and long vertical that challenges any expert.

Big vertical at the far reaches and back bowls of many resorts demands a tactical skill set that prevents your engine from blowing a gasket and keeps enough fuel in the tank to eke out every last bit of terrain. Efficiency is the buzz word for enduring the rigors of long, steep descents. Tactics for back bowls include good body alignment over wide, rockered skis; big, open turn shape; turns that slash across the snow; and floating. When used together, these tactics will let you scrub speed while drifting sideways and buttering! Back bowls often house large powder stashes. If you visit these areas several days after a storm, the powder will probably be hammered into large bumps or chopped-up snow. In any case, back-bowl skiing allows you to run your skis in big, round turns through untouched snow. See figure 5.12 for an example of a skier in a back bowl.

The muscular and aerobic stamina needed for skiing back bowls comes from a strong motor that can withstand the paralyzing evils of oxygen debt. Once you have reached the limits of your aerobic capacity, your ability to move athletically will be compromised. Even the best technique and tactics in the world will not help. We all have felt like our legs were made of jelly on those long back-bowl runs. This sensation comes from lack of oxygenated blood to the leg muscles, forcing you to lean on the stiff plastic of the back of the boots and to lean back on your uphill pole,

FIGURE 5.12   Freedom of the hills is found in back-bowl skiing.

Lines for Back Bowls

The most common lines in back bowls are the classic, ridge, flute, and pillow lines.

Classic Line

The classic line takes the most direct and open path down the center of the bowl. This line provides speed consistency and symmetrical turn shapes. For intermediate skiers, the classic line is a great starting point.

Ridge Line

Choose the ridge line to avoid unstable snow and avalanche threats. The ridge line provides safety by moving over firmer snow at an angle lower than the critical pitch of 30 to 40 degrees where most avalanches occur. It is a moderate line for skiers who want a casual run. Watch out for exposed rocks, since the wind-scoured surface will have less snow. Make short turns that keep you on the ridge and maintain a safe distance from the corniced edge.

Flute Line

The flute line develops from wind blasting wet snow against a steep face. This creates vertical ridges running down the face of a steep slope. To ski this line, alternate turns from one side of the flute to the other. This back-and-forth action will keep your speed in check, but may release snow sloughs that can knock you off balance if you get caught in their path.

Pillow Line

In this line, you ski from one pillow of snow to the next, sometimes dropping from one to the other. You will skim and smear from one huge pillow, or mogul, to the next, using active extension and retraction. In deep powder, you can take a straighter line and can drop from pillow to pillow like a gradual waterfall of huge soft bumps. Review your mogul (bump) technique before attempting this line.

trenching it into the snow behind you. If your cardio training is rock solid, you have the agility and muscle function to play with a variety of different tactics for back-bowl mastery. The following sections provide more detail about the qualities of each level for back bowls.

Score of 3 for Back Bowls

You have a solid foundation of speed management, line choice, and turn shape for deep snow. You can ski in deep snow with several turn types and intensities and can see the best line and apply the right combination of tactical choices for maximum performance. You are ready to progress to a professional or competitive venue. Retesting is recommended every four to six weeks.

Score of 2 for Back Bowls

You will experience new and exciting freedom as you move from groomers to the world of off-piste skiing. Although you have already made great strides in ungroomed conditions, moving into back bowls is a milestone that opens up new terrain. You have a wide variety of powder tactics that will open up more terrain and conditions as you continue to master skills. Your skills include skimming the surface and diving deep into the snow. Higher speeds help you generate the energy to glue your dynamic movements together.

Score of 1 for Back Bowls

The surfing feeling you get in powder will be enhanced as you let the skis ride up and over the soft snow. You will experiment with a wide range of movements to create a consistent ride.

See table 5.4 for information on scoring and tactics drills for back bowls.

TABLE 5.4   Scoring and Tactics Drills for Back Bowls

Scoring	Related tactics drills
SCORE OF 3 Give yourself a 3 if the following apply: • Strong, deep turn mechanics are present at faster speeds that are complemented by a synchronized pole swing and directional touch. • You can change the shape and tempo of the turn at will to avoid obstacles and to adjust line. • You can switch tactics as needed, depending on snow condition, depth, and consistency. • You can improvise to develop a playful and flowing image. • Your tactical skill set includes buttering, slashing, high-speed turns, and smear turns.	• Redirecting focus, page 164 • Pushing the envelope of speed and tempo, page 171
SCORE OF 2 Give yourself a 2 if the following apply: • Consistent parallel-turn mechanics are present at faster speeds using a large-turn radius. Pole plant is present. • You can reduce and increase speed by changing turn radius and intensity. • You know basic powder and deep-snow tactics, including buttering, slash turns, and high-speed turns. • You can ski with consistent, high energy down a long, open run.	• Unlocking freeze frame, page 164 • Getting the right amount of edge angle, page 166 • Checking your speed, page 171
SCORE OF 1 Give yourself a 1 if the following apply: • Basic parallel-turn mechanics are present with a regular pole plant. • You can maintain consistent speed and turn shape in deeper snow. • You can react to changes in the snow, but may have to stop to regroup after half a run. • You understand advanced tactics of back bowls but are unsure how to best apply them. • You know the dangers of deep snow.	• Anticipating terrain changes, page 164 • Facing the line, page 173 • Getting into gear, page 171

Trees

Skiing in a quiet, peaceful glade next to snow-covered trees that are perfectly spaced to match your tempo, speed, and mood is much more appealing than ramrodding through a dense thicket of underbrush. Ski resorts have begun to manicure their arboreal areas to match the turn intensity of the average off-the-groomed skier, leaving enough room for the occasional missed turn or poor line choice. A realistic game plan in the trees will produce bigger openings, real or imagined, and a safe passage through this natural obstacle course. Solitude on a winter mountain comes from being in the right place at the right time. Having the skill to go in the challenging places that others avoid provides new opportunities and sacred moments.

Foot speed and mental commitment are needed for success in the trees. Training with slow movements will make you slow in the trees. Try to add quick stop-start lateral, diagonal, forward, and backward movements to your program to ingrain ballistic and varied movement patterns. Visual skills are also important for good tactics in the trees, both because you need to see the trees in order to avoid them and because it is the first link in good coordination among your eyes, hands, and feet. Reading the terrain improperly or misinterpreting important cues can greatly affect your performance in the trees. Your balance will also be affected if your vision is compromised. To test this, balance on one leg with your eyes closed.

Lines for Trees

The most common lines in trees are the mixed line, the tight line, and the round line.

Mixed Line

The ability to enter a tree run with the confidence to shape any turn comes from commanding the mixed line. Most trees runs are not equally and symmetrically spaced. Rather, they include a mixture of species, sizes, spacing, and density. The ability to vary turn length gives you more options.

Tight Line

A tight tree line requires quick reaction and a proactive approach that includes looking ahead, reading the needed sequences of turns before you arrive, and moving the lower body with precision. Avoid any movements that take you out of the rhythm or disrupt your flow through the trees.

Round Line

The round line is used in trees that are widely spaced and easy to navigate. It requires a wide, round turn that begins above the tree you are turning around, gradually rounding to a C–shape, and checking your speed to set up for the next turn. The round line is a great way to start the descent for beginners because it provides a wide berth around trees. It also lets you control your speed to manageable levels.

The perceptual skills needed for effective tree skiing are as ingrained as the movements you use when dodging a ball that has been chucked at you. As you see the ball coming, you instinctively move your head and core out of the line of fire and prepare for the next strike. The only difference in skiing trees is that you are the ball, so prepare your plan of attack before you enter the glades. A good skill set for tactical tree skiing includes visualizing the line through the trees, proactively executing several turns in your mind's eye before you reach the eye of the needle, planning your tempo so that the turn zigs around the tree rather than zagging into it, and keeping your descent in the fall line. The following section lists the qualities of each level when skiing trees.

Score of 3 for Trees

You have the ability to change turn shape, tempo, and line at will. Tactical competency at this level allows you to navigate any challenge found in the trees with creativity and confidence. You are ready to train in a professional or competitive venue. Some of my past students have competed in ski races and free-ride competitions, while others have gained professional certifications as ski instructors or guides. Retesting is recommended every four to six weeks.

Score of 2 for Trees

You can navigate basic and intermediate tree lines. You also make lane changes in the trees and have speed and directional control. In easier tree runs, you maintain a continuous flow down the fall line with blended turn speeds.

Score of 1 for Trees

You are testing and sampling the tactics that best fit your ability and skill set. You feel most comfortable with a round line that allows a wide berth around trees. You like to stay in the lower phases of your speed range with time to plan your attack as you navigate through the trees.

See table 5.5 for information on scoring and tactics drills for trees.

TABLE 5.5   Scoring and Tactics Drills for Trees

Scoring	Related tactics drills
SCORE OF 3 Give yourself a 3 if the following apply: • Strong parallel-turn mechanics are present at faster speeds with coordinated suspension movements, edging movements, and synchronized pole plants. • You can change the shape and tempo of the turn at will, resulting in immediate control of speed and direction. • You can switch tactics and rhythm to adjust to asymmetrical growth patterns in the trees. • You can improvise as obstacles change from trees to bushes, rocks, and back to trees.	• Redirecting focus, page 164 • Creating symmetrical patterns in turns, page 165 • Pushing the envelope of speed and tempo, page 171
SCORE OF 2 Give yourself a 2 if the following apply: • Consistent parallel-turn mechanics are present at faster speeds. Pole use is present. • You can reduce and increase your speed as trees close in or open up. • You know when and where to begin a turn to avoid arcing back into the tree. • You can ski proactively through tighter trees with flow and rhythm.	• Unlocking freeze frame, page 164 • Choosing the correct tempo, page 171 • Avoiding gridlock, page 173 • Getting out of a rut, page 173
SCORE OF 1 Give yourself a 1 if the following apply: • Basic parallel-turn mechanics are present at faster speeds. • You can maintain a consistent speed and rhythm on moderate pitch with widely spaced trees. • You can react to changes in snow while maintaining rhythm and flow. • You understand tactics for trees but must think before executing them. • You can maintain momentum down the fall line. • You know the safety precautions for skiing trees.	• Having a plan B, page 165 • Facing the line, page 173 • Anticipating terrain changes, page 164

Safety in the trees comes from adopting an attitude of basic awareness and becoming attuned to your external environment. Keep the following points in mind when skiing trees:

- *Remove your pole straps.* If your pole gets caught on a branch or snag, it can dislocate your shoulder or knock you off balance. Some brands of poles have detachable straps.

- *Wear a helmet.* Wearing a helmet in the trees provides protection and gives you the confidence to ski your chosen line.

- *Choose a line appropriate for your skill level.* Skiing in tight trees before you are ready is a poor choice.

- *Stay clear of tree wells.* These are deep moats that form around the tree base during heavy snow falls. Skiers have died from suffocation after falling into these wells, since the new snow falls in around them, rendering them helpless.

- *Ski with a buddy.* If you get into trouble in the trees, a partner who can assist you or go for help is essential.

The variety of terrain and conditions found on any mountain requires a wide range of tactics for successful and safe runs. This is the thinking part of your skill set, in which you recognize a situation, survey your options, and execute your total package of skiing skills. Study, analysis, and practice of these tried and true tactical game plans will give you everything you need to attack the mountain.

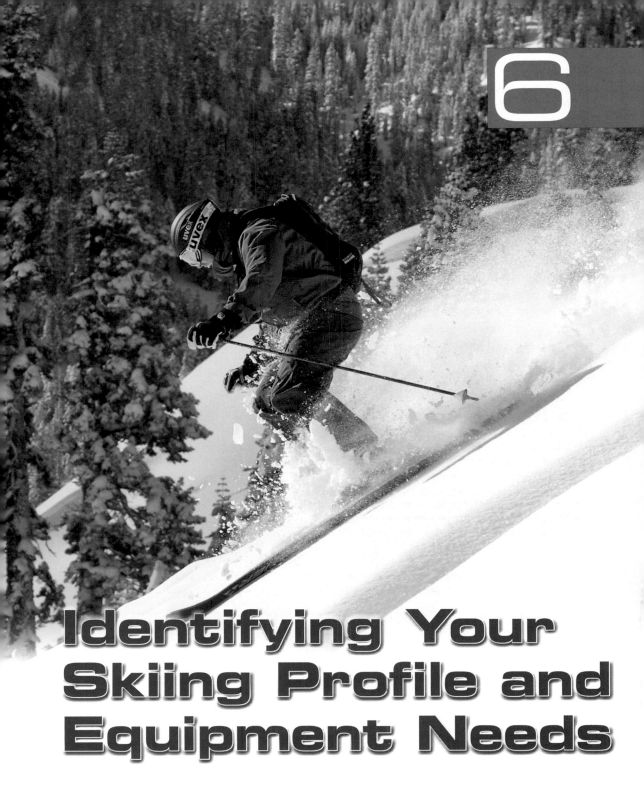

Identifying Your Skiing Profile and Equipment Needs

When asked to classify themselves, most skiers refer to their usual terrain or their level of skiing aggression. Examples include a black-diamond skier, a cruiser, or an aggressive, all-mountain skier. Skiers rarely describe themselves in terms of their physical attributes or limitations. Understanding the physical components that make up your fitness profile will speed up the improvement process and help you pinpoint the areas of development for the fastest results.

Each skier brings a unique package of physical, mental, and motivational parameters to the mountain. This is part of the reason I still teach skiing—it's fun because it is always changing. Each student provides a fresh experience and a clean palette to create with. Over the years, identifying the strategies for effectively helping students has culminated in this book. The better your conditioning, the better you will ski. Tuning in to your equipment allows you to interact more efficiently with the snow. Knowing where and how to change direction, speed, and intensity to match the demands of the terrain and your personal desires helps, too!

For those who are interested in taking a closer look at their overall strengths and weaknesses, volumes of new information have emerged due to advanced equipment, changing attitudes toward sport fitness, active lifestyles, increased access to mountains, and a growing desire to perform well as we age. Wading through all this information can be challenging. With the right combination of specific sport knowledge and customized practice concepts, you can quickly reach a higher level of skiing performance. An approach that is too broad can suck up valuable chunks of your training time with unreliable results. Most avid skiers opt for the most direct route to improvement, which begins with understanding their profile.

Building a program that addresses all aspects is paramount for achieving maximum performance. A well-balanced program incorporates the exercises and drills that fill in the holes identified in the screens. It also makes any necessary equipment adjustments. This approach is truly customized, not one size fits all.

What Type of Skier Are You?

The personal attributes of body type, strengths and weaknesses, movement preferences, and symmetry all combine to help determine skier type. By identifying which category you fall into, you will be able to simplify your process when developing a comprehensive training program, making it specific and streamlined for your individual needs. Instead of focusing on technique or equipment alone, this type of customized training addresses total athletic performance. By adapting the exercises to your performance needs, you will be able to practice your skiing both on and off the slopes. A prescribed at-home series of exercises and drills for mobility, stability, aerobic capacity, agility, and power will deliver big paybacks in performance and will increase the fun factor on the slopes.

The assessments in chapters 2 through 5 alert you to your areas of strength and weakness and prescribe specific drills and exercises for improving your overall movement in each tier of the pyramid. These results will help you design an effective program that culminates with noticeable improvement on the hill. Start by reviewing your assessments in each of the four pyramid blocks, starting with functional movement and progressing through fitness, technique, and tactics. Enter the drills and exercises on the summary sheets from chapters 2 through 4. Finally, reflect on the following questions.

1. Where were my left- and right-side imbalances?
2. What were my lowest scores? What limitations did they indicate?
3. What was my weakest link? Is there a common theme around that result?
4. Were my weakest results in the block of functional movement, fitness, technique, or tactics?
5. What connection can be made between the compensations in the blocks of functional movement and fitness and the affectations or misjudgments in the blocks of technique and tactics?
6. Is my choice of equipment negatively affecting my stance, balance, or leg turning?

The Performance Pyramid and Skier Types

The components of the performance pyramid correspond to four different types of skiers: overpowered, underpowered, underskilled, or combination. To calculate your scores from the assessments in chapters 2 through 5, divide your total score in each block of the pyramid by the number of tests in the block. Use these numbers to determine your type.

- If your lowest scores are in functional movement, you are an overpowered skier.
- If your lowest scores are in skiing fitness, you are an underpowered skier.
- If your lowest scores are in technique and tactics, you are an underskilled skier.
- If your scores span across several blocks, you can classify yourself as a combination skier. Most of us fall into this category. In this case, you will identify your weaknesses and select exercises that build strengths in those areas.

For example, if you consistently scored a 1 or 2 in the functional-movement assessments, a 2 or 3 in the tests for skiing fitness, and a 2 in technique and tactics, you should classify yourself as an overpowered skier. This is not a negative thing—it's just where your strengths lie. If you're an overpowered skier, your program should fill in the gaps with stability and mobility exercises. Very few skiers completely fit into a single category. Most display the traits of two different types, thus requiring specific exercises to meet their needs.

To progress, take inventory of what is working for you and what is holding you back. Since overpowered athletes rely on the fitness block to get through most skiing challenges, convincing them to focus on mobility and stability exercises is sometimes a chore. However, revisiting basic

Performance Pyramid for the Optimal Skier

Our ultimate goal is to eventually become optimal skiers, maintaining balance in each of the pyramid blocks (see figure 6.1 for an example). Optimal skiers exhibit ideal functional movement and keen body awareness in all planes of movement. They react to terrain changes with body adjustments and refined agility skills. The solid foundation of functional movement supports higher levels of training and skill refinement. These skiers can pick up new skills quickly and are rarely sidelined with injuries. Quality training comes with intense, precise practice. As soon as fatigue sets in, most skiers compensate, straining their connective tissue. Optimal skiers can withstand longer outings to ingrain quality movements and can practice for longer periods due to good overall alignment, mobility, and strength.

This skier looks relaxed. All joints are slightly flexed and aligned with the body parts. The stance of optimal skiers is never overly crouched or contrived; instead, they maintain an athletic posture as they stand in their ski equipment. Movements are timely and well blended with the speed and terrain. The skill and power needed are equally supported by both functional mobility and stability.

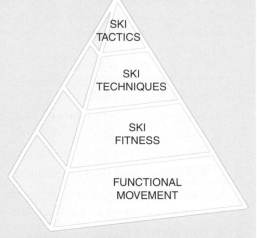

FIGURE 6.1   Optimal pyramid in which all blocks are balanced.

elements of functional movement raises the ceiling for their improvement. Underpowered skiers sometimes balk at the thought of focusing on strength training and aerobic fitness, preferring to stick with yoga. It is human nature to focus on what we are good at and gloss over what is hard for us. Although it is not always fun, working on weaknesses is a shortcut to improvement. Underskilled skiers do well in the areas of functional movement and fitness, but have not logged the miles on snow needed to progress. To ingrain skiing movements, you must repeat specific sequences many times before they stick. The strengths and weaknesses of combination skiers show up in all blocks of the pyramid. Since most of us fall into that category, test thoroughly to find all your gaps. Once you have successfully filled in the holes in your profile, you will be an optimal skier.

Performance Pyramid for the Overpowered Skier

The overpowered skier is fit, using good mobility and stability to deal with terrain challenges. They often use the big muscles that can generate fast, ballistic movements in order to ski well. Even skiers with adequate skills can go a long way with a powerful, muscular frame. Imagine the snow-covered pitch at your favorite resort, with its natural dips, rolls, banks, and curves. You may even venture into the moguls or off the groomed snow into cut-up powder or the trees. To ski this run well, you need both a fundamental set of skiing skills and a physical system that can withstand the rigors of the downhill route. Any chink in your armor will limit your possibilities and thwart the best-laid plans. If you are overpowered, expect to experience difficulty in any terrain configuration that requires a full range of motion in all planes of balance. Since turn tactics are always compromised by poor mobility, compensations will arise.

Overpowered skiers are powerful to the point of being blocky. Their muscular and tight bodies can be explosive while turning, but they lack a full and effective range of motion. They can resist huge forces, but are as stiff as a statue. They lack joint mobility, especially in the hips, as well as fluid core movement and finessed leg movement. Although they have a good overall stance, when flexion and extension are required, their range of motion is limited. Movements are often rushed and will appear forceful, due to their muscular frame. They use gross movements to get the job done. See figure 6.2 for an example of a pyramid for the overpowered skier.

The overpowered skier exhibits the following inefficiency cues:

- Skis with a stiff outside leg
- Body follows skis during turning
- Hops skis around turns
- Upper body rotates first when beginning a turn
- Upper body dominates the movement pattern
- Rhythm is choppy and asymmetrical
- Places heavy, clumsy pressure on the skis due to dominant but powerful leg movements
- Stiff upper body

To remedy these inefficiencies, improve mobility and stability in the hip, torso, and shoulders for a better stance and overall alignment. Your hips support the pelvic area and are crisscrossed with muscles, tendons, and ligaments that align the body's frame. Working these areas with essential movement

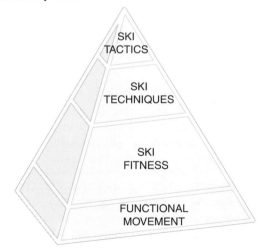

FIGURE 6.2 The overpowered skier's pyramid shows an exceptionally solid fitness block but a disproportionately small functional-movement block.

exercises will improve your movement and balance. It will give you the elasticity to reach the far end of your functional-movement patterns in case of a fall.

Performance Pyramid for the Underpowered Skier

Underpowered skiers have good mobility and core stability, but lack the component of overall fitness, causing them to get tossed around by building forces in the turn. They also lack the endurance needed for longer, sustained runs. Their technique is affected by their inability to deal with the physical demands of dynamic skiing. If you are an underpowered skier, you will demonstrate both a broad base of movement patterns and a good range of athletic movements. Your skiing skills are adequate for meeting on-hill challenges with dynamic balance, but you lack the athleticism needed to effectively perform power moves. Quality-movement patterns break down quickly as your muscles fatigue and external forces increase. To improve, you must get your power-output system in order. You can greatly increase your overall performance and ability to recover by building your strength, power, agility, and speed. Whether you are naturally flexible or have acquired agility through training, your mobility component is in good shape. However, if flexibility is your only strength, you will always be limited to undemanding terrain and conditions.

Underpowered skiers look nimble and agile on their skis, sometimes resulting in too much range and the inability to hold on to the dramatic angles they create. Their stance silhouette is lanky or gangly, with bigger angles throughout the body. Some angles may look asymmetrical due to an A-frame alignment of the lower legs or an overflexed stance that causes the hips to settle back and the spine to stand up straight. Underpowered skiers can absorb varied terrain deeply when they are fresh, but tire quickly and must rely on the stability of the hard, plastic shell of the boot or the tail of the ski. They display finesse and have a good feel for the snow; however, they lack the crucial power for recovering quickly or avoiding an obstacle. See figure 6.3 for an example of the underpowered skier's pyramid.

The underpowered skier exhibits the following inefficiency cues:

- Feels balanced for the first half of a run but quickly tires and leans on the uphill ski and pole
- Lacks the ability to power into a turn with the leg muscles and instead waits for the turn to come, resulting in late edging and an uncontrolled skid
- Takes a wide path across the hill when turning
- Allows quick-twitch muscles to become muted by fatigue and lack of agility

To remedy these inefficiencies, you must build strength and power, beginning with the core and working outward. This process is similar to the way a child develops. As your core strength builds, you will be better prepared to tap into the smaller, more-specific skiing muscles as well as increase your flexibility and agility. Since skiers must function in many different planes at once, your focus in strength training should be multidimensional.

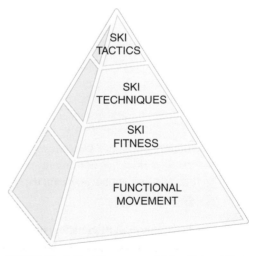

FIGURE 6.3 The pyramid for the under-powered skier is centered on functional movement, but lacks development in the fitness block.

Performance Pyramid for the Underskilled Skier

Underskilled skiers show great ability in the blocks of functional movement and fitness, but lack technical and tactical skill. Skiing is a sport that requires repetition of movement patterns, and underskilled skiers have not gone through all the paces yet. If you are an underskilled skier, you are the bread and butter for skiing schools around the world. You have a good base of functional performance, but you are weak in the skills department. Unfortunately, most ski schools think that everyone is underskilled. They focus primarily on skill improvement but fail to address physical limitations. If you are truly an underskilled skier, you will be both agile and strong, but will struggle with movement patterns due purely to your lack of quality miles on the snow. If you are in good shape, you will usually know it, because you must work at it. You are probably active in other sports that demand good range of motion, strength, and endurance.

Underskilled skiers look athletic when standing over the skis. They can make quick changes to technique and tactics because their bodies can withstand the continuous attempts to get it right. They stay fresh longer and can operate at peak performance for several hours. Their weak link is their lack of fundamental skills and inability to apply them to specific situations. They surprise people because their sporty appearance doesn't match up with their lack of skill. Skiing has a steep learning curve that requires the body to stand up to many physical demands. Fortunately, yours can! See figure 6.4 for an example of the underskilled skier's pyramid.

Underskilled skiers exhibit the following inefficiency cues:

- Meet on-hill challenges with pure athleticism, muscling their way through tough conditions due to durability
- Performance ceiling is often due to lack of skill rather than lack of physical capabilities
- Easily ingrain bad habits since their fitness level allows for repeated inefficient movements
- Movements are often forceful and ballistic, resulting in snow coming off the skis all at once

Fixing these inefficiencies requires more time on the snow. Developing a base of fundamental skills and tactics comes from a carefully guided program that pays attention to precision, execution, and quality practice miles. Like a blank slate, the underskilled skier has not ingrained years of habits that must be unlearned before going to the next step.

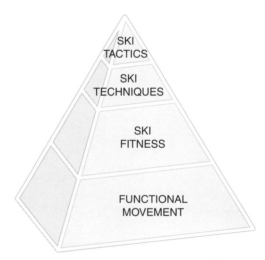

FIGURE 6.4 The underskilled skier's pyramid has well-balanced and proportionate blocks of functional movement and fitness, but small and disproportionate blocks of techniques and tactics.

Performance Pyramid for the Combination Skier

Although the combination skier's pyramid may seem balanced at first glance, it is easy to pick out the holes in the total package. This pyramid can actually differ depending on the individual skier. The combination platter, as we like to call this skier, has a variety of strengths and weaknesses that do not necessarily fall into classic categories. This skier type includes several combinations of limitations in more than one block of the pyramid. When you see limitations in the technique and tactic blocks, you can often make a direct correlation to difficulty with a certain movement or skill. For example, asymmetrical parallel turns as noted in the skill test could be caused by poor rotational mobility in the hip.

Combination skiers commonly pull from several pyramids, since their areas of strength and compensation span the entire spectrum. Some skiers have huge aerobic engines that allow them to climb for hours, but lack the specific leg strength and core stability to power through difficult snow. The summary sheet for combination skiers may look like a jigsaw puzzle with random pieces missing. However, the beauty of this category is that combination skiers only need to work on their areas of weakness. See figure 6.5 for an example of a combination skier's pyramid.

Combination skiers exhibit the following inefficiency cues:

- Asymmetries between left and right turns
- Lack of finesse when executing balance maneuvers, such as single-leg skiing
- Poor stance due to leaning backward or forward
- Impaired timing of movements, such as lack of synchronicity between pole and leg movements

To remedy these inefficiencies, combination skiers must first understand that their limitations will vary depending on their unique combination of weaknesses from several blocks. The screens for functional movement, fitness, technique, and tactics will identify the holes in their profile. They must seek diverse solutions.

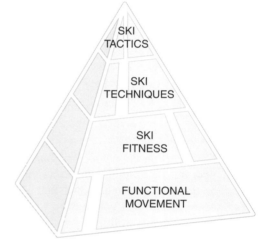

FIGURE 6.5   A combination skier's pyramid may look like a jigsaw puzzle with a few pieces missing. Gaps in several blocks can throw off the pyramid's balance.

The process of identifying your category will make you aware of your total package, whether functionally good or bad. Your process should be thorough with attention to the details of your personal pyramid's makeup. These movement areas and exercises will constitute your program according to type. See part III for more details.

Equipment Needs

Customized equipment is the glue that brings all the blocks of the pyramid together. Establishing the correct connection between your body and your equipment sets you up for success by helping you ingrain solid skiing movements and clean mechanics. It is just as important to identify inadequacies in your equipment as in your physical makeup.

Options for skiing equipment are continually evolving, making it easier to ski in a variety of conditions and terrain. The sport has exploded in terms of new ski boot and binding designs. The days of skis of a single width, shape, camber, or purpose are gone. Countless new products have sprung up in their place. Now, skiers can choose contemporary skis, bindings, and boots to match their personal styles. The hard part is wading through the mountains of information out there in order to select a ski boot and binding that is right for you. The following sections will help you narrow down your search, providing insights on matching your skier type and terrain preferences.

Boots

The ski boot is most often overlooked when matching skiers with equipment. This piece of equipment is your contact to the ski and snow. Without a proper fit, alignment, and compatibility with your skier type, it is very difficult to improve. Besides your body, your boots are the most important piece of equipment you will acquire, so when purchasing, choose a model with the right fit that can be adjusted to your physical needs. Transfer of energy from the body to the ski comes from a combination of good alignment and a properly fitted boot. A good boot fitter will help you navigate through the multiple brands available to find a boot that is right for your personal profile.

Boot Fit

Once you begin skiing more of the mountain, you will tend to pack out your boot liners, and that fresh-out-of-the-box feeling will go away. If you were properly fitted at the shop, this initial process will only improve the overall fit. If you begin to experience problems when the liner packs out, you must troubleshoot your fit. The following symptoms indicate a fit that is less than optimum:

- *Toenail turns black.* This is a common symptom for a boot that is too big, since your foot slides back and forth, jamming your toenail into the front of the boot. Short of buying a shell a size smaller, you can get a customized foot bed or put a shim under your foot bed to take up space.
- *Numbness on the top of your foot.* Your boot may be too big, causing you to overtighten your buckles, which pinches nerves on the top of your foot. Your boot shell could also be one size too small, which can be easily fixed by wearing a lighter pair of socks. It's also possible that you need to grind out more room in the shell, which should be done by an expert boot fitter.
- *Numbness along the sole and sides of the foot.* A shell that is too narrow for your foot restricts movement and causes aching and general discomfort. You can expand the volume of the boot with some grinding or by lifting the foot bed.

Remember that manufacturers make products to serve a mass audience. It is impossible for these big companies to design a boot or ski specifically for you. Although companies do address the needs of market segments and take feedback from selected focus groups, the results do not always satisfy specific needs. Your needs are based on two important questions. Are you capable of the physical performance needed to operate that specific boot design? Do you possess the skill set required to maximize the design characteristics of that specific boot? Knowing the answers to these questions can save you time and frustration as you try to figure out which boots are right for you.

Foot Beds

A foot bed is a skiing-specific inner sole that comes in every boot. However, their generic design makes them soft enough to conform to any foot sole. For a foot bed customized for your foot, see a certified pedorthist or a highly recommended boot fitter. Standard foot beds that come with boots are mostly for comfort, but customized foot beds provide the best mechanical advantage by addressing your unique profile. They address compensating movements due to a poor connection between your foot and the boot and make your stance more consistent by positioning your foot in the same way every time you put your boots on. Without customized foot beds, skiing is a hit-and-miss experience, since you may struggle with balance and stance. Customized foot beds let your foot relax rather than working to create support and alignment, making you better prepared to attack mountain challenges as they arise. The following symptoms indicate poor foot-boot interplay:

- Poor response from your equipment as you struggle to articulate your feet and ankles
- Cramping and tightness in your leg muscles due to searching for the neutral spot in the boot
- Sloppy and uncomfortable feeling in the fit due to foot changes over time

Manufacturers cannot accommodate every possible foot configuration, so it's up to you to address your personal needs in order to enhance your enjoyment and improve your overall performance.

Cuff Flex

Cuff flex measures how much the plastic cuff moves and bends as you flex your boot forward from a basic stance. If the cuff is too soft, you lose precision; if it is too stiff, you lose forgiveness. A cuff that is just right aids performance and provides comfort. Some stock boots come with adjustable cuffs, but most high-performance boots must be cut by a boot fitter to soften them or augmented to stiffen them. Specific red flags exist for each type of skier that indicate problems with cuff flex.

Overpowered Skier

Overpowered skiers may feel as though their feet are crashing into the front of the boot, causing a feeling of bottoming out, or they may feel as if they have no ankle support. If your lower boot contorts as you flex forward, your boot flex may be too soft for your power. Lack of response or sloppiness without ankle support while skiing also indicate that the boot is too soft.

Underpowered Skier

Underpowered skiers may feel that they can't move their ankles, that their boots are too stiff, or that their cuffs prevent them from flexing. If the front of your boot makes you feel like you are pushing up against a brick wall as you bend your ankle, your boot is probably too stiff. While skiing, if you bend excessively in the hips with a straight lower leg, you may be suffering from a stiff boot or a lack of muscular ability. Junior racers often wear boots that are too rigid for their physical development or ability level.

Underskilled Skier

Underskilled skiers may feel as though they have no lateral stability. They may also experience calf pain from overtensing their legs in response to new sensations. Underskilled skiers are often fitted with a boot that is too big. This is the fault of the boot fitter. They should be aware that shoe size differs from boot size. Ski boots should feel snug, but not painful. A boot that immediately feels comfortable in the shop is not always the right fit. A boot that needs adjustments here and there might seem too small, but is often the right fit.

Combination Skier

For the combination skier, the variables inherent in the cuff profile range from too stiff to too soft. Close evaluation is required for proper customization. A progressive flex is the goal for all skiers, but combination skiers may have several different needs that can fall under either category (too stiff or too soft).

Lateral Cuff Adjustments

The upper cuff should be set to match the alignment of the lower leg. This basic adjustment can be done with the help of a friend. Remove the boot liner and loosen the rivets located on the sides of the boot at ankle height. Next, place your foot beds on the boot board inside the plastic shell. Step into the boot and have a friend check that the plastic of the upper cuff is the same distance away from your leg all the way around. This process only takes 10 minutes and sets you up for a solid foot-boot connection. Again, several red flags indicate issues with lateral cuff alignment based on each skier type.

Overpowered Skier

Overpowered skiers may experience shin rubbing or calf pain due to excessive pressure on the outsides of the cuff. They often have stockier frames with lower legs that bow outward (as opposed to angling inward). Although this is not always the case, if the plastic touches the outside of your shin, you must make lateral cuff adjustments.

Underpowered Skier

Underpowered skiers may experience poor circulation in their feet due to pinching or restriction in the upper cuff. They often present an A-frame configuration in the lower legs. If the A-frame causes the shins to bang against the inside of the boot, they will experience discomfort and irritation in the lower legs and feet. Once adjustments are made, they can perform better and can relax the lower legs.

Underskilled Skier

Underskilled skiers may feel out of balance due to misaligned cuffs that impede the natural stance. Proper alignment starts with the foot bed, works its way up through the boot cuff, and moves up through the body. Eliminating as many variables as possible allows underskilled skiers to concentrate on the core skills of the sport, leading to faster results.

Combination Skier

For combination skiers, problems with cuff alignment range from too far inside to too far outside. Alignment can vary between feet, presenting diverse problems, such as one boot that is too far inside and another that is too far outside. This is common with asymmetrical leg alignment. Balanced alignment is the goal for all skiers, but combination skiers may present alignment imbalances that will be revealed during the process of cuff adjustment.

Boot Balancing

Boots that are aligned with the natural geometry of your lower body produce a quick response when you move. You should be able to move your legs sideways, forward, and backward without activating your big muscles. Well-balanced boots improve your balance, touch, and comfort over prolonged skiing sessions. In boot balancing, material is grinded off the bottom of the boot, either inside or out, to align the center of knee mass to the center of the boot. This process changes the geometry to produce a harmonious relationship between skier, equipment, and snow. For some people, the difference is dramatic; for others, it is negligible. The following red flags, listed by skier type, may indicate issues with boot alignment.

Overpowered Skier

Overpowered skiers may experience knee pain and leg wobble as they force the skis to the side to release the edges. Their stance looks bowed in the lower legs. They often feel stuck on edges because their bowed stance overcompensates normal tipping movements needed for a turn. With the proper grind, their skis will react more smoothly and they can transition between turns without force or hesitation.

Underpowered Skier

Underpowered skiers may knock their knees into the top of the opposite boot, resulting in bruising on the inside of the knees. Their stance takes on an A-frame position in the lower legs. They often struggle to get their skis on edge. This is an unnerving feeling, since it is hard to feel the edge bite until the leg and boot have tipped to an extreme angle. If they have made cuff adjustments but their lower legs still angle inward, they must make grind adjustments.

Underskilled Skier

Underskilled skiers may experience irritation of the patellar tendon and inconsistent reactions when they try to engage their edges. They do not have enough mileage to know what they should feel, so any inconsistencies in boot alignment will compound the problem, leading to overuse of the muscles and tendons in the lower body. As they become more proficient, they will learn to apply the right amount of pressure at the right intensity.

Combination Skier

For combination skiers, the variables of cuff profile will range from several degrees inside to several degrees outside. They can be identified during boot balancing. Aligned lower legs that are symmetrical and balanced are ideal for all skier types, but the combination skier may present several different needs, such as one leg that is tipped in more than the other or one leg that bows out while the other bows in. This is common if an injury like a broken leg or a damaged knee joint has occurred. The solution must address the misalignment of each leg for a symmetrical and balanced stance.

If you have any of these symptoms, the center of your knee's mass is probably misaligned either inward or outward with the center of your boot and ski. A few millimeters of change can have dramatic results. This problem should be addressed before moving on. The most effective and permanent way to make the proper adjustments is by planing the bottom of your boots to meet the optimal degree of correction. Choose a ski shop that specializes in this service.

Boot Rotation

Equipment faults and fixes are easy to identify in the lateral and fore-aft planes. However, equipment problems in the rotational plane are more difficult to identify. The most common affectations that can play a role in the ability to rotate the foot and leg are biomechanical issues like a pigeon-toed stance, duck-feet stance, or a rail flare. The outward or inward rotation of normal stance affects turning of the legs in one of two ways: the feet either flare out, causing misalignment and loss of turning power, or they flare in, disrupting the natural foot-to-boot setup. The following red flags, listed by skier type, indicate problems with rotation.

Overpowered Skier

Overpowered skiers have a slightly pigeon-toed stance. Their feet point in and their knees often track inside. However, this problem is often addressed by the stock geometry in most boot designs. When they try to fit into a new boot, they often feel pressure in their insteps and as though their toes are twisting inward. Minor adjustments to the footbed or lateral grinding will remedy these compensations.

Underpowered Skier

Underpowered skiers often have an A-frame position in the lower legs, which leads to a duck walk. The average adult has 4 to 10 degrees of abduction in the stance, or duck-foot positioning. Several boot designs address this problem to promote easier turning. However, no two boot manufacturers agree on the amount of abduction needed or how it should be obtained for the best results. Body development can also play a role in the asymmetry, since the bones of younger skiers may grow faster than their muscles and tendons, resulting in misalignment and overuse injuries.

Underskilled Skier

Underskilled skiers may either bow their legs out or turn their knees in to compensate for lack of feel for proper alignment. Every boot has a rail or toe-and-heel counter for the binding's attachment. The shoe that encases your foot is above the rail. The center of the rail sits slightly inside the center of the shoe, giving the skier the mechanical advantage of moving over the inside edge. This offset is known as rail flare. Each boot has different degrees of flare. Bowlegged skiers do better with less flare and knock-kneed skiers should have more flare. Underskilled skiers with standard anatomy do best with less flare.

Combination Skier

Combination skiers exhibit a range of issues. One foot may be splayed out, both may be splayed, or one may be splayed out while the other rotates in. These unique alignment issues are best addressed by a professional boot fitter. The goal here is to identify the stance abnormalities. Close evaluation is required for proper customization.

Skis

Skis play an important role as you develop your personal signature on the slope. Choosing a ski with the right design for the terrain you want to master is a process that begins with answering a few questions about your personal style. You must also understand the basic parameters that will assist you in your developmental journey. As you answer the style questions, you will begin to see a pattern which will segue into the needs identified for your skier type. Follow up by learning about proper skis for your desired terrain and conditions and types that match your physical and technical profile.

- *Do you want to master one type of terrain before moving on to another challenge?* If so, consider a ski that excels on your favorite part of the mountain. For example, powder-specific skis float and turn easily in the deep stuff, but don't perform well on hard pack.
- *Do you prefer to move around the mountain and spend a little time in each challenge, mixing it up as you explore?* Look for a versatile ski that can be your workhorse, meeting many challenges at one time. The all-mountain carving ski performs well in most conditions and terrain.
- *Do you want to build a quiver of skis that you can choose from, depending on the conditions of the day?* Select the overachiever skis in each category to prepare for whatever may come.
- *Do you want to ski out of the boundaries in the morning and then cruise the groomers in the afternoon?* This requires an all-mountain ski that can slay the powder and carve groomers. You can also choose two different types and switch skis at lunch.

Depending on the answers you provided for the equipment questions, you will be closer to choosing a ski that fits your personal needs. The following descriptions of ski design will help you decide what shape and type of ski matches your chosen terrain. As you read the list, note your personal preference and continue to ask yourself which ski design makes most sense for you.

All-Mountain Skis

All-mountain, or multipurpose, skis run the spectrum in terms of design quality. Begin by weighing the advantages and disadvantages of ski weight, quickness, and stability. Tight situations that require quick, precise movements call for a ski that is nimble and responsive. Any extra weight that makes it slow to edge will work against you when the terrain gets narrow. Deeper snow conditions require a slightly fatter ski. Consider all the snow conditions you like and the terrain where you spend the most time to find your perfect fit.

All-mountain skis are fat enough to float in powder, but quick enough from edge to edge to elicit dynamic reactions for tight terrain. They are typically as tall as your forehead, which helps with maneuvering in challenging terrain like bumps and narrow steeps. In bumps, shorter skis (below forehead height) are more reactive, but you should expect to lose some of the Cadillac feel you get from a longer ski when you want to open up the throttle in open, flat terrain.

All-Mountain Performance Skis   All-mountain performance skis are your one-ski quiver choice. The best terrain for these skis are bumps, steeps, trees, and powder. Their versatility gives you carving capabilities on groomers, the ability to float in powder, and momentum in cut-up slush or heavy, wet powder. This forgiving ski can do everything, but it will not achieve the highest marks in special situations.

Basic Vocabulary for Ski Design

- *Tip*—This is the bend in the front of the ski. Powder skis have more bend and carving skis have less.

- *Shovel*—This is the widest portion of the tip. The more the shovel tapers to the waist, the quicker the initiation will be.

- *Waist*—This is the middle of the ski, or the portion that fits under your foot. Narrower waists are better for quick and precise turning on hard pack, but wider ones are better for deep snow flotation.

- *Tail*—This is the bend at the end of the ski. The more the ski tapers from the tail to the waist, the quicker it will finish the turn. Rear taper is straighter than front taper for smooth finishes.

- *Camber*—The bend designed into a ski helps distribute the skier's weight equally along the entire length for maximum holding power and control. The bow created by placing the bases of two skis together is traditional camber. A ski with traditional camber is best for carving on ice and for all-mountain skiing, but a duel camber with early rise or a reverse camber (rockered ski) is better for big, smeared turns in the deepest snow.

- *Sidecut*—This is the taper from tip to waist and waist to tail. Skis with a deep sidecut are good for holding on firm snow and arcing tight turns. A shallow side cut is good for big turns in powder and deep snow.

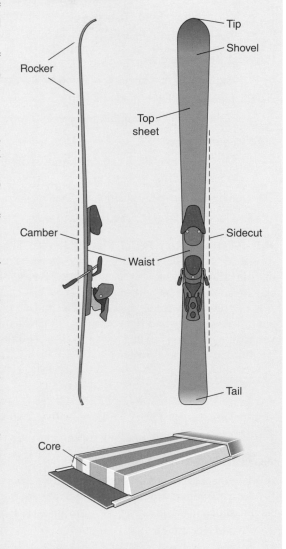

- *Core*—This wood or foam material stabilizes the ski. Wood cores can vary in stiffness and durability, but generally feel reactive and resilient coming out of a turn. Foam cores are less expensive and tend to feel damp underfoot.

- *Taper*—This is the difference between tip width and tail width. If the widths are close, the tail will follow almost the same arc as the tip, creating a tight turn. If the widths vary, the tail has less effect on the exit of the turn.

- *Top sheet*—This is the top layer of material on a ski, or the skin that highlights the graphics. It can be an important element when purchasing skis for many people. Boutique-ski manufacturers make personalized top sheets.

Ski Specifications

- *Waist width*: 70 to 85 millimeters
- *Turn radius*: 18 to 30 meters
- *Camber*: Traditional, early-tip rise rocker, or shovel rocker

Physical Requirements

1. Agility and quickness to respond to the changing conditions and terrain
2. Upper- and lower-body mobility to facilitate separation between the two
3. Controlled power output for explosive movements and quick directional changes

Skill Requirements

1. Versatility that allows you to switch easily from heavy-edge carving movements to softer, smearing turns
2. Stable upper-body position with independent leg turning for tight terrain and fall-line skiing
3. Good pole timing for rhythm and flow

All-Mountain Mid-Fat Skis   This ski is closely related to the all-mountain per-formance ski, but slants toward powder-specific skis. It is for people who want to ski more powder than anything else, but also want some carving ability on the groomers. The best terrain for these skis is variable terrain with soft, deep snow and changeable conditions. They also allow for front-side carving on groomed, open runs. The mid-fat ski is not as wide as a full-rocker powder board, but it is wide enough to float through soft powder and to provide a nice platform in the crud. Its versatility gives you holding power in firm conditions. It can be used as a multitask ski if you are simplifying to a one-ski quiver.

Ski Specifications

- *Waist width*: 75 to 112 millimeters
- *Turn radius*: 17 to 21 meters
- *Camber*: Traditional, full rocker; early-tip rise rocker; shovel rocker

Physical Requirements

1. Power production is needed for skiing diverse landscape. If you lack serious power, choose a ski with a softer flex profile that is shorter for easier swing weight.
2. Endurance for extended energy output is fundamental. If it is lacking, you will compensate and risk injury.
3. Strength will allow you to push, pull, and resist the terrain, conditions, and natural forces coming your way.

Skill Requirements

1. Movement basics of powder skiing, including two-footed balance and steering
2. Knowledge of all-mountain tactics and strategies for diverse situations
3. Off-the-groomed carving for good touch with the snow

Carving Skis

High-performance skiing relies on the elements of a carved turn. To match the tool with the tech-nique, you must pick out the ski with the right parameters. For maximum carving capabilities, choose a ski with a waist that is 63 to 75 millimeters wide and a turn radius of 12 to 15 meters. The narrow waist makes snappy turn initiations and will draw a tight, arced circle during turns. This carving ski will want to turn everywhere. If you are not ready for it, this ski can be a real workout.

Performance Carving Skis The exhilaration of carving clean arcs on an untouched groomer and looking back at your double trenches is incredible. Performance carving skis can give even underskilled carvers the feeling of increasing g-force as they balance through the tight arc of the turn. Underskilled skiers can use these specialized skis to improve the fundamental movements needed for high-performance skiing. The best terrain for these skis is groomed slopes, with consistent conditions and even terrain. I always start the season with a short carving ski because it brings me back to my fundamental-movement patterns. This is a good place to start for beginners and experts alike. However, performance carvers are not as stable at higher speeds and do not float well in deeper snow.

Ski Specifications

- *Waist width*: 65 to 75 millimeters
- *Turn radius*: 12 to 18 meters
- *Camber*: Traditional and traditional with early-tip rise

Physical Requirements

1. Hip mobility to engage edges and absorb forces through the turn
2. Core strength for balance and stability in the arcing phases of the turn
3. Lateral stability in the joints for progressive edging movements

Skill Requirements

1. Basic carving skills matched with a balanced stance over the outside ski
2. Ability to guide skis through a tight arc without slipping sideways or chattering off the edge

Racing Skis Racing skis feel rock solid underfoot. They carve with scalpel-like precision. The best terrain for these skis is groomed, firm snow that provides an even, consistent surface. Slopes that have been salted or watered overnight are a good testing ground for racing skis. Pack and rolled, corduroy-covered slopes can also provide a forgiving practice surface for learning the subtleties of a thoroughbred racing ski. These skis are real carving tools that perform well at higher speeds on firm snow with maximum edge grip. Besides being monsters on the firm pack, racing skis can improve your overall athleticism and dynamic-skiing skills just by using them. Logging miles on real racing skis promotes efficient movements and muscle memory.

Unlike powder and all-mountain skis, racing skis don't like to float (due in part to their narrow waist). If you do find yourself in deep snow, kick up your speed and power through it. When riding a racing ski, be prepared for a workout. They require constant attention and precise movements. Edge contact with the snow is predictable and constant. It will feel solid underfoot and will give you confidence in firm conditions. Exits out of turns are dynamic and committed, with a lot of pop!

Ski Specifications

- *Waist width*: 62 to 70 millimeters
- *Turn radius*: 12 to 40 meters
- *Camber*: Traditional

Physical Requirements

1. Proper posture for aggressive fall-line skiing
2. Movement efficiency with a focus on dynamic balance
3. Hip stability in the extended and flexed positions

Skill Requirements

1. Side-cut awareness and ski-design turning
2. Edge and pressure applications to tighten and open the turning arc
3. Leg turning independent of upper body

Free-Ride or Big-Mountain Skis

The good news is that more people can ski powder well than ever before. The bad news is that after a fresh dump, the mountain is tracked out by noon. If you can't beat them, you might as well join them. Free-ride or big-mountain skis will help you gain valuable mileage in the powder, without the steep learning curve typical with narrow-waisted skis.

The modern off-the-groomed ski culture is all about free-ride and big-mountain tactics that include huge-radius, high-speed turns, floating tactics on the surface of the powder, buttering the ski sideways to scrub speed, slashing over various terrain features, big air, and spinning and skiing backward in powder. The best terrain match for these big-mountain powder skis is ungroomed conditions where you can choose your own lines, such as big, open bowls with a ton of vertical drop. The terrain has a variety of pitch angles, but the snow density will seem more consistent due to the flotation properties found in wider skis.

Free-ride skiers are flocking to new designs that include wider overall footprints with straighter forebodies for consistency in powder and in deep, cut-up snow. These skis allow you to avoid all the irregularities under the snow by floating on the surface layer. Rockered skis look like water skis, with the tip and tail lifting out of the snow. This helps initiate the turn, since the ski floats and exits easily. The reverse camber also facilitates smearing the turn in the powder. Ski manufacturers are experimenting with a variety of different designs that vary in camber, shape, stiffness, and taper. The flat to cambered ski feels like what most of us expect from a powder ski. However, the half-rocker and full-rockered skis are now becoming the norm.

Ski Specifications

- *Waist width*: At least 80 millimeters
- *Turn radius*: 28 to 40 meters
- *Camber*: Reverse, hybrid, early-tip rise, early-tail rise, and a full rocker

Physical Requirements

1. An established endurance base and efficient body alignment for longer, more-demanding runs
2. Precise athletic stance (not muscle strength) to align your skeleton and hold you in place
3. Flexibility for energy transfer and leg retraction in high-speed powder turns

Skill Requirements

1. Aggressive commitment to the fall line and a balanced stance with your hips over the outside ski
2. Tactical awareness to build effective game plans and strategies for big terrain
3. Leg turning independent of upper body

We all have unique bodies and athletic profiles. Dreaming of a magic pill that will cure any difficulties in functional movement, fitness, technique, tactic, or equipment is naïve. Assess your skier type and take some time to choose equipment that is right for you. This is the most efficient path toward improvement. Remember, rushing through this process will only stunt your development and frustrate you as you struggle to build performance and durability. Taking the time to enjoy the process will deliver sounder, longer-lasting results.

7 8 9

PART II

Training, Drills, and Exercises for Ski Performance

Functional-Movement Exercises

As chapter 2 explains, developing the functional-movement block of the performance pyramid is the first step toward becoming a great Alpine skier. Without a solid foundation, advanced technical skills and power movements will only mask your compensation areas, leading to problems later on. Developing good daily habits and strengthening your problem areas benefit your overall athletic performance.

The way you move in your everyday routines creates habitual movement patterns that either help or hinder your performance. Tight muscles, weak joints, and imbalances between the sides of your body all seem natural after a while if you neglect to address them. You may begin to wonder what happened to your athleticism. Many chalk it up to the aging process or to a chronic injury, failing to differentiate between what is permanent and what can be reversed. Take full advantage of off-season training to create a balanced body that can handle the rigors of skiing once the snow begins to fall.

The following sections provide exercises that relate to the functional-movement assessments in chapter 2. For example, if your results from the overhead-squat assessment indicate weakness or immobility, seek out the specific exercises for improving those movements in this chapter. If you fail to address weaknesses in your movement patterns, you will never reach the range of motion needed for skiing moves in that plane of your body. Building strength and power around a faulty framework is counterproductive and will only reinforce your compensations. Therefore, exercises for proper mobility and stability will set you on the right course for long-term gains.

Overhead-Depth Squat

The overhead-depth squat test on page 11 in chapter 2 assesses the bilateral, symmetrical, and functional mobility and stability of your hips, knees, ankles, and spine. Table 2.1 on page 12 provides exercises for stability and mobility related to your score on this test. As chapter 2 states, if you score a 3 on an assessment, your only requirement is to revisit the test every four to six weeks to monitor your skill level.

Stability Exercises for the Depth Squat

To further improve or to maintain stability for scores 1 through 3 of the depth-squat test, practice the following exercises.

Depth-Squat Progression

SCORE OF 2

Tightness in your glutes and hamstrings throws off the balance of opposing muscles, causing joints to overload, especially the knee. Many ACL injuries are attributed to the combination of fatigue and this common imbalance. This exercise stretches your glutes, hamstrings, and spine.

To perform this exercise, stand with your feet parallel and hip-width apart. Squat into a deep, flexed position with your knees over your feet and your chest up, then extend your arms overhead. Stand up again.

a   b

EASIER VARIATION

- Execute the same movement with the help of a block, raising your heels 2 inches (5 cm).

Dumbbell-Assisted Squat

SCORE OF 2

The turning forces created by speed and terrain increase the amount of pressure felt through the legs. Adding weight also adds power to your mobility. Therefore, when you are faced with a high-energy turn, you will be accustomed to the intensity of the sensations. This exercise stretches your glutes, hamstrings, and spine with a counter-balance of added weight.

To perform this exercise, stand with your feet parallel and hip-width apart. Hold the dumbbells in front of you at the level of your chest. Squat slowly and deeply, then return to a standing position. Lower yourself with your hips, legs, and glutes, rather than with your back.

a   b

Depth Squat With Lowered Heel

SCORE OF 2

Stiff Achilles tendons can greatly affect your ability to properly flex your ankle and ski boot. Performing a depth squat while progressively raising and lowering your heels both lengthens these tendons and creates muscle memory for a proper squat.

To perform this exercise, stand with your feet parallel and hip-width apart and with the heel raised to a position between 1.5 and 2 inches (4-5 cm). Squat into a deep, flexed position, holding your knees over your feet and your chest up. Extend your arms out for balance. Next, return to a standing position. Repeat this movement, progressively lowering the heels with increasingly smaller shims. Note that you will notice that your range of motion and balance are dramatically affected with toes lifted as seen in the photo. You can also use this as an awareness exercise to identify any ramp-angle abnormalities in your boot setup.

a   b

Miniband Walking Routine

SCORE OF 1

The friction created by heavy snow or by forces from a fast turn requires resistance training. In this routine, the constant tension from the miniband prepares your glutes and legs for the opposing forces found on the mountain. The interaction between skis and snow creates resistance, resulting in a game of tug-of-war. This exercise works your glutes and core stabilizers.

a   b

> continued

> *continued*

To perform this exercise, assume a quarter or half squat and wrap a miniband around your legs, above the knees. Step forward, swinging your opposite arm. Step with the other leg while swinging the opposite arm. Keep the miniband taut throughout these movements. Repeat the movement forward, backward, and to both sides.

Mobility Exercises for the Depth Squat

To further improve or to maintain mobility for scores 1 through 3 of the depth-squat test, practice the following exercises.

Toe-Touch Progression
SCORES OF 2 OR 1

The touch receptors in your feet help you manage your position and control the pressure along the length of your foot that transfers to the length of the ski. This exercise helps you acquire the awareness and flexibility needed for active foot movements. It stretches the hamstrings, Achilles tendons, lower back, and glutes.

To perform this exercise, stand upright with your toes elevated 2 inches (5 cm) on a block, and reach for the sky. Flex your waist and touch the tops of your feet. If you cannot touch your toes, go as far down as you can without strain. Keep your legs straight and flex the hips, not the lower back. If you find that your knees track outward or inward, place a rolled towel between your knees to keep them over your feet. Repeat the same movement, elevating your heels.

a   b

Hurdle Step
SCORE OF 2

Coordinating and stabilizing your hips and torso in rough snow conditions and over bumpy terrain requires functional movement that is symmetrical and aligned through the ankle, knee, and hips. This exercise stabilizes your core, builds mobility in your hips, and addresses imbalance between the left and right sides of your body.

To perform this exercise, stand directly behind a hurdle or string. It should be in front of your knees, no higher than the bottom of your patellar tendon. Balancing on one leg, lift the other leg over the hurdle and place it down on the other side. Touch the ground with your foot and then bring it back over the hurdle without touching it.

a   b

Butterfly Wall Sit

SCORE OF 2

Open hip flexors and supple groin muscles increase hip mobility and recovery range for unexpected loss of balance or for greater mobility during leg turns or flexion. This exercise stretches the hip flexors and the gracilis and sartorius muscles, otherwise known as the groin muscles.

To perform this exercise, sit with your back against a wall and the soles of your feet touching each other. Allow the weight of your legs to slowly widen the gap between your knees, and then pull your feet toward your groin as much as you can. If you have trouble keeping your back straight, s t on a yoga block.

Depth-Squat Stretch

SCORE OF 2

The mobility gained through this stretch will increase your range of motion for deep flexion during terrain absorption. This exercise stretches the glutes and hamstrings and increases lower-back mobility.

To perform this exercise, stand in an upright position with your feet at least hip-width apart. Bend at the waist and grab your feet, then lower your buttocks to your ankles, keeping your chest up. Holding your feet, use your hips to extend back up, straightening your legs as you do so.

Stretch for Quads and Hip Flexors

SCORES OF 2 OR 1

Repeated firing of the quad muscles tightens the IT (iliotibial) band. If it is not stretched out, knee pain can result. This exercise helps balance and stretch the muscles that tighten from repeated movements. It stretches the quads, the IT band, and the groin muscles and increases dorsiflexion on the forward foot.

To perform this exercise, start in a half squat, bending one knee and resting the top of the other foot on a stability ball. Lunge forward slightly until you feel a stretch. To open the groin muscles and the hamstrings, keep your back straight and your chest high.

Thoracic 90-Degree Stretch

SCORE OF 1

Some skiers can easily dissociate the torso from the hips for precise leg turning, while others struggle with stiffness. This exercise loosens the hip flexors and allows the legs to easily move to either side.

To perform this exercise, lie on your back and extend your arms out to the side. Raise your legs to assume an L-position, with your back flat on the floor. Keeping your core tight, lower your legs to one side, return them to the middle, and then lower them to the opposite side.

Reach, Roll, and Lift on Stability Ball

SCORE OF 1

When skiing, your shoulders and chest muscles are in constant action as you plant and push with your poles and stabilize your core. At the end of the day, these areas feel stiff. Working on mobility helps your recovery and performance. This exercise works your back, shoulders, and core.

To perform this exercise, kneel behind a stability ball and extend your arms on top of the ball with your palms up. Roll the ball forward lengthening your back and stretching your arms forward.

HARDER VARIATION

- For a deeper stretch, lower so that you are sitting on your heels.

Single-Leg Squat

The single-leg squat test on page 13 in chapter 2 assesses knee stability and hip mobility when full body weight is applied. Table 2.2 on page 14 provides stability and mobility exercises that are appropriate for each score. As chapter 2 states, if you score a 3 on an assessment, your only requirement is to revisit the test every four to six weeks to monitor your skill level.

Stability Exercises for the Single-Leg Squat

To further improve or maintain stability for scores 1 through 3 of the single-leg squat test, practice the following exercises.

Single-Leg Squat Progression
SCORE OF 2

In skiing, single-leg balance is essential for maintaining alignment with the outside ski for maximum edging and pressure. The single-leg squat builds strength and stability in a full range of movement.

To perform this exercise, stand with your feet hip-width apart, center your weight over one leg, and extend your arms out to the sides. Balancing on one leg, slowly lower yourself into a squatting position, bringing your extended leg parallel with the floor. Begin by supporting your opposite leg on a bench and squat halfway. As you progress, remove support from your opposite leg and move to a full squat. Keep activation in the glute muscle and avoid stress on the patellar tendon of the bent knee.

Single-Leg Squat With Medicine Ball
SCORE OF 2

The single-leg squat is less stable than the double-leg squat. If your quads and hamstrings are out of balance, your knees can wobble and angle in or out. This exercise prepares you for the variable conditions and terrain of the mountain. It stretches the quads, calves, lower back, and the glutes.

To perform this exercise, stand and extend a medium-weight medicine ball out in front of you at chest level. Perform a single-leg squat, going as low as you can. Rise slowly by stabilizing your hips and your weighted leg. Switch legs and repeat. You will find that the medicine ball adds counterbalance, making this exercise easier than a single-leg squat without weights.

Single-Leg Squat With Miniband

SCORE OF 2

Adding a miniband as resistance to a single-leg squat supports your improvement in the three-dimensional environment of skiing. This exercise builds balance and functional range of motion in the lower body.

To perform this exercise, wrap a miniband around your knees. Lower yourself into a single-leg squat, maintaining tension on the band. As you stand up again, maintain equal spacing between both legs and consistent resistance on the band. Keep activation in the glute muscle and avoid stress on the patellar tendon of the bent knee.

Single-Leg Balance

SCORES OF 2 OR 1

Focusing on spatial awareness keeps your senses sharp for the ever-changing playing field.

To perform this exercise, stand on one leg and close your eyes. Adjust your ankle joint for balance without the help of your vision. Try to keep your lifted foot off the ground for 15 seconds, then repeat the movement on the other leg. Repeat the exercise with your eyes open, turning your head to the left and to the right. Repeat for both legs.

HARDER VARIATION

- Perform this exercise while moving your head from side to side with closed eyes.

Indoor Stork

SCORE OF 1

Single-leg stability helps you balance on the outside ski during the stages of a ski turn, from the initiation to the apex. Shifting your weight between skis during the turn fragments your turn shape, resulting in poor contact with the snow. When your skeleton is aligned and your muscle groups are balanced, they work together to keep the skis tracking through the snow. When they are not aligned, you fight against the imbalance or compensate with poor technique. This exercise stretches your glutes, quads, hamstrings, and hip flexors.

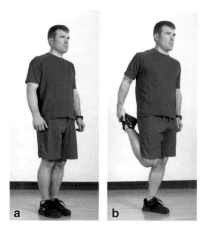

To perform this exercise, stand with your back straight and your arms at your side. Lift your right foot behind you until it touches your buttocks, then grab it with your right hand. Maintain good posture by keeping your back straight and your eyes focused straight ahead.

Knee-and-Ankle Grab

SCORE OF 1

The stability you gain by keeping your upper body aligned as your leg twists outward is essential for recruiting your glutes during turns. Clearing the inside leg (in this case, the lifted leg) allows for a deep range of lateral motion with the extended (weighted) leg. This exercise stretches your hip flexors and glutes.

To perform this exercise, stand with your back straight and your arms at your side. Lift your right leg and grasp your knee with one hand and your ankle with the other, allowing your knee to splay outward. Lower your leg and repeat on the other side.

Standing Split Squat

SCORE OF 1

Skiing involves a series of movements that require balance and strength in the hip and leg muscles. As you enter a tight turn, your core stabilizes when your legs turn, shaping the radius of the arc. This exercise helps you find balance as your legs become active.

To perform this exercise, step back into a lunge and lower your core to the ground, touching your back knee to the floor. Your front leg should maintain a 90-degree angle and your chest should point up and forward. You will feel the muscles engage in your hips and lower back. Keep your back erect and your front knee from sliding over the front toes.

Single-Leg Squat With Opposite-Hand Reach

SCORE OF 1

Coordinating opposing sides of your body is essential in skiing because you continually counterbalance one quadrant of your body with the opposite one.

To perform this exercise, step forward into a lunge and lower your core to the ground, touching your back knee to the floor. For an extra balance challenge and stretch for the upper shoulder and arm, raise the arm that is opposite to the forward leg. Your front leg should maintain a 90-degree angle and your chest should point up and face forward. You will feel the muscles in the hips and lower back engage. Keep your back erect and your front knee from sliding over the toes.

Single-Leg Squat With Assistance Line

SCORE OF 1

Outside-leg dominance is essential for precision, balance, and edge hold during any change in direction. As you flex your inside leg more deeply, you must maintain balance over the outside ski, where the majority of the weight is centered. This exercise stretches the quads, ankles, and glutes.

To perform this exercise, stand holding a line that is attached to a post or stationary object. Perform a single-leg squat, extending your arms in front of you. Flex slowly down to your point of resistance without bending at your waist. Rise up, pushing through your heel.

Mobility Exercises for the Single-Leg Squat

To further improve or to maintain mobility for scores 1 through 3 of the single-leg squat test, practice the following exercises.

Single-Leg Bridge for Glutes

SCORE OF 2

Activating the glutes for leg flexion and turning movements prevents excessive lower-back muscle recruitment, which leads to overuse injuries in the back. This exercise stretches your glutes, hamstrings, and back. It also builds stability in your hip flexors.

To perform this exercise, start with your back on the floor and your knees bent at a 90-degree angle. Engage your glutes and project your pelvis toward the ceiling, keeping your heels and shoulders planted on the ground. Next, extend one leg to form a straight line from your shoulder to your ankle. Shift all your weight to the leg firmly planted on the ground. Hold this position, then lower yourself slowly until your buttocks are just above the floor.

Leg Drops

SCORES OF 2 OR 1

The ability to move opposite sides of the body with control serves as a fundamental pattern for advanced moves. Many skiers establish a strong side that throws off their balance and mobility, causing inefficient, asymmetrical movements and potential overuse injuries. Coordination in all planes of the body rounds out any one-dimensional favorites, leading to balanced movements for synchronizing turns and building rhythm. This exercise stretches your hamstrings while at the same time building stability to support your lower back. It also builds core stability and body symmetry.

To perform this exercise, lie on your back with both legs extended to form a 90-degree angle with the floor. Slowly lower and raise one leg, keeping your hips level and your lower back on the floor. Repeat the movement with the other leg.

EASIER VARIATION

- Perform this exercise with a resistance band wrapped around your foot.

Standing Split Squat With Dumbbells

SCORE OF 1

Mobility and strength form a key combination for precision movements. This exercise requires balance in the fore-aft plane. Maintaining the split-squat position requires hip mobility and stability.

To perform this exercise, stand holding light dumbbells to build stability and strength in your hips and glutes. Step back into a lunge and lower your core to the ground, touching your back knee to the floor. Your front leg should maintain a 90-degree angle and your chest should point up and forward. You will feel the muscles in the hips and lower back engage. Keep your back erect and your front knee from sliding over the toes.

Backward Stretch for Quads and Hip Flexors
SCORE OF 1

The lowest point of your flexion range requires stability in the glutes. Without it, aggressive terrain or the forces in a turn will push you to the ground.

To perform this exercise, stand with your arms raised and your fingers interlocked behind your head. Step backward with your leg, engaging your glutes. Keeping your back knee aligned with your rear foot, lower that knee to a position just above the floor. Hold this position, continuing to engage the gluteal muscles. Push back up to a standing position by extending your lowered leg and pulling up with the other. Repeat this movement on the opposite side.

Stretch for Frontal Range
SCORE OF 1

Although recoveries and purposeful dynamic movements are cousins, both can push you to the limits of your range of motion. Unlike the wild situations ahead of you on the mountain, this exercise engages your full range of movement in a controlled and safe manner. It stretches your hamstrings, groin, shoulder, and lower back.

To perform this exercise, assume a forward-lunge position, extending your back leg straight behind you. Flex your front leg, keeping your knee behind your toes. Reach both hands forward and place the palms on the floor inside your flexed knee. Reach your outside arm around and toward the ceiling and hold the stretch. Switch arms and reach your inside arm to the ceiling. Return to the lunge position and repeat the movement on the opposite side.

Rotational Stability

The rotational-stability test on page 15 in chapter 2 assesses proper cross-body coordination with core stability. Table 2.3 on page 15 provides exercises that are appropriate for each score. If you score a 3 on an assessment, your only requirement is to revisit the test every four to six weeks to monitor your skill level. To further improve or to maintain stability for scores 1 through 3 of this test, practice the following exercises.

Forward Plank With Alternating Arm Lift

SCORE OF 2

Power initiated from the core can begin as isometric torso stabilization, but can quickly change to a powerful core release that redirects the skis into the next turn. This exercise works your shoulders, core, and glutes.

To perform this exercise, begin in a push-up position. Twist around to a side plank position and extend your right arm toward the ceiling. Stabilize your torso and lower back. Repeat on the other side.

HARDER VARIATION

- Begin in a push-up position. Lift your right leg toward the ceiling. Stabilize your torso and lower back. Repeat on the other side.

Plank Progression

SCORE OF 2

All movements in skiing begin in the core, and the best skiers generate power with stable torsos and highly mobile hips. Without a solid center for stabilization, you are as ineffective as a rag doll. You can only coordinate opposing extremities if your core is strong.

To perform this exercise, lie facedown in push-up position, resting on your forearms. Stabilize your torso and hold the position for 90 seconds (see figure a for an example of the plank). Avoid sagging or arching the middle of your body. Maintain a straight line through the midpoint of your body. Next, lie on your side, supporting yourself with one of your forearms

so that your body forms a straight line. Balancing on the outside edge of your bottom foot and your forearm, hold the position for 90 seconds, then switch sides (see figure b for an example of the side plank). If you would like an additional challenge, perform both exercises at the same time by starting in the front-plank position and lifting into the side-plank position, holding each for 90 seconds. To increase the intensity in the side plank, lift your top leg and hold your feet hip-width apart for 90 seconds before switching sides.

Lunge Chops

SCORE OF 2

Rotational ability is improved by strengthening the shoulders, arms, torso, and glutes. The core stability that results from an exercise like this one creates an anchor in the middle of your body that your extremities can work against. This exercise works your shoulders, core, and arms.

To perform this exercise, move into a lunge position, with your forward leg next to and perpendicular to a pulley machine. Grab the handle, pull the cable down to your chest, and rotate away from the pulley. Start facing the machine and finish the rep with your back to the machine.

Half-Kneeling Dowel Twist

SCORE OF 1

The ability to move the torso separately from the legs helps with dynamic turning and powerful core-body movements. The angling essential for edging skills is enhanced as the torso balances above the tilted lower body. This exercise stretches the lower back, hips, and shoulders.

To perform this exercise, start by bending one knee and hold a dowel across your shoulders. Keeping your upper body erect, twist your torso toward your front leg. Hold the position for 30 seconds and repeat in the other direction.

Hip Crossover

SCORE OF 1

Symmetry in turns requires equal mobility on both sides of your body. This exercise indicates differences between your left and right sides, strengthens your core, and builds mobility in your midsection, a necessary element for upper- and lower-body separation.

To perform this exercise, lie on your back and extend your arms, palms up. Bend your legs to a 90-degree angle, with your knees up and your feet off the floor. Keep your back and shoulders on the ground as you rotate your knees to one side. Return your knees to the center and then lower them to the opposite side. Your knees should maintain the 90-degree angle at all times.

EASIER VARIATION

- Perform this exercise while gripping a volleyball or a ball of similar size with the inside of your legs. Roll your legs and the ball to one side, and then swing them back to the opposite side, keeping the ball in contact with the ground as you move from side to side.

Circus Pony

SCORE OF 1

Opposing body parts, such as your right leg and left arm, are often engaged simultaneously, providing a counterbalance for maintaining body alignment. This exercise develops both core stability and bilateral coordination. It works your torso, shoulders, and glutes.

To perform this exercise, lie on your stomach on a stability ball. Anchor the ball with your core before engaging your arms and legs. Extend one leg out, simultaneously extending the opposing arm. Slowly lower them and switch legs and arms.

Knee Plank

SCORE OF 1

Core stability gives you control of your dynamic strength and improves your movement efficiency. Imagine a house of cards that collapses when a heavy object is placed on it. The same thing happens to your strength if you lack core stability. This exercise works your torso, shoulders, and back.

To perform this exercise, lie facedown in push-up position with your knees and forearms on the floor. From this position, stabilize your torso and hold the position for 90 seconds. Your knees, back, and shoulders should form a straight line.

Stability-Ball Twist

SCORE OF 1

Transitions between turns may feel awkward if you do not engage the ski edges due to temporary loss of stability. Strong abdominal muscles that hold the center in place can briefly stabilize the body. This exercise stretches the core and back muscles.

To perform this exercise, lie faceup on a stability ball with your legs bent to a 90-degree angle. Slowly twist your torso to the right while stabilizing the ball, keeping your abs contracted. Twist with your shoulders and torso, not with your hips and legs. Return to the starting position and then slowly rotate to the left.

Seated Rotation

SCORE OF 1

Torso mobility facilitates directional changes and efficient stops. Lower-back stiffness can limit the range of motion needed for turning. Without upper-body mobility, the entire body moves as one unit, limiting athletic movement. This exercise stretches your core and torso rotators.

To perform this exercise, sit on the floor with your legs crossed and hold a dowel across your chest. Keeping your spine erect and your shoulders and the dowel level, twist your torso to the left. Return to the center to face straight ahead and repeat the movement on the opposite side.

Lateral Lunge

The lateral-lunge test on page 16 in chapter 2 assesses your lateral range of motion in the hips. It also tests your ability to keep your torso upright as you extend your outside leg and flex your inside leg. Table 2.4 on page 17 provides related stability and mobility exercises for each score on this test. If you score a 3 on an assessment, your only requirement is to revisit the test every four to six weeks to monitor your skill level.

Stability Exercises for the Lateral Lunge

To further improve or to maintain stability for scores 1 through 3 of the lateral-lunge test, practice the following exercises.

Backward Lunge With Arm Raise

SCORE OF 2

Engaging the gluteal muscles stabilizes and lengthens the hip flexors, which flex and extend the leg muscles. This exercise stretches the hip flexors, glutes, quads, shoulders, and core stabilizers.

To perform this exercise, stand with your legs together and your arms at your sides. Lunge backward with one leg and engage your glutes, keeping your back toe in alignment with your back knee and your chest up. Raise the arm that is opposite to your front leg.

Push back up to standing position and switch legs and arms.

Straight-Arm Lateral Lunge With Dumbbells

SCORE OF 2

Strong quads, hip flexors, and calves are needed to lower the center of gravity when your movements become more dynamic. A low center of gravity requires that you hold your chest up and in a ready position, rather than bending at the waist.

To perform this exercise, stand with your feet about hip-width apart and hold dumbbells out in front. Step to the side with one leg and keep that leg extended as you lower yourself over the bent leg until your thigh is parallel with the floor. Hold the position and

stretch the dumbbells out in front of you at chest height. Push back up to the starting point. Repeat on the opposite side.

Resistance-Band Rotation

SCORE OF 1

The resistance created by heavy snow or a steep pitch requires you to release and reengage the skis. If your knees struggle and shake from the band's resistance, remember that the same thing can result from the dynamic forces in a ski turn. You can avoid wobbly legs if you have conditioned your legs to move through resistance. This exercise stretches and stabilizes your glutes, adductors, and abductors.

To perform this exercise, assume a half-squat position and wrap a resistance band around your legs above the knees. Keeping your left leg stable and your hips and shoulders pointed forward, move your right knee back and forth. Switch legs.

Hip Stretch With Resistance Band

SCORE OF 1

Balancing securely on one leg while moving the other gives you versatility and independence. Skiing requires a wide range of movement that challenges balance in all planes. This exercise stretches and stabilizes the glutes, adductors, and abductors.

To perform this exercise, attach one end of a resistance band to a post and the other to one of your ankles. Stand with your hands on your hips and engage your core. Extend the leg attached to the band to the side and then move it back. For maximum burn, engage and release the band slowly. Switch legs.

Lateral Lunge on Stability Ball

SCORE OF 1

Dynamic movement in the lateral plane involves flexing one leg while extending the other. This skill can be seen at almost all levels of ability. However, it is most visible in the advanced level, since skiers use a long-leg, short-leg technique in the turn's apex. This exercise stretches the quads, hip flexors, and calves.

To perform this exercise, sit on a stability ball and assume a squatting position with your feet wide apart. Slide laterally and flex one leg while extending the other leg and lowering your stance. Keep your chest up and use the ball to maintain correct position in the lateral lunge. Be careful not to hang on it or lean against it. Return to the starting position and repeat on the opposite side.

Lateral Lunge With Arm Reach

SCORE OF 1

Strong quads, hip flexors, and calves are needed to lower the center of gravity when your movements become more dynamic A low center of gravity requires you to hold your chest up and in a ready position, rather than bending at the waist.

To perform this exercise, stand with your feet about hip-width apart and your arms down. Step to the side with one leg and keep that leg extended as you lower yourself over the bent leg until your thigh is parallel with the floor. Keep the extended leg straight and the foot planted on the floor. Both feet should point straight ahead. Reach the arm on the same side as the outstretched leg up to the ceiling. Hold the position and push back up to the starting point. Repeat on the opposite side.

a    **b**

Mobility Exercises for the Lateral Lunge

To further improve or to maintain mobility for scores 1 through 3 of the lateral-lunge test, practice the following exercises.

Drop Lunge

SCORE OF 2

Every ski turn involves flexing and extending the legs. These movements require lateral and rotational mobility. Most of our everyday movements occur in a straight line, making the hips and IT bands unbalanced and stiff. Flexibility in the lateral plane provides fine-tuning movements needed for edging and for releasing the skis. This exercise stretches the hips, glutes, and IT bands.

To perform this exercise, stand with your feet hip-width apart, raise your arms, and clasp your hands behind your head. Reach your left leg behind your right leg and point your hips and shoulders straight ahead. Lower into a squat, keeping your right heel planted on the ground. Keep your toes pointed **a** **b** straight ahead. Return to a standing position and switch legs.

Stretch for Adductors and Abductors With Resistance Band

SCORE OF 2

Hip mobility is necessary for steering your skis across the hill with short turns and instant breaking movements. It also helps you dissociate your upper body from the lower body. This exercise stretches the glutes and the IT bands.

To perform this exercise, lie on the floor on your back, extend your legs, and wrap a resistance band around your foot. Hold both ends of the band with the opposite hand and pull your extended leg over the other one as far as it will go without pain. Hold this position for three counts. Then pull the extended foot to the opposite side of your body and hold for three counts. Repeat on the other leg.

Inchworm

SCORE OF 1

Stabilizing your shoulders and core improves the internal blocking needed for short-radius turns, long turns, and fall-line skiing. Solid pole plants also help with external blocking; however, internal stability must be developed. This exercise stretches the glutes, hamstrings, and calves and builds stability in the lower back.

To perform this exercise, flex your waist and touch the floor with your hands, keeping your legs straight. Move from a pike position by walking your hands out in front of your head. Continue moving your hands until you assume a standard push-up position or beyond. Keeping your legs straight, walk your feet toward your hands, back into the pike position.

Ankle Stretch

SCORE OF 1

Symmetrical forward and diagonal movements of the lower leg assist shin-boot contact for better leveraging over the front of the ski. Forward leverage helps you engage the front of the ski for smooth turn initiations. This exercise stretches the calf muscles and the Achilles tendons.

To perform this exercise, start in a half kneeling position and place a dowel next to the outside of your foot. The dowel will keep the knee tracking over the foot. Flex forward, aligning your knee over the middle of your foot. Your heel should stay on the floor.

Stretch for Quads

SCORE OF 1

Repeated skiing movements stiffen the hip flexors and quads and shorten support muscles like the psoas, putting stress on the lower back. This exercise stretches the quads, the IT bands, and the groin, and increases dorsiflexion on the forward foot.

To perform this exercise, assume a half-squat position, with one knee bent and the other leg folded behind you. Rest the top of the foot of the back leg against a wall. Press your shoulders against the wall, allowing your leg to fold behind you and your foot to touch your buttocks and the wall. Lunge forward slightly until you feel a stretch. Switch legs and repeat.

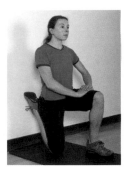

Lateral Hip Adduction With Resistance Band

SCORE OF 1

Balancing securely on one leg while moving the other gives you versatility and independence. Skiing requires a wide range of movements that challenge balance in all planes. This exercise stretches and stabilizes the glutes.

To perform this exercise, attach one end of a resistance band to a post and the other to one of your ankles. Stand with your hands on your hips and engage your core. Extend the leg attached to the band to the side and then move it back. For maximum burn, engage and release the band slowly. Switch legs.

You will clearly feel the results of these exercises as you move throughout the day with fluid hips and a solid, balanced core. Your torso will be more erect and you will move deeper as you bend down to perform daily tasks. Once you're out on the snow, you will observe better balance and greater control of your extremities. It will be easier to make long-lasting technical changes that are rooted in good body mechanics. Now that you have addressed the chinks in your functional movement, you are ready to participate in a variety of strength and power-building activities that will provide the full picture of fitness needed for skill development.

Fitness Training and Exercises

This chapter goes hand in hand with the assessments from chapter 3, providing workouts and drills that strengthen and build your level of skiing fitness so you can effectively execute the next two blocks of the pyramid, technique and tactics. Without proper functional movements, you build on a weak foundation. The same principle applies to the second level, the fitness block. Without identifying the exercises necessary for cardiorespiratory fitness, muscular fitness, and strength and power fitness, you build on shaky ground.

You may feel excited as you approach the technique and tactics blocks, since you will soon connect with your improved strength and cardio capacity, enhancing your confidence and preparation for the challenges of the mountain.

Cardiorespiratory Training

The following workouts can be performed with the aerobic activity of your choice. They are broken down into the three types of cardiorespiratory-fitness assessments from chapter 3—aerobic, anaerobic threshold, and anaerobic power. Each provides detailed information about training, using specific workout zones that target the different cardio levels.

As you work toward the heart-rate (HR) goals that align with your cardio objectives for each workout, remember that it takes a while to increase your HR. Your HR may not always reflect the intensity of your activity. Chapter 3 introduces the idea of rate of perceived exertion (RPE) as a way of aligning your intensity with your HR zones. This concept is particularly important at the start of a workout or interval because you must rely on your RPE to determine your intensity until your HR can catch up and relay its own information. After that, the shorter the interval, the more important RPE monitoring becomes. You may not have enough time to raise your HR into the target zone, at least during the first few intervals. However, as your workout time progresses, your HR will increase more rapidly, allowing you to move into the zones more quickly. The easiest way to monitor and regulate your HR while exercising is on a treadmill, stationary bicycle, or elliptical trainer. Mountain biking, trail running, hiking, road cycling, cross-country skiing, and backcountry skiing are all wonderful ways to enhance your cardiorespiratory endurance; however, they require a little more work to keep you in the zones prescribed by the workout.

As you perform the following workouts, remember that you might find it hard to physically push yourself into zones 2 or 3 during the first three intervals. As you fatigue, your HR easily climbs into the higher zones, but the relationship may not accurately reflect your intensity. In some cases, muscular prefatigue limits your ability to reach higher zones. Balancing your program in terms of cardio and muscular training will correct this type of weakness.

Aerobic Workouts (Zone 1)

Many people are familiar with aerobic workouts that get the heart going and continue the same pace for 40 to 60 minutes. You come home experiencing the endorphins that tell you that you've worked out, and you feel satisfied until the urge hits you again. Working in this zone is important, but it's only one piece of the puzzle. Once you have incorporated the full cardiorespiratory program, this aerobic level serves as the cruising gear that allows you to shift into the higher gears of the anaerobic zone.

As the aerobic assessment in chapter 3 (see page 31) illustrates, workouts for aerobic fitness are performed at zone 1. Your goal in these routines is to extend the duration of nonstop work in an activity you enjoy and actually look forward to doing. (Table 3.1 provides sample prescriptions for the popular activities of running and cycling.) The key to these workouts is tracking your HR and making sure you stay within your training intensity for zone 1. This ensures that you only work on the output of your aerobic system. Refer to table 3.1 on page 31 for specific time guidelines for aerobic workouts based on your score (3, 2, or 1).

Anaerobic Workouts (Zones 2 and 3)

Passing from the aerobic zone to the anaerobic zone is important for skiing, but you must train at levels that raise your HR for short durations. The following workouts outline strategies for moving into zone 2. The demands of skiing require more than one cardiorespiratory level. Training for aerobic, anaerobic threshold and anaerobic power fitness gives you the complete cardio package.

Workouts for the Anaerobic Threshold (Zone 2)

The workouts for the anaerobic threshold consist of bursts of moderate energy, or intervals ranging from two to five minutes within your zone-2 HR. (See the anaerobic assessment on page 32 for more information.) Your goal is to increase the amount of work before lactate begins pooling in your system, causing muscle burn and fatigue. These interval workouts pay off on long slopes that require continuous muscle firing. They also teach your body to handle overloads of lactate by converting it into fuel, extending your window of precision movements and postponing fatigue.

Assess your anaerobic threshold at least once every two weeks to monitor your progress. You can choose from any of the workouts for training your anaerobic threshold. Each provides guidelines based on your score from chapter 3. Always start with a 5- to 10-minute warm-up to get your HR into zone 1.

Base Workout for Anaerobic Threshold

This workout is identical to the anaerobic-threshold assessment in chapter 3. You should do it at least once every two weeks to monitor your progress. Perform as many three-minute interval cycles as possible, following the instructions on page 32. Remember to keep your HR within zone 2 and to conclude your workout when it can no longer drop to zone 1 during the two-minute period of active recovery.

Once you can complete four intervals, follow the workout guidelines for a score of 2. Once you can complete seven intervals, follow the workout guidelines for a score of 3. See table 3.2 on page 33 for more information.

Intensity Workout for Anaerobic Threshold

In order for workouts in zone 2 to be effective, you must maintain the same intensity over the entire interval. Your goal is to hone in on this intensity, through both RPE and HR monitoring, and maintain it over the duration of the interval. Start with 5 to 10 reps of 2-minute intervals of your chosen activity (preferably a treadmill or bike), resting actively in zone 1 for 1 or 2 minutes between reps. Check your HR at the end of each recovery time. When it can no longer recover to zone 1 by the end of the rest period, the workout is over. Once you can complete 10 two-minute intervals, build your capacity by adding 30 seconds to the interval portion, starting over with a goal of five reps. You can also decrease the period of active rest between intervals if you recover more quickly than the allotted 2 minutes.

Ladder Workout for Anaerobic Threshold

This workout builds your capacity to work in zone 2 over a longer period of time. Skiing on a long racecourse, in heavy snow, or over steep bumps involves prolonged, intense muscular effort similar to the requirements of this workout. This type of training allows you to gradually increase the length of your runs and exercise more dynamic control. Your objective here is to start on the low end of the interval range prescribed in your score (see table 3.2 on page 33). Increase your time with each interval until you reach the high end of your range. This workout is called the ladder because it climbs from bottom to top. You will recover for two minutes between intervals, but will complete all intervals whether or not your HR has recovered by the end of the rest period.

SCORE OF 3

If you currently have a score of 3 for anaerobic threshold, do two fewer intervals than you can normally complete in the base workout for anaerobic threshold. Equally distribute the intervals between 3 and 5 minutes. For example, if you are currently completing seven 3-minute intervals as your base workout, do five intervals for this workout (one of 3 minutes, one of 3.5 minutes, one of 4 minutes, one of 4.5 minutes, and one of 5 minutes).

SCORE OF 2

If you currently have a score of 2 for anaerobic threshold, do one less interval than you can normally complete in the base workout for anaerobic threshold on page 117, equally distributing the intervals between 3 and 4 minutes. For example, if you currently complete four 3-minute intervals in your base workout, do three intervals for this workout (one of 3 minutes, one of 3.5 minutes, and one of 4 minutes).

SCORE OF 1

If you currently have a score of 1 for anaerobic threshold, do one more interval than you normally complete in the base workout for anaerobic threshold, equally distributing the intervals between 2 and 3 minutes. For example, if you currently complete two 3-minute intervals in your base workout, do three intervals for this workout (one of 2 minutes, one of 2.5 minutes, and one of 3 minutes).

360 Workout for Anaerobic Threshold

As with the ladder workout for anaerobic threshold, this routine builds your capacity to work in zone 2 for longer periods of time. It differs in that you will start and end with the same interval time, allowing the workout to come full circle, or 360 degrees. Perform the middle portion of the workout at the time on the high end of your score (see table 3.2 on page 33). You will recover for two minutes between intervals, but will complete all the intervals whether or not your HR recovers by the end of the rest period.

SCORE OF 3

If you currently have a score of 3 for your anaerobic threshold, do two fewer total intervals than you can normally complete in the base workout for anaerobic threshold on page 117. Start with a 3-minute interval, build up to five minutes, and work back down, ending with another 3-minute interval. For example, if you currently complete seven 3-minute intervals in your base workout, do five total intervals (one of three minutes, one of 4 minutes, one of 5 minutes, one of 4 minutes, and one of 3 minutes).

SCORE OF 2

If you currently have a score of 2 for anaerobic threshold, do one less interval than you can normally complete in the base workout for anaerobic threshold on page 117. Start and end with a 3-minute interval and perform the rest of the intervals for 4 minutes. For example, if you currently complete five 3-minute intervals in your base workout, do four intervals in this workout (one 3-minute interval, two 4-minute intervals, and one 3-minute interval).

SCORE OF 1

If you currently have a score of 1 for anaerobic threshold, do one more total interval than you can normally complete in the base workout for anaerobic threshold on page 117. Start and end with a 2-minute interval and perform the rest of the intervals for 3 minutes. For example, if you currently complete three 3-minute intervals in your base workout, do four intervals in this workout (one 2-minute interval, two 3-minute intervals, and one 2-minute interval). The number of 3-minute intervals will always be one fewer than those in your base workout.

Workouts for Anaerobic Power (Zone 3)

These workouts use high-intensity intervals that range from 20 to 120 seconds and are performed in zone 3. (See the anaerobic assessment on page 32 for more information.) Your goal is to increase the amount of time in which you can produce an all-out effort. These interval workouts train you to both perform at your highest intensity for longer periods of time and to produce power bursts for finishing strong or getting out of trouble on the hill.

Perform the assessment for anaerobic power at least once every two weeks to monitor your progress. The following base workout is actually the same as the assessment in chapter 3. Otherwise, you can choose from any of the workouts for training anaerobic power. Each workout matches your score from chapter 3. Always warm up for 5 to 10 minutes in zone 1 before starting.

Base Workout for Anaerobic Power

This workout is the same as the anaerobic power assessment in chapter 3. Perform it at least once every two weeks to monitor your progress. Perform as many 30-second interval cycles as you can, following the instructions on page 32. Remember to keep your HR in zone 3 and to conclude the workout if it no longer drops to zone 1 during the two minutes of active recovery. When you can complete five intervals, follow the workout guidelines for a score of 2. Once you can complete eight intervals, follow the workout guidelines for a score of 3.

Intensity Workout for Anaerobic Power

As in zone-2 workouts, in order for zone-3 workouts to be most effective, you must maintain the same intensity over the entire interval. Your goal is to hone in on this intensity through both RPE and HR monitoring and to maintain it over the duration of the interval. Start with 4 to 12 reps of 20-second intervals of your chosen activity, actively resting in zone 1 for 2 minutes between each rep. Check your HR at the end of each recovery time. When it can no longer recover to zone 1 by the end of the rest period, the workout is over. Once you can complete 12 intervals of 20 seconds, build your capacity by adding 5 seconds to the interval portion. Begin again with a goal of four reps.

Ladder Workout for Anaerobic Power

This workout builds your capacity to work in zone 3 for a longer period of time. Your objective is to start at the low end of the interval range prescribed for your score (see table 3.3 on page 33), increasing your time with each interval until you reach the high end of your range. As mentioned previously, this workout is called the ladder because it climbs from bottom to top. You will recover for two minutes between intervals, but will complete all intervals whether or not your HR has recovered by the end of the rest period.

SCORE OF 3

If you currently have a score of 3 for anaerobic power, do three fewer intervals than you can normally complete in the base workout for anaerobic power, equally distributing the intervals between 30 and 120 seconds. For example, if you currently complete eight 30-second intervals in your base workout, do five intervals for this workout (a 30-second interval, a 55-second interval, a 75-second interval, a 95-second interval, and a 120-second interval).

SCORE OF 2

If you currently have a score of 2 for anaerobic power, do two fewer intervals than you can normally complete in the base workout for anaerobic power, equally distributing the intervals between 30 and 60 seconds. For example, if you currently complete six 30-second intervals in your base workout, do four intervals for this workout (a 30-second interval, a 40-second interval, a 50-second interval, and a 60-second interval).

Mixed-Cardio Workouts for Zones 1 and 3

These workouts target both anaerobic power (zone 3) and aerobic capacity (zone 1) through circuits with at least 5.5 minutes of continuous activity.

WORKOUT 1
Repeat this 12-minute circuit until your HR no longer recovers to zone 1 during the last 2-min. interval. A good goal is 4-6 repetitions.

- 5-min. warm-up
- 1 min. in zone 2
- 1 min. in zone 3
- 30 sec. in zone 1

- 1 min. in zone 3
- 30 sec. in zone 1
- 1 min. in zone 3
- 2 min. in zone 1

WORKOUT 2
Repeat this 13-minute circuit until your HR no longer recovers to zone 1 during the last 2-min. interval. A good goal is 4-6 repetitions.

- 5-min. warm-up
- 1 min. in zone 2
- 1 min. in zone 3
- 1 min. in zone 1

- 1 min. in zone 3
- 1 min. in zone 1
- 1 min. in zone 3
- 2 min. in zone 1

WORKOUT 3
Repeat this 7.5-minute circuit until your HR no longer recovers to zone 1 during the last 2-min. interval. A good goal is 2-4 repetitions.

- 5 min. warm-up
- 20 sec. in zone 3
- 10 sec. in zone 1

- Repeat 8 times
- 2 min. in zone 1

WORKOUT 4
Repeat this 10.5-minute circuit until your HR no longer recovers to zone 1 during the last 2-min. interval. A good goal is 4-6 repetitions.

- 5-min. warm-up
- 1 min. in zone 2
- 30 sec. in zone 3
- 30 sec. in zone 1

- 30 sec. in zone 3
- 30 sec. in zone 1
- 30 sec. in zone 3
- 2 min. in zone 1

Mixed-Cardio Workouts for Zones 2 and 3

These workouts target the spectrum of anaerobic benefits (anaerobic threshold and anaerobic power in zones 2 and 3) while working aerobic capacity (zone 1) through circuits of at least seven minutes of continuous activity.

WORKOUT 1
Repeat this 12-minute circuit until your HR no longer recovers to zone 1 during the last 2-min. interval. A good goal is 4-6 reps.

- 5-min. warm-up
- 1 min. in zone 2
- 1 min. in zone 3

- 3 min. in zone 2
- 2 min. in zone 1

WORKOUT 2
Repeat this 12-minute circuit until your HR no longer recovers to zone 1 during the last 2-min. interval. A good goal is 4-6 reps.

- 5-min. warm-up
- 2 min. in zone 2
- 1 min. in zone 3

- 1 min. in zone 2
- 1 min. in zone 3
- 2 min. in zone 1

WORKOUT 3
Repeat this 12-minute circuit until your HR no longer recovers to zone 1 during the last 2-min. interval. A good goal is 4-6 reps.

- 5-min. warm-up
- 1 min. in zone 2
- 2 min. in zone 3

- 2 min. in zone 2
- 2 min. in zone 1

WORKOUT 4
Repeat this 12.25-minute circuit until your HR no longer recovers to zone 1 during the last 2-min. interval. A good goal is 4-6 reps.

- 5-min. warm-up
- 2 min. in zone 2
- 1 min. in zone 3
- 1 min. in zone 2

- 30 sec. in zone 3
- 30 sec. in zone 2
- 15 sec. in zone 3
- 2 min. in zone 1

Exercises for Muscular Fitness, Power, and Agility

Once you have addressed the fundamentals of mobility, stability, and endurance, glue it all together with training for strength, power, and agility. Strength training for skiing focuses on performing better in the varied challenges of the mountains. Increasing your strength ultimately gives you long-range power output without sacrificing precision or effectiveness. Power is essential for all-mountain skiing, since you use strong legs and a stable torso to attack the steep, bumpy terrain. Stability comes from strong, balanced torso muscles that let you control your arms and legs during dynamic skiing.

Agility training improves your ability to react to outside stimuli and to quickly engage your muscles. The following exercises increase your ability to quickly and effectively move in all planes of the body. Agility exercises also stimulate your central nervous system, helping with quick directional changes, acceleration, and deceleration. This component pulls together all the necessary aspects of skiing performance, including functional mobility, stability, endurance, strength, and power.

Exercises for Muscular Fitness

Although Alpine skiing engages both halves of the body, the lower-body muscles of the hip flexors, quadriceps, hamstrings, calves, ankle, and foot are primarily responsible for turning. Strength training for skiing must specifically involve the major muscle groups used for turning and managing terrain. The workouts must also be broad enough to keep the body balanced for recovering and making symmetrical movements in all planes. Although the muscle groups of the lower body are bigger, absorbing most of the direct force of terrain and snow, the upper body is just as important when it comes to balance, pole use, and stability. Without an equal marriage of the two halves of the body, you are susceptible to technique flaws and muscular imbalances.

Many Alpine ski teams have conducted kinesiology testing and movement experiments indicating that the muscle groups of the lower body are the primary movers for athletic skiing. The tests and corresponding exercises focus on the ability of the upper and lower body to effectively move in multiple planes. Core and upper-body strength round out the total performance with complementary muscle groups and torso stabilization. The abs, lower back, and upper torso work with the lower body as the legs twist and tip to manipulate the skis. The shoulder and arm muscles are involved in pole plants and balancing movements. Although the muscles of the lower body are key, well-balanced skiers have muscular symmetry in the upper body as well. Once you have completed the assessments in chapter 3, meet your strength, agility, and power needs with the following exercises.

When transitioning from easy to difficult terrain, you move from two-dimensional skiing to three-dimensional skiing. Crossover strength training that involves simultaneously balancing in several different planes and moving weights is best for advanced situations. Although exercises that work a muscle group in one direction can be helpful for learning a movement pattern, multiplane exercises, such as those performed on ski simulators or on other devices that challenge your balance while lifting, are preferable once you have learned proper form and execution techniques. The exercises for a score of 1 are primarily one-dimensional and those for a score of 3 are primarily three-dimensional.

Exercises for Upper-Body Strength

Upper-body strength keeps your body effectively positioned for balance and pole use as the energy builds throughout ski turns. To further improve or to maintain upper-body fitness for scores 1 through 3, practice these exercises.

Push-Up

SCORES OF 3, 2, OR 1

Forces transmitted from the mogul, through the ski pole, and up to your shoulder can be powerful enough to damage your shoulder joint if your supporting muscles are not strong enough to stabilize the ball and socket.

To perform this exercise, assume a push-up position with your shoulders seated in their joints. Maintaining a straight line from your ears to your heels, lower your body until your chin and chest touch the floor simultaneously. Push back up and repeat the process until you have completed the recommended number of reps. Your shoulder muscles must stay engaged to keep your shoulder blades from flaring out and your abdominal and gluteal muscles must stay activated to keep your waist from sagging.

VARIATIONS

- *Easier.* Perform the push-up with your hands on a bench.
- *Harder.* Perform the push-up with your feet on a bench.

Push-Up on Stability Ball

SCORE OF 3

Although outside influences are always static when working in a gym, dynamic movement with simultaneous balance adjustment makes skiing unique. Therefore, you must train accordingly. The stability ball adds another dimension to this exercise, moving both side to side and back and forth.

To perform this exercise, assume a push-up position, with your shins balanced on a stability ball and your hands placed on the floor shoulder-width apart. Keeping your body stable, slowly lower yourself to the floor and then forcefully push back up to the starting position. Pushing with purpose adds a power component to this exercise. You should keep your body aligned to aid stabilization on the

ball. Don't pike your body as you return to extension.

VARIATIONS

- *Easier.* Perform the push-up with your knees on the ball.
- *Harder.* Perform the push-up with your ankles or toes on the ball.

Bench Press With Dumbbells

SCORES OF 3 OR 2

While skiing, you constantly use your arms, chest, and shoulders to push up slight inclines or up to the lift, to stabilize pole plants, and to recover balance with pole plants.

To perform this exercise, lie on your back on a bench, holding weights straight above your shoulders. Make sure you are aligned from your shoulder to your knee. Working one side at a time, lower the weight and then push it back up immediately. Repeat this process with the other arm and continue for the recommended count. You should use your full range of

motion as you extend and flex your arms. Keep your abdomen engaged to avoid arching your back as you push the weight up.

VARIATIONS

- *Easier.* Perform the exercise by moving both dumbbells together or by using a barbell.
- *Harder.* Perform the exercise by using different weights in each hand or by holding a weight in one hand.

Supine Row With Feet Elevated

SCORES OF 3 OR 2

When you fall, your natural reaction is to extend your arm to protect your head and core. Without upper-body strength, you lose the ability to resist the forces from a fall. The most common skiing injuries are thumb sprains due to arm-extension recoveries.

To perform this exercise, set the bar at waist height on a squat rack or a smith machine. Lie on your back with your heels elevated on a stability ball. With your core engaged and your shoulder blades flat against your back (not flaring out like chicken wings), pull up until your chest touches the bar and then lower yourself back down, keeping

your heels on the stability ball. Avoid breaking at the waist. Keep your body line straight and the bar at a height that allows for full-arm extension.

VARIATIONS

- *Easier.* Perform the exercise with your feet placed on a step.
- *Harder.* Perform the exercise while lowering your chest to a position below your feet.

Kneeling Single-Arm Row

SCORES OF 3 OR 2

As the forces of wild terrain try to bend and twist you into a pretzel, your core muscles stabilize you, keeping you balanced and aligned for efficient movements. If these muscles are weak, you may get pushed and shoved around the hill. If they are strong, you have the stability needed to push back when you are challenged.

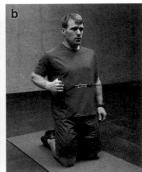

To perform this exercise, kneel in front of a cable machine with both knees on a pad and your back straight. Grab the pulley with one arm and pull as if you were rowing. Move as much weight as possible without shifting your torso in any direction. Repeat for the prescribed number of reps and then switch sides. Lower the weight until your arm is extended and keep your spine parallel to the floor. Also, to keep your torso from twisting, engage your abdominal and gluteal muscles.

VARIATIONS

- *Easier.* Perform the exercise on one knee, bringing the other knee out in front of you.
- *Harder.* Perform the exercise while sitting on a stability ball.

Chest Press

SCORE OF 1

In skiing, strong chest muscles support your stance and promote an athletic posture for dynamic movements. Underdeveloped chest and shoulder muscles lead to slumping, which requires your lower back and hips to compensate, causing pain and injury.

To perform this exercise, lie down or sit on the bench with the bar grips at chest level. Grab the bar with an overhand grip and extend your arms toward the ceiling. Return the bar to the starting position, feeling the stretch in your pectoral (chest) muscles. Keep your grip wide enough to maintain mobility through your shoulders. Return the weight slowly to benefit from the cocontraction, or negative portion of the exercise.

Horizontal Row

SCORE OF 1

Stabilizing your core and working your chest and arms builds the strength needed to coordinate multiple body parts. In skiing, core strength lets your legs and arms work efficiently and correctly time movements for the right application.

To perform this exercise, stand in front of a bar and bend your knees slightly. Keeping your back straight, bend over and grab the bar. Pull it to your waist, engaging your core and back muscles. Lower the bar until your arms are extended. Keep your knees bent slightly and your back straight. Stiff hamstrings often cause the back to round.

Lat Pull-Down

SCORE OF 1

Skiers pull and push with their arms and lats to control their ski poles when turning and propelling themselves from one point to another.

To perform this exercise, sit on the bench facing the weight rack. With a wide grip, grasp the horizontal bar attached to the cable. Pull the bar to your chest and return it until your arms are extended. Repeat this movement for the prescribed number of reps. Keep your grip wide enough to ensure shoulder mobility, but not so wide as to limit movement. Also, return the bar slowly to benefit from the cocontraction, or negative portion of the exercise.

Core-Strength Exercises

Core strength will help you move efficiently and precisely. Since all movements start in the center of the body, the core is the center of the body's universe. The function of the extremities depends on core strength. If your core is stable and strong, you will be able to effectively and dynamically incorporate your arms, legs, glutes, and the rest of the outer muscle groups. To further improve or to maintain core fitness for scores 1 through 3, practice these exercises.

Medicine-Ball Toss With Sit-Ups

SCORES OF 3 OR 2

Quick core responses for adjusting balance or executing ballistic moves are mandatory for all-mountain skiers. The coordination of the core and the extremities is fundamental to skiing success. This exercise strengthens the back and torso and the toss makes this a great core-body power exercise.

To perform this exercise, lie on your back with your knees bent and hold a medicine ball over your head. Use a chest-pass technique to throw the ball to a partner. As your partner catches it and immediately tosses it back, let your torso rock back and reload for another trunk-propelled pass. Avoid using your arms for all the work and stay focused on the pass so that the ball doesn't slip past your hands.

VARIATIONS

- *Easier.* Perform this exercise using an overhead pass.
- *Harder.* Increase the weight of the ball.

Medicine-Ball Side Toss

SCORES OF 3 OR 2

Lateral-leg movements require the core to stay countered and primed for energy bursts. Skiers who lack this power often use their whole bodies to move their skis from side to side. Tipping and turning the legs laterally under a stable upper body is much more efficient. This exercise strengthens the obliques and the toss also makes this a great core-body power exercise.

To perform this exercise, stand parallel to a brick or concrete wall, assume a half squat, and hold a medicine ball with both hands. Load your torso by turning away from the wall with your shoulders, and then fire the ball against the wall

with all your core power. Finish the movement with your torso facing the wall. Catch the ball as it bounces back. Maintain stability, initiate the throw with your hips, keep your chest up, and rotate through your upper back and arms rather than your lower back.

Hanging-Leg Hip Raise

SCORE OF 3

You will ski with greater control if you have strength-ened your abdominals and hip flexors because fore-aft control during finite leg movements depends on a strong core.

To perform this exercise, grasp a high bar and hang with your legs straight. Raise your knees to your chest by flexing your hips until your knees move toward your shoulders. Lower your legs until your hips and knees hang in a straight line. Don't arch your back. You should stabilize your pelvis, keeping your abdomen and glutes tight.

Stand-Up Paddle Board

SCORES OF 3, 2, OR 1

Sometimes getting out of the gym is the best thing you can do during intense periods of indoor training. Consider getting out on the water. Paddling is a great core and cardio workout since your ability to propel the paddle through the water with a powerful stroke is determined by your gross strength. This movement also mirrors driving skis through thick, heavy snow. Stand-up paddle boarding on flat water strengthens the core, improves balance, stabilizes muscles, and sharpens nerve endings for skiing.

The basic paddling stroke requires a straight arm and an upper-body rotation technique that applies well to skiing. The lower body balances the board as the upper extremities propel you and the board through the water.

To perform the exercise, pull your bottom arm toward your hip for the downstroke. Be careful not to pull past your hip, which wastes movement by pushing water up rather than propelling you forward. Straighten your top arm to combine arm movement and body weight into the stroke. If your top arm is bent, strength only comes from your arms. Keep the stroke parallel to the board to propel yourself in a straight line.

Supine Leg-Ups

SCORES OF 2 OR 1

Any core-strength drill that isolates the upper and lower body is a good exercise for skiing. This exercise requires you to stabilize your upper body with a bench as you engage your hip flexors, pulling your legs toward your hips and then toward the ceiling.

To perform this exercise, lie on a bench on your back and extend your legs out over the end. Raise your legs until your thighs are vertical and bend your knees. Lift your pelvis off the bench and try to touch your

a   b

> continued

> *continued*

feet to the ceiling. Return your pelvis to the bench and repeat the movement. The deeper you flex, the more you work the lower abdominals. Make sure this activity does not stress your back. Remember to keep your back stable and strong so your pelvis can stabilize any fore and aft movements.

VARIATIONS

- *Easier.* Perform this exercise on the floor.
- *Harder.* Perform this exercise while keeping your knees extended. You can also add ankle weights.

Sit-Ups

SCORE OF 1

Core stability helps you handle forces in all directions as you move between ski turns. Sit-ups and variations like crunches, side crunches, and weighted sit-ups are useful because they build core strength or core stability.

To perform this exercise, lie on your back and bend your knees to a 90-degree angle. Raise your upper body as a single unit, holding your arms across your chest. As you rise off the floor, lift with your waist and hips rather than by curling your back.

VARIATIONS

- *Easier.* Have a partner hold your feet down as you rise up.
- *Harder.* Place the small of your back on a stability ball and hands behind your head and rise up. You can also twist your torso to one side as you rise up.

Exercises for Lower-Body Strength

Lower-body strength helps you maintain balance, efficiently rotate and edge your skis, adjust to bumpy terrain, and execute recovery moves. The biomechanical chain that makes up the lower body's stability, mobility, and strength provides a platform for addressing all skiing challenges. If these components are missing or out of balance, out on the mountain you may feel like you are shooting a cannon from a canoe—you can land upside down in an instant. To further improve or to maintain lower-body fitness for scores 1 through 3, practice these exercises.

Split Squat

SCORES OF 3, 2, OR 1

Skiers need hip mobility combined with core stability and complemented by timed movements. A good skier displays a quiet upper body while actively turning with the legs. This exercise opens the hip flexors while keeping the spine and chest erect.

To perform this exercise, stand with your hands interlocked behind your head. Begin your squat by flexing the knee and hip of your front leg until your back knee is close to the floor. Repeat the movement and switch legs. Keep your chest up and engage your glutes. Also, keep your front knee tracking over your foot as you flex.

a   b

VARIATIONS

- *Easier.* Perform the exercise with your hands at your sides.
- *Harder.* Rest the top of one foot on a step behind you. Wear a weighted vest or hold a barbell, dumbbells, or kettle bells. To add another dimension to the exercise and allow for more abdominal work, hold a weight in one hand while elevating the foot.

Lateral Lunge

SCORES OF 3, 2, OR 1

Skiers require a large range of movement for dynamic moves from side to side. This exercise opens your hip flexors and stretches your hamstrings and quads.

To perform this exercise, stand with your feet hip-width apart. Step out to one side and squat back on that leg. Make sure your feet are pointing ahead as you flex down over your foot. Your flexed knee should track over the foot and your trail leg should be

a   b

completely straight with the foot planted on the ground. Push back up to a standing position and repeat the exercise for the prescribed number of reps. Switch sides. As you flex, focus on moving down and back, flexing the hips rather than the spine.

VARIATIONS

- *Easier.* Hold weights at your sides as you perform the exercise.
- *Harder.* Hold dumbbells at your sides and press them over your head as you stand up.

Bridge on Stability Ball

SCORES OF 3, 2, OR 1

Since skiing challenges both range of motion and balance, practicing indoors with a stability ball may help your skill on the snow. In this exercise, the instability of the ball challenges the bridge movement.

To perform this exercise, lie on your back and place both heels on a stability ball. Engage your glutes and raise your hips toward the ceiling. Your shoulders, hips, and knees should always form a straight line. Repeat the exercise for the prescribed number of reps. You should feel your glutes and lower back engage when you lift your hips.

VARIATIONS

- *Easier.* Perform the exercise with your heels on a bench.
- *Harder.* Perform the exercise with one or both heels on a stability ball. As you lift, flex your legs to draw the ball close to your glutes. If you elevate only one leg, bring the thigh of your free leg toward your chest as you flex.

Romanian Deadlift

SCORES OF 3, 2, OR 1

In skiing, recovery movements depend on your ability to balance at the boundaries of your range of motion. Exercises that extend your range of motion and require coordination while lifting weights build your zone of possible recovery movements.

To perform this exercise, stand with your feet about shoulder-width apart and hold a barbell with both hands. Hinge forward at your hips, lowering yourself toward the ground. As you bend over, keep your shoulders, hips, and head aligned and your back straight. Return to an upright position. Repeat the movement. As you bend over, try to sit back, distributing your weight evenly over your entire foot.

VARIATIONS

- *Easier.* Perform this exercise without weights, focusing on engaging your hamstrings and glutes.
- *Harder.* Perform this exercise with increased weight.

Exercises for Power and Agility

Power and agility exercises are important to the skiing-fitness block of the performance pyramid because they help you feel comfortable making dynamic movements while skiing fast. When skiing moguls, narrow chutes, slalom courses, or through tight trees, quick and proactive moves can mean the difference between starting and stopping with a frustrating rhythm or successfully navigating through the challenges with flow and confidence. Most technical challenges demand explosive power and an equal amount of finesse. Combining these moves adds needed speed to your skiing.

Power Exercises

Power in skiing is a unique combination of acceleration and deceleration movements that look and feel like a rhythmic dance down the slope. In slow motion, these movements don't look rhythmic at all. They are an on-again, off-again blend of fore-aft and lateral adjustments for balance, movement down the slope and into the next turn, twists and turns for alignment, and countermovements to balance upper- and lower-body rotation. These quick movements are hard to identify unless you really analyze them. Power-movement exercises enhance your ability to store energy and use it to explode at will. Without this component, movement delivery can be mechanical and contrived. To further improve or to maintain power for scores 1 through 3, practice these exercises.

Lateral Box Blast

SCORES OF 3, 2, OR 1

In skiing, the explosive power generated as the glutes, hamstrings, and quads coil and release builds stamina for long, hard runs. Big, vertical runs require you to make continuous, linked arcs down the slopes.

To perform this exercise, find a box that is 6 to 16 inches (15 to 40.5 cm) high. Place one foot on the floor and the other on the box. Jump laterally across the box, switching foot position for the landing (the foot that started on the box lands on the floor and the foot that started on the floor lands on the box). Bound immediately back to the starting position. Repeat this process for the number of repetitions that corresponds with your score (see table 3.7 on page 38).

Reactive Step-Up

SCORES OF 3, 2, OR 1

Fore-aft adjustments keep you aligned over the ski for good balance. This exercise focuses on independent leg action, an important ingredient for advanced skiing.

To perform this exercise, find a box that is 6 to 16 inches (15 to 40.5 cm) high. Assume a semisquat, with one foot on the box and your arms in a ready position. Jump up, extending your ankle, knee, and hip joints. Switch feet in the air and then land with your opposite foot on the box. Maintain good posture with your chest up and coordinate arm swings as if you were running. Resting your foot on the box for as little time as possible, repeat the explosive movements for the prescribed number of repetitions for your score (see table 3.7 on page 38).

Tuck Jump

SCORES OF 3, 2, OR 1

Explosive movements from the bottom to the top of your range of motion are needed for dynamic movement as well as for recovery and escape moves. Tuck jumps help you realign and regain balance.

To perform this exercise, start in a tuck position with your thighs parallel to the floor. Hold the squat for 30 seconds and then explode into a full-body extension. Land softly with flexed legs and return to the squat position. Repeat this process for the number of repetitions prescribed for your score (see table 3.7 on page 38).

Lateral Hurdle Jump

SCORES OF 3, 2, OR 1

Jumping over any object builds leg spring and agility; however, moving laterally while hopping is akin to the movements you make when springing from one turn to the next. This exercise helps you build quick response in lateral movements.

To perform this exercise, find a hurdle that is 6 to 16 inches (15 to 40.5 cm) high. Hop over the hurdle and land in a stable position, then recoil back over the hurdle and land in a balanced position on the opposite foot. Use your hips and arms to generate power for moving up and over the hurdle. This also helps coordinate total-body movement. Repeat the exercise for the number of repetitions appropriate for your score (see table 3.7 on page 38).

Uphill Running and Downhill Hiking

SCORES OF 3, 2, OR 1

The combination of running uphill and walking downhill is a great superset for skiing. The resistance of the uphill slope works the explosive action of your hamstrings, calves, glutes, and hip flexors. The downhill portion strengthens the quads and hamstrings in the other direction. Again, getting out of the gym is key for maintaining interest. Choose outdoor activities like running or hiking for a change of pace.

To perform this exercise, pick a destination at the top of a nearby hill or a steep incline. Run uphill, taking short, quick steps, keeping your feet in motion, and moving your arms backward, forward, and up. Keep your breathing relaxed and consistent and focus on the top of the hill rather than on your feet, which undermines posture and morale. After reaching the top of the hill or incline, hike down the hill. Walking downhill with a weighted backpack creates eccentric contractions of your leg muscles. Your quads will lengthen and your hamstrings will retract as you step on the downhill foot. This muscle contraction is almost identical to what happens in your leg muscles during a powerful ski turn.

Agility Exercises

Agility allows you to store and release energy efficiently while skiing. During a short turn in which the upper and lower body twist against each other, energy is stored and primed like a coiled spring, ready for a dynamic release. When skiing movements store and release energy, the released tension propels you from one turn to the next like a slingshot. The alternative is bogging out and starting from scratch on each turn. Reactive and dynamic, explosive energy (commonly known as agility) also plays a role in applying technique adjustments, technique execution, terrain tactics, and recovery movements to the slopes. To further improve or to maintain agility for scores 1 through 3, practice these exercises.

Agility Ladder

SCORES OF 3, 2, OR 1

The varied footwork patterns in this exercise mix up the most ingrained default moves. Changing your ballistic movements on the fly is the best training for the unpredictable surface of a mountain. Surprising conditions and terrain require quick changes that must happen within seconds. Practicing a variety of movements pays off on the snow.

To perform this exercise, you will need an agility ladder, or duct tape placed on the floor. Change your technique with one of the following variations, based on your score (see table 3.8 on page 39).

IN-IN-OUT-OUT

SCORE OF 1

In skiing, you continuously make microadjustments with your feet to maintain balance in rough or bumpy terrain. This exercise requires quick forward and backward adjustments as you move in and out of the ladder.

To perform this exercise, face the ladder from the side. Quickly step your right foot into the first square, followed by your left foot to the count of "one, two."

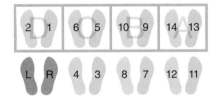

Quickly move your right foot out of that square, followed by your left. Spring into the second square with your right foot, followed by your left. Lead with your right foot out of that square, followed by the left. Repeat the pattern for the appropriate number of reps.

ICKEY SHUFFLE

SCORE OF 2

In skiing, accurate lateral-foot placement adds precision to edging movements. This exercise requires attention to foot placement in the lateral plane.

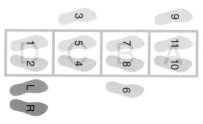

To perform this exercise, face down the ladder and stand to the right side of the first square. To the count of "one, two, three," place your left foot into the first square, followed by your right foot, then jump outside of the second square, landing on your left foot. Next, spring into the second square, landing on your right foot, followed by your left foot. Jump out again and land on your right foot. Repeat the pattern for the prescribed number of reps.

CROSSOVER ZIGZAG

SCORE OF 3

In skiing, the ability to separate leg and hip movement is crucial. Practice differentiating your movement with this exercise.

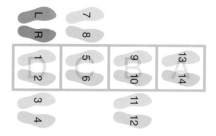

To perform this exercise, stand to the left of the first square and face down the ladder. Step into the first square with your left (outside) foot, followed by your right (inside) foot. Step outside of the first square with your left foot, followed by your right. Step into the second square with your left foot, followed by your right foot, and then step outside of the second square, first with your left foot and then with your right. Repeat the pattern.

Jumping Rope

SCORES OF 3, 2, OR 1

Jumping rope is one of the best training exercises for skiing because it incorporates foot speed, ballistic foot and ankle moves, and arm and hand timing. The rhythmic sequences of foot-to-foot hops and well-timed hand movements match the timing of fall-line skiing.

To perform this exercise, you will need a jump rope. When jumping, keep your spine erect, your abs tight, and your ankles and wrists in continuous motion. You can vary your technique by using one of the following variations for the prescribed amount of time for your score (see table 3.8 on page 39):

CLASSIC SWING

The basic pattern of one rotation with a two-foot jump is the classic routine for beginners. Hold the grips at waist height with the rope placed behind you. Swing the rope over your head and then use both feet to jump over it as it brushes the ground. Start with 10 seconds on and 10 seconds off, repeating for 5 minutes. When you improve, add more time to the work load (note that the rest is always half of this up to 5 total minutes), working up to 5 consecutive minutes, then progress to a double swing, which is a great power exercise.

SLALOM

Begin with the classic two-foot jump, then imitate slalom moves by hopping from side to side with your feet together. Try for 15 seconds on and 20 seconds off for 3 to 6 minutes.

DOUBLE SWING

The double swing is more difficult than the classic single rotation. It works both agility and endurance and is a great power exercise. Hold the grips of the jump rope at your hips and place the rope behind you. As you jump, swing the rope over your head, in front of you, and under your feet twice before landing. When progressing to doubles, go back to 10 seconds on and 10 seconds off, as mentioned previously for the classic swing, starting with a goal of 1 to 2 minutes, and again working up to a total of 5 consecutive minutes.

Practicing drills that remedy your weaknesses is the only way to manage your progress. Any random exercise can improve your stability, mobility, strength, or endurance. However, exercises that pinpoint solutions to specific problems build fitness more effectively. Once you have balanced your overall fitness program and have incorporated it into your regular routine, you will be equipped for technique and tactics.

9

Technique and Tactics Drills

As in any endeavor, learning to ski requires realistic goals and maximized training time. This book aims to alter perceptions about how to reach a skill level that lets you experience the exhilaration that lures die-hard skiers back to the slopes each year. Another purpose is to provide step-by-step directions, or how to get from here to there. There really isn't a shortcut to skiing mastery. The journey toward proficiency is based on fundamental skills.

Drills for Skiing Technique

Ingraining alignment patterns and efficient movements inherent in good skiing takes practice. Glossing over these fundamental techniques will only result in bad habits. Practicing flawed techniques eventually hinders your innate ability and natural progress. The following drills correspond with the techniques in chapter 4.

Technique Drills With Neutral Stance

The basic neutral-stance assessment on page 45 of chapter 4 focuses on spine and shin angle, symmetry between the left and right sides of the body, and equal weight distribution between skis. Look at your score to see your particular areas for improvement. The following section includes the drills that are prescribed to maintain a score of 3 or to improve scores of 2 or 1. These drills will help you develop balance in several planes of movement as you learn how to maintain an athletic, neutral stance in all situations.

Lateral-Step Drill

SCORE OF 3

This drill develops lateral awareness and agility while supporting the integrity of the basic neutral and engaged stance. It also strengthens fundamental edge control by practicing basic pressure, eventually leading to skating movements and carved turns.

To perform this drill, stand in a balanced position with your weight equally distributed over both feet. Push off onto a slight grade, then step straight out to the right with your right foot, followed by your left foot. Continue stepping as you glide through the turn. Repeat this sequence as you turn to the right and left. Focus on cleanly transferring your weight between skis. A complementary dryland exercise for this drill is the lateral box blast on page 133.

Hop Drill

SCORE OF 3

This drill equalizes the joints in your lower extremities so you can attain an athletic ready position. Once you are balanced over the skis, your movements will become more efficient.

To perform this drill, assume a neutral stance and prepare for a straight glide. Simultaneously bend your ankles, knees, and hips and hop off the snow. Land softly with balance, progressively flexing your ankles, knees, and hips. Hop up again immediately. Complementary dryland exercises for this drill are the tuck jump on page 134 and the reactive step-up on page 133.

a   b

Shuffle Drill

SCORE OF 2

This drill develops fore-aft alignment and centers you over the skis. These skills are essential because during skiing, forces push and pull along this axis.

To perform this drill, stand in a balanced position over both skis, flexing all joints slightly. Shuffle your feet back and forth while gliding in a straight line (this can later be done in a turn). Focus on moving your legs under stable hips. A complementary dryland exercise for this drill is the plank progression on page 105.

a   b

High-Low Drill

SCORE OF 1

Vertically extending and flexing the body while maintaining balance and a neutral stance are vital to managing terrain and pressure. This drill develops a wide range of vertical movements needed for absorbing terrain.

    To perform this drill, assume a balanced position and prepare to flex all your joints simultaneously. Push off onto a slight grade, lower your hips, and touch your ankles with your hands. Rise back up to a tall position and repeat the movement. Focus on keeping your chest and head up. Complementary dryland exercises for this drill are the single-leg squat with opposite-hand reach on page 101 and the single-leg squat with assistance line on page 102.

Marching Drill

SCORE OF 1

Shifting from foot to foot while maintaining the neutral stance widens your base of support and provides a platform for balancing and turning movements. This drill develops awareness for symmetrical alignment on both sides of the body.

To perform this drill, stand balanced over both skis, comfortably extending your arms just below your chest. After pushing off on a slight grade, lift one ski off the ground, followed by the other. Alternate your feet in a sequential stepping motion, keeping your hips level. Try to increase the space between the ski and the snow with each step, focusing on lifting your legs without moving your hips. A complementary dryland exercise for this drill is the indoor stork on page 100.

Pole-Spin Drill

SCORE OF 1

Spinning your poles in front of your face as you ski aids balance and hand position, stabilizes the upper body, and coordinates upper- and lower-body movements.

To perform this drill, glide down the slope and begin to spin your poles in front of you, keeping your eyes ahead. As you develop a rhythm with the spinning poles, begin to make some turns. This drill requires concentration, but after several miles, the results will pay off. Complementary dryland exercises for this drill are the circus pony on page 107 and the single-leg squat with assistance line on page 102.

Technique Drills With Engaged Stance

The engaged-stance assessment on page 46 of chapter 4 focuses on maintaining an athletic, balanced position while moving and tipping the skis. It also highlights lateral alignment and the relationship of the feet, knees, hips, hands, and shoulders when balancing on slopes of varying degrees. Technique drills for the engaged stance are important because they serve as the foundation for all lateral movements in advanced skiing. High-edge angle with upper-body control and balance are vital for high-speed turns and carving movements. Engaged-stance drills also help you coordinate your upper and lower body, helping you stay aligned during the arc of the turn and transitions between turns. Your score in this assessment highlights areas for improvement in the engaged stance. The following drills will help you maintain a score of 3 or improve scores of 2 or 1.

Engaged Stance at Higher Speeds

SCORE OF 3

Practicing the engaged stance at higher speeds will help you develop dynamic balance on tipped edges.

To perform this drill, assume the engaged stance, keeping both edges embedded in the snow. Allow your skis to travel through the natural arc across the hill and stop with your skis facing uphill. Look back at your tracks. When done correctly, this drill results in two clean, pencil-thin lines etched in the snow behind you. A complementary dryland exercise for this drill is the plank progression on page 105.

Traverse Drill on Steeper Terrain

SCORES OF 3 OR 2

Moving on steep terrain requires greater angles in the lower body that are counterbalanced with the upper body. This relationship is important for high-speed turns and steep slopes.

To perform this drill, move around the mountain and look for steep terrain to traverse across. As you find steeper slopes, increase your edge angle by tipping your legs into the hill and countering your upper body over the downhill ski. Complementary dryland exercises for this drill are the backward lunge with arm raise on page 109 and the plank progression on page 105.

Traverse Drill

SCORE OF 3

This drill develops a connection between each side of the body. Leaving two clean lines in the snow requires good alignment, balance, equal tipping of both skis, and making contact between the edges and the snow.

To perform this drill, assume an engaged stance with your poles pressed against the back of your pelvis and glide across the hill, leaving two clean tracks in the snow. When you have reached the opposite side of the slope, turn and recreate the tracks in the opposite direction. Complementary dryland exercises for this drill are the indoor stork on page 100 and the stability-ball twist on page 108.

a   b

Traverse and Reverse Traverse Drill

SCORE OF 2

This drill links two traverses in the engaged stance, ingraining the movements and leg turns of the position. The stability felt in the core as you release and guide the skis into the next traverse is the same that is inherent in all transitions between turns.

To perform this drill, traverse across the hill in the engaged stance. As you approach the opposite side of the trail, flatten your skis, turn with your legs to pivot them, and reengage the edges to traverse in the opposite direction with the same stance. Complementary dryland exercises for this drill are the hip crossover on page 107 and the stability-ball twist on page 108.

a   b

Engaged Stance on One Ski

SCORE OF 1

This drill develops alignment and balance on the outside (downhill) ski in the engaged stance. Balancing on one leg pressures and bends the weighted ski, creating a tighter arc as you move across the hill.

To perform this drill, lift your uphill leg off the snow while maintaining an engaged stance to leave one clean track in the snow. Balance on the ski until you come to a complete stop. See how long you can elevate the uphill ski. Be prepared to quickly redirect it back up the slope. Complementary dryland exercises for this drill are the indoor stork on page 100 and the knee-and-ankle grab on page 101.

Engaged Stance With Low-Edge Angle

SCORE OF 1

This drill develops a wider range of edge engagement and disengagement in the traverse position and the range of sensitivity needed to moderate edge hold and to regulate intensity of the turn radius.

To perform this drill, assume an engaged stance and move across the slope with flat skis, leaving a smeared track. Maintain your weight on both skis and place the uphill side of your body slightly ahead of the downhill side. Quickly reengage your edges and repeat the movement several times. A complementary dryland exercise for this drill is the circus pony on page 107.

a   b

Technique Drills for Leg Turns

The leg-turn assessment on page 49 of chapter 4 reveals strengths and weaknesses in this area. The drills in this section help ingrain the movements and skills necessary to turn the legs without moving the torso, such as awareness of hip position. Your score in this assessment highlights necessary areas for improvement. The following drills will help you maintain a score of 3 or improve scores of 2 or 1.

Leg Turn on One Ski

SCORE OF 3

This drill develops strength in the muscles required for turning your skis without your upper body. This technique is needed for linking continuous turns in all-mountain skiing.

To perform this drill, assume an athletic, engaged stance and lift one ski off the snow. Start gliding and begin to turn the ski that is still in the snow, using your leg to guide it. Keep your hips facing downhill as you turn the ski across the fall line. Focus on good flexion and extension movements to maintain balance on one ski. Complementary dryland exercises are the hip crossover on page 107 and the drop lunge on page 111.

a

b

c

Clock-Face Drill

SCORE OF 3

As your rotational range increases, your ability to guide the skis without moving your hips also grows, allowing you to move the skis into or out of the fall line at will.

To perform this drill, face down the hill in a basic neutral stance. Think of the position straight down the hill as 12 o'clock and the areas across the hill to your left and right as 9 o'clock and 3 o'clock, respectively. As you turn your skis, point your tips toward 10 and 2 o'clock. Gradually increase your range of motion, moving your skis to the 9 and 3 o'clock positions. Focus on turning both legs simultaneously while facing your upper body downhill. Complementary dryland exercises for this drill are the seated rotation on page 108 and the hip crossover on page 107.

a   b

Leg Turn With Feet on Bindings

SCORE OF 2

This drill, similar to the rotational-movement exercise 2 shown on page 23, develops the sensation of foot and leg rotation from a static position, allowing you to focus on the skill without the distractions of speed or terrain. Begin by securing your skis on a level surface.

To perform this drill, start in a neutral stance with feet free of bindings, but balanced on top of the toe pieces of the bindings. Use your poles for balance and slowly pivot your feet without

a   b

moving your hips. Turn both feet at the same time and then turn them both back in the opposite direction. Repeat this motion several times to ingrain the feeling of turning with your feet. Take care not to slip off the bindings while pivoting. Complementary dryland exercises for this drill are the knee-and-ankle grab on page 101 and the hip crossover on page 107.

Hands-on-Hips

SCORE OF 2

Over time, you develop awareness of when your legs turn independently of your hips. Use these valuable movement cues to begin each turn. Turning with your hips is less efficient than turning with your legs.

To perform this drill, assume a balanced stance with your hands on your hips. Turn your legs left and right without turning your upper body. Keeping your hands on your hip bones, draw your awareness to the parts of your body that are moving. Continue turning without rotating your hips. Linking these turns helps create muscle memory for short-radius, fall-line turns. Complementary dryland exercises for this drill are the stability-ball twist on page 108 and the circus pony on page 107.

a   b

Wedge Leg Turn

SCORE OF 1

This drill develops leg-turning movements needed for parallel turns and for advanced carving turns at slower speeds.

a   b

> continued

> *continued*

To perform this drill, glide in a wedge position, keeping the tips of your skis together and the tails apart. Use your poles to push off onto a slight incline and guide one foot through a crescent-moon shape while positioning the other foot in the converging position. After changing direction, begin to shift your weight to the opposite foot and guide that ski through a crescent arc of equal size. You will feel the action of the leg turn through your leg and up into the ball-and-socket joint in your hip. Complementary dryland exercises for this drill are the plank progression on page 105 and the hip stretch with resistance band on page 110.

Cross-Hill Leg Turns

SCORE OF 1

This drill develops parallel leg movements at the end of a turn and allows you to ingrain active leg turning without the added pressure of moving down the fall line. It helps you practice continuous leg turning and master parallel finishes.

To perform this drill, start in a slight wedge position, applying more weight to the downhill ski. Make small turns across the slope, keeping the uphill ski parallel to the downhill ski when both skis are turned uphill. Flatten your skis, let them drift back downhill, and then make another turn uphill, letting your skis move into a parallel position. Focus on turning with your legs rather than with your hips. Complementary dryland exercises for this drill include the resistance band rotation on page 110 and the plank progression on page 105.

a   b

Technique Drills for Parallel Turns

The parallel-turn assessment on page 51 of chapter 4 reveals strengths and weaknesses in the areas of single-leg pivoting, independent leg action, pole planting, and edge release. Parallel turns are the foundation for redirection of your skis. The use of well-timed muscular force will apply torque to the skis, resulting in turning action. Turning both legs simultaneously while maintaining dynamic balance over the skis will produce the most efficient turns. If the upper body becomes the major source of turning power, rather than the legs, then efficiency is lost. Your score will highlight necessary areas for improvement in parallel turns. The following drills will help you maintain a score of 3 or improve scores of 2 or 1.

Stepping Through the Turn

SCORE OF 3

This drill develops the combination of leg turning and edging movements needed for the parallel turn.

To perform this drill, place your skis across the hill in an athletic, engaged stance. Glide across the hill and then begin to turn, making miniature changes in direction as you step the tips toward the new turn. After taking several steps, leading with the outside edge of your downhill ski, you will have made a full turn. Apply pressure to the outer edge of the downhill ski to flatten it and draw your body through the arc. Complementary dryland exercises for this drill are the single-leg balance on page 100 and the leg drops on page 103.

Pole Plant and Release

SCORE OF 3

An incorrect ski pole swing can interrupt your flow from turn to turn, especially if it rotates around your body. It can become a helpful device for timing and direction when the pole is swung in the direction of the new turn.

To perform this drill, start in the fall line and extend your arms, ready to make a pole plant. Use the swing of the pole as a directional aid by diagonally flicking your wrist and forearm in the direction of the apex of the new turn. Focus on swinging the pole basket from your wrist. Complementary dryland exercises for this drill are the forward plank with alternating arm lift on page 105 and push-up on stability ball on page 124.

a   b

One-Leg Pivot

SCORE OF 2

This drill develops the mental commitment and release movements needed to execute and initiate a pure parallel turn.

a   b

c

d

To perform this drill, place your skis across the hill with the tail of your downhill ski on the heel piece of your uphill ski's binding. The skis should now be perpendicular to each other. Move your hip over your feet, allowing your uphill ski to release and realign with your downhill ski, and finish with a parallel turn. Focus on moving your hips over your feet as you release the uphill ski. Complementary dryland exercises for this drill are the indoor stork (with eyes closed) on page 100 and the plank progression on page 105.

Two Skis to One Ski

SCORE OF 2

This drill develops balance over the outside ski at the end of the turn, helping you transition into full single-ski turns in which all weight is balanced on the outside ski.

To perform this drill, begin a turn while balancing on both skis. As you steer the skis through the arc, redistribute your weight to the downhill ski. As you finish the last part of the arc, center all of your weight on that ski. Complementary dryland exercises for this drill are the backward lunge with arm raise on page 109 and the lateral lunge on stability ball on page 110.

a

b

Simultaneous Edge Change

SCORE OF 1

This drill helps you initiate all turns with parallel skis. The ability to transition into a turn from sequential to parallel movements requires confidence that comes from feeling comfortable with speed. Until you are willing to go through the transition a little faster, you will have to start every turn with a sequential stem move. Going faster will help you move your body across your skis, resulting in a flattening of the ski. This is often called the "floating stage." Your skis will drift and release for a moment until you apply a downhill tipping movement with the feet, as seen in figure b. If you can feel that both skis are flat in the transition, this is a good indicator that you are performing it correctly. You can check yourself by looking at your ski tracks in the transition. If you see two equally flat tracks in the transition area without edge or skidding marks, then you have completed a successful simultaneous edge change.

To perform this drill, stand on the side of the hill in an engaged stance and push off. Once you are up to speed, flatten your skis, releasing both edges at the same time. Lean forward, weighting the front of both skis. The skis will naturally seek the fall line and will begin to turn. Use this downhill momentum to continue the turn. Complementary dryland exercises for this drill are the seated rotation on page 108 and the plank progression on page 105.

a

b

c

Parallel-Turn Garland

SCORE OF 1

This drill develops the end and beginning of each turn, which is good for people who fear the fall line.

To perform this drill, do a series of turns across the hill. Focus on making easy initiations and quick finishes without entering the fall line. Complementary dryland exercises for this drill are the plank progression on page ‾05 and the seated rotation on page 108.

Hand on Hip and Hand in the Air

SCORE OF 1

This drill is excellent for sensing the moment for edge release and initiating the subsequent turn.

To perform this drill, place your downhill hand on your downhill hip and raise your uphill hand in front of your uphill shoulder. This puts you in a strong position to initiate the parallel turn by flattening the skis. Allow them to drift downhill and then quickly edge them, placing pressure on the front of the outside ski. The ski will react and arc through the turn. As you finish the turn, release the edges and let the tips fall back down the hill. Place the hand that is now facing downhill on your downhill hip and raise the outer hand in front of your uphill boot. You will immediately feel the benefit of having your hips on a level plane as you seamlessly transition from turn to turn with power, balance, and precision. This exercise will enhance the balance at the finish of the turn, smooth out transitions, produce easy edge changes, and enhance proper upper body alignment through the turn. A countered and aligned upper body position will facilitate effective parallel turn movements. Repeat this movement several times. You will soon feel the seamless engagement and release of both skis. A complementary dry-land exercise for this drill is the knee-and-ankle grab on page 101.

a   b

Technique Drills for Carved Turns

The carved-turn assessment on page 52 of chapter 4 reveals strengths and weaknesses in the areas of balance over the ski edges, weight distribution over both skis, and lateral movements that involve the ankles, knees, hips, and spine. To solidify the movements needed for edge-to-edge carved turns, you must practice angling drills and master edging movements. Your score in this assessment highlights necessary areas for improvement in carved turns. The following drills will help you maintain a score of 3 or improve scores of 2 or 1.

Short-Turn Pole Touch

SCORE OF 3

Balancing over tipped-up skis while carving an arc requires upper- and lower-body coordination. The muscles on the side of your torso will fold like an accordion.

To perform this drill, assume an engaged stance and hold the grips of your poles, resting the shafts on your shoulders. Make a short turn, keeping your skis parallel and tipping your knees into the slope. Extend your outside pole tip to touch the snow in line with your downhill boot at the apex of your turn. As soon as the pole touches the snow, return the shaft to your shoulder and release the other pole. Touch the snow on the opposite side as you shape that turn. Focus on a two-beat rhythm during this drill. Touch the pole tip to the snow on the count of one and return the pole shaft to your shoulder on the count of two. Continue this rhythm as you repeat the action on the opposite side. Complementary dryland exercises for this drill are the straight-arm lateral lunge with dumbbells on page 109 and the single-leg squat progression on page 99.

a

b

c

Carved Turn With Hands on Knees

SCORE OF 3

Precision carving is rooted in tipping the lower leg, which is also known as knee angulation. Without the fine movement skills of ankle and knee flexion, we rely too much on big joints and muscles to tip the skis on edge. This process is slow and inefficient. Isolating the knees for specific lateral movements develops the fine tuning needed to shape a carved turn. It also quiets any upper-body affectations that disrupt leg activity.

To perform this drill, reach down and grasp both knees with your hands, keeping your chest up. Maintaining your grip, begin to turn by tipping both knees into the hill, and then push them with your hands. Both knees should simultaneously bend and flex in equal amounts. Release and push to the other side. Focus on keeping your chest up and your eyes ahead. Make your foot movements quick. A complementary dryland exercise for this drill is the miniband walking routine on page 95.

a

b

Long Leg, Short Leg

SCORE OF 2

Changing your leg length means flexing and extending your legs sequentially. The stability from aligning the outside leg during extension increases your holding power and range of motion,

a

b

which is necessary for higher carving speeds. The inside, flexed leg helps provide a balanced platform. Clear that leg out of the way for a greater range of motion.

To perform this drill, assume a wide, engaged stance, placing most of your weight on the downhill ski. Begin to turn by tipping your legs downhill. Balance on your edges, ready to carve. As you pick up speed, extend your outside leg (which started as the uphill leg) and flex the inside leg so that it is shorter than the other leg. As you transition into the next turn, redistribute your weight to the new outside leg, which is now the shorter leg. Progressively alternate the weight between legs. Focus on s multaneously flexing the inside leg as you lengthen the outside leg. Complementary dryland exercises for this drill are the straight-arm lateral lunge with dumbbells on page 109 and the hip crossover on page 107.

Advanced Railroad Track

SCORE OF 2

Proper alignment and balance on the edges gives you a clear line of control through your body, down through the skis, and into the snow. Leaning too far over the front, too far to the back, or too much to the side causes you to lose control. Lowering your center of gravity gives you room to move your skis efficiently in the lateral plane, making essential turning movements for carving easier.

To perform this drill, assume a stance that is slightly wider and more compact for stability and a light, precise touch. Tip your ski edges simultaneously and with equal pressure to create half-moon tracks in the snow. Focus on quick lower-body moves with your feet and ankles to engage, flatten, and reengage your edges. Try to do this without skidding. Complementary dryland exercises for this drill are the hip crossover on stability ball on page 107 and the in-in-out-out agility ladder on page 135.

Traverse Edge Change

SCORE OF 1

Quick edge-to-edge movements are important for transitioning between turns. This skill has many applications for advanced skiing. Early-edged initiation is an important element in successful carving. Although this is a stationary drill, it is challenging and can be used to test your ability to achieve the high early edge needed for carving turns. Notice in photo a the upper body has repositioned to angle over the uphill ski, which is now the new outside ski. Using the poles while stationary is critical to avoid falling over. This exercise will also require a focus on your feet and skis, keeping your feet parallel and both skis tipped at the same edge angle. Tipping the feet will correspond with repositioning the upper body. Once you begin to incorporate this movement into your turns, you will be better prepared to address the challenges of carving a complete turn. Tipping the skis to a high edge angle early in a carved turn requires two components: speed through the turn transition and body commitment across the skis. Without these two important elements your edges will only engage later in the turn, causing the skis to skid. Once the movements of tipping the feet and skis are matched with the corresponding upper-body counter, you will see your work pay off with carving turns that are efficient and dynamic. The early edge change is an important milestone in carving technique.

To perform this drill, start on a gradual, groomed slope in a neutral stance. Tip your skis from one set of edges to the other without pausing. Use your poles to balance over your skis. Practice moving back and forth until you can change edges without feeling stuck on a flat ski. Focus on progressively tipping both skis at the same time. Complementary dryland exercises for this drill are the lateral hurdle jump on page 134, the Ickey shuffle agility ladder on page 136.

Outside Pole Drag

SCORE OF 1

As your upper body counterbalances over the outside ski, you attain a higher edge angle, producing a cleaner and tighter arc. If your upper body tips too much into the hill, you will lose both edge grip and lateral balance. This drill helps your counterbalance alignment by forcing you to stay over the outside ski. When this exercise is done correctly, you will feel your bottom rib touch the top of your hip bone on the same side as where the pole touches the snow. This is similar to the feeling of a side crunch that you do in the gym. As you begin to feel this side crunch, your upper body will be properly countered and prepared to carve the skis. Most people will feel this sensation, but only in the later stages of the turn. Tipping the feet early corresponds with tipping or crunching the upper body to match alignment. If you are performing this drill on flat terrain, the angles will not be as acute, but as speed and pitch increase, your ski edge angle and body angles become greater. Practicing this exercise on diverse slopes and at varying speeds will quicken the learning curve and ingrain this key movement for carving technique.

To perform this drill, assume an engaged stance and extend your arms to the sides, holding your poles like swords. In the fall line, reach over the outside ski and etch an arc in the snow with your pole tip and your skis. Focus on curving your spine toward the downhill ski and reaching with your pole. Complementary dryland exercises for this drill are the seated rotation on page 108 and the drop lunge on page 111.

a

b

c

d

Tuck Turn

SCORE OF 1

Low tucks isolate the lower legs, ankles, and knees, ingraining tipping action without involving the upper body. This gives you quick, efficient carves without extraneous movement.

To perform this drill, assume a tucked position, flatten your skis, and point them down the fall line. Begin by tipping your skis from one set of edges to the other, allowing enough time on each set to make a shallow, carved turn. Keep your legs flexed and your upper body balanced over the downhill ski. Focus on maintaining equal pressure and angle as you tip both skis. Complementary dryland exercises for this drill are the single-leg squat with medicine ball on page 99 and the tuck jump on page 134.

a

b

c

d

Practicing Basic Terrain Transitions

Skiers need to develop a feel for ski-snow contact during terrain changes like dips and rises, depressions and mounds, or concave and convex areas. This awareness is a key tactile component for touch and finesse. To practice the feel of varying terrain, ski over gentle undulations on a slope, absorbing the peaks and valleys with your ankles, knees, and hips while maintaining a basic stance. Allow your ankles, knees, and hips to flex and extend, keeping your weight centered over both skis. As you progress, you will encounter the following terrain and condition changes.

Gentle to Steep Slopes

Whether the transition between slopes of different grades is gradual or abrupt, the change requires responsive and precise stance adjustments. When moving from a gentle slope to a steep one, prepare by making a few body adjustments before the breakover. Perform this movement from an athletic stance and prepare to change terrain by matching the angle of your ski with the pitch of the hill. You must also position your upper body prior to moving through the breakover. Remember to keep your hands ahead and to equalize pressure throughout the full length of the ski. Skiing from a gentle slope to a steep one too fast launches you into the air. To prevent this, moderate your speed and lean forward to keep the tips of the skis on the snow. To anticipate the acceleration of the skis ahead of the body, pull your feet in line with your hips. Changes in pitch are not the only factor that causes changes in speed. Variable conditions may also be responsible. Your skis will also accelerate when skiing from deep powder to a groomed slope. Prepare for this acceleration by keeping your core strong and by moving your upper body toward your tips.

Just as your skis accelerate when you hit the steeps, your skis will decelerate as you move onto a flatter slope. This is also known as *compression.* Prepare yourself by slightly flexing your joints and anticipating a quick, downward pull. Absorbing the initial shock will help you maintain balance and will prepare you for extending and recentering.

Groomed to Ungroomed Snow

You will also experience compression when you ski from a groomed slope to a deep-powder slope and from powder to groomed snow. All these transitions require balance adjustments. Perform the needed movements by first anticipating the effect the upcoming change in condition will have on your skis. Pull or push your skis backward or forward, depending on what is required prior to entering the transition. When moving from groomed snow to powder, push your feet forward. When transitioning from powder to groomed snow, pull your feet back.

Firm to Soft Snow

For steep, firm snow, shift your focus to actively steering a turn with a healthy mix of edging and rotary to facilitate turn shape. As the snow softens and becomes more forgiving, you can play more with the amount of edge that you use throughout the turn. Remember that speed increases with more carving on firm snow. The connection between edge pressure and skidding is a theme that skiers must consistently moderate by feeling the interaction between skis and snow. In addition to direction of travel, your primary responsibility is continuous adjustments to speed and turn shape in response to the obvious cues.

Wet to Dry Snow

When the snow melts in the spring, you are sure to encounter sections of the hill where your skis literally stop because of suction from the wet snow. Although it may be difficult to anticipate these spots, skiing in shaded areas where the snow stays colder and dryer provides consistent glide. When you ski out of the shadows into a sunny slope, prepare for your skis to slow down. If they slow dramatically, lift one out of the snow to reduce the suction effect. Place it back down lightly and lift the other.

Drills for Skiing Tactics

Tactical drills will help you avoid skiing aimlessly from slope to slope without a game plan or an idea of your desired outcome for the run. These drills will give you the awareness and ability to apply different tactics to any situation, beginning with reading terrain and moving on to the application of turn type, speed management, and line choice. As you build solid tactics, you will soon realize that they separate good skiers from great ones.

Tactics Drills for Reading the Terrain

Chapter 5 helps you identify your strengths and weaknesses in applying the tactic of reading the terrain. Look at your score in the terrain assessments to identify areas for improvement. The following drills are prescribed in order to maintain a score of 3 or to improve scores of 2 or 1.

Redirecting Focus

SCORE OF 3

Nervousness on steeper terrain and at higher speeds creates tunnel vision and brings your speed down to a crawl. Overanalyzing the situation makes your movements fragmented and incomplete. As your speed increases, slightly redirect your focus down the hill to anticipate the approaching terrain. This is similar to looking down the road while you are driving: if you only look in front of the bumper, you can't anticipate upcoming changes. Holding on to the turn too long by traversing across the hill will make you feel indecisive, as if you are shopping for turns. A good rule of thumb is if you have not yet started the turn by the time you go past the midpoint of the trail, you are too late. You have probably lost all your rhythm.

Unlocking Freeze Frame

SCORE OF 2

If you find that you are staring down a steep slope longer than it would have taken you to ski down, you have reached the freeze-frame zone. Don't do this to yourself! Relax, briefly scope your line, take a deep breath, and let your skis release onto the slope. If you can't let go, count down from three to one, then go and don't look back! If you are still caught in the freeze zone, stem your uphill ski out into the fall line, keeping your downhill ski across the hill and on edge. This positions the stemmed ski to point toward the halfway point of the next turn. You can then redistribute your weight to the outside ski and finish turning the ski across the hill, completing a successful turn.

Anticipating Terrain Changes

SCORE OF 1

As your skis bend and twist with the varied terrain, the resulting forces can quickly knock you off balance. Anticipate changes in terrain by picking your head up and scanning the topography. Keeping your eyes on the prize will help you balance by making premeditated adjustments. Holding your head down will throw off your total alignment and will cause you to fall backward in rough terrain.

Having a Plan B

SCORE OF 1

Backing off from steeper terrain is not a party foul by any means. It's better to have a plan B than to do something beyond your capabilities and end up in the medical clinic at the bottom of the hill. Before skiing a steep slope, survey your options and make a decision about your game plan before you commit to a course of action. Most accidents happen when skiers commit to a line, but then have second thoughts and lose their confidence. If this happens to you, keep your skis on! Never try to climb out wearing only boots on your feet. Your skis are the best tool for gripping firm snow.

Tactics Drills for Applying Turn Shape

Chapter 5 explains the strengths and weaknesses in applying the tactic of turn shape when faced with different terrain. Look at your scores in the terrain assessments to determine your areas for improvement in applying turn shape. The following drills are prescribed for maintaining a score of 3 or improving scores of 2 or 1.

Matching Turn Shape With Conditions

SCORE OF 3

Bumps in the warm spring often equal softer lines! In the spring, the moguls get soft due to rising temperatures. This opens up opportunities to ski more direct lines like the zipper. The colder and harder the snow is, the faster your ski reacts to it and the quicker you must respond. Early in the morning when the snow is hard and crunchy, pick lines that are easier and more forgiving. As the snow begins to soften in the afternoon, try lines that are straighter and more demanding. In soft conditions, the ski reacts more slowly, giving you a little more time to think and respond to the demands of your bending skis. Choosing the right time of day will broaden your options for technical lines in the bumps!

Creating Symmetrical Patterns in Turns

SCORE OF 3

Skiing an asymmetrical zigzag pattern from one side of the chute or gully to the other is not rhythmic or graceful. Instead, this practice only creates confusion and doubt about what to do next. Toss a snowball down the chute and watch the path it takes. This natural fall line should lie somewhere in the middle of the chute. Use this line as your path, turning from one side to the other. A good, consistent turn shape that is symmetrical and rhythmic will produce the best results.

Fishhook Ending in a J-Shape

SCORE OF 2

The straight part of the J-shaped turn is easily executed. The difficult part is the end, the part that links turns, especially on steep terrain. Skipping the end is a common fault that results in a fragmented transition between turns. Turning the skis too soon prevents energy from being generated and results in slow, choppy turns. Adding a fishhook ending to the J-shape turns the legs and pivots the skis to finish. The legs are then pivoted again in the opposite direction to transition into the next turn. Anticipate the finish and begin to tip the skis and turn the legs halfway through the J. This makes the end precise and facilitates the link with the next turn.

Regulating Pressure and Edge on Turns

SCORE OF 2

In skiing, the term *touch* means allowing your body to relax and maintaining just enough functional tension to move with agility. Being too stiff and rigid results in harsh movements, skis that chatter or bounce away, and a loss of grip. On the other hand, keeping your joints too supple compromises your balance. The key to developing touch on steeps is to soften your toe grip on your foot bed, letting the foot become supple. Your foot can now become part of your boot's suspension system. This practice helps you learn how to switch to and from the different turn shapes. Concentrate on regulating the amount of edge and pressure you apply to the ski.

Maintaining a Strong Finishing Turn

SCORE OF 2

The biggest killer of the round turn is failing to finish the arc. Letting the ski straighten at the finish results in gradually increasing speed to the point of losing control. This fault is almost the opposite of the windshield wiper, since the skis never really come across the hill. Keeping the shape round from beginning to end will equalize speed and increase control. High marking is a great way to feel a complete turn finish. As you start on one side of the slope, hold one turn until you come completely across the hill before progressing to a stall out. The ski will engage, gradually climbing uphill as you move from one side of the slope to the other. As you stall, stop and take note of your high mark.

Establishing Turn Shape With Ski Placement

SCORE OF 2

Not knowing how to get into the line is the first barrier to any sequence of turns. Your first turn sets you up for a path that is strategically correct. If you miss it, you play catch up for the remainder of the run. Make your first turn the best one by sighting your entry target, releasing your skis toward the entry point of the line, and moving your skis into the line. Your vision must be at least a turn ahead in order to see where you should go next.

Getting the Right Amount of Edge Angle

SCORE OF 2

Carving technique is the foundation for good skiing, however in deep snow, a more smeared turn works best. With wider, softer skis in powder, overedging only makes the skis dive and bog out. Stay on top of the skis and use a blend of carve and smear to find the best turning tactic in deeper snow. Making big angles with your joints, as in carved turns, only overpowers the edges, causing them to dig in. Stay positioned over the center of both skis for a big platform that can be used for big-mountain and back-bowl tactics. On the other hand, if you smear with too little edge, you will drift sideways without control. This can be fun, as in a power slide, but at this level, it is better to apply a bit of an angle to induce friction as you slide.

Ingraining the C-Curve

SCORE OF 1

If you tend to overturn or underturn your C, apply a progressive and continuous turn to your skiing by placing a hula hoop or a rope in a rounded shape on the snow. Ski a turn around the hoop or rope, focusing on rounding the turn. Match the rotation of the skis with the curve of the object.

Avoiding a Windshield Wiper in the C-Turn

SCORE OF 1

Although the windshield wiper is an effective drill for speeding up leg-steering skills, it can also be a fault when making progressive, C-shaped turns. Skiers sometimes instinctively use this technique when they are intimidated by terrain, rushing to get their skis across the hill. Instead, reduce the speed of your leg turn and focus on gradually guiding your legs throughout the entire turn. Progress beyond the visual aids in the snow and practice allowing the length of at least one ski to pass while pointing the skis downhill. Next, turn them across the slope. This practice is a good reminder to keep the turns round.

Setting Pace for Turns

SCORE OF 1

Reactive and defensive leg turns into a static position on the skis are counterproductive, encouraging slipping and a choppy rhythm. Set your pace with the first two turns and match your leg turning with a solid pole plant. Keep turning and moving down the hill. Coming to a stop will kill your flow. Remember not to hold on to the edges for too long. This bad habit brings you too far across the hill, taking you out of rhythm and out of your line. To keep their bodies in continuous motion, many skiers practice their turns with a chant, such as "one and two and three, cha, cha!"

Centering on the Ski

SCORE OF 1

Although incorrect, many skiers position themselves far back over the skis in powder. Some instructors even coach students to lean back in powder. Instead, balance over the midpoint to distribute your weight along the entire length of the ski. You can center yourself by flexing your joints in your first two turns. Next, push off in the powder and quickly flex both ankles, knees, and hips, moving down and then up. A centered stance makes you more comfortable with speed in deep snow and prepares you for directional changes and speed adjustments.

Turn Management Practice

Older skis only allowed for one type of turn, but skis with new designs have created a host of new turns for deep snow, including slashing, scrubbing, buttering, skidding, carving, scarving, and slicing. The following powder tactics will expand your deep-snow options.

Slashing

Slashing is a hybrid turn for powder that combines edging and pivoting to deflect off features found in back bowls, letting you ride on wind lips, straddle fluted vertical ribs, slice over cornices, and blast through snow pillows. They also kick up a huge spray of snow. To slash, spot your feature and gauge your speed as you enter the terrain. Start the turn by smearing the skis, allowing them to float over the top of your intended target. Once you're on the feature, embed your edges with a slight tipping motion. Finish the turn by carving out the bottom of the lip, cornice, or pillow (see figure *a*).

Slashing requires equal pressure from tip to tail. Too much forward energy early on in the turn loads the front of the ski, disrupting your balance. Instead, allow your weight to bend the ski. As the ski flexes, the tip and tail will bend simultaneously for a rounded, carved finish.

a

Scrubbing

Scrubbing helps you control speed in powder while maintaining flotation, which is easier with a fat, rockered ski. To slow your speed on groomed slopes without losing momentum, tip your skis and round the turn in an hourglass shape. Higher-edge angles drive skis deeper into the snow. Instead, flatten and pivot your skis to scrub the top layer. Your tracks should look smeared (see figure *b*).

b

Buttering

Buttering, or the action of the ski as it smears the top layer of snow, is similar to surfing, but requires considerably less effort. Flatten wide skis in powder and make wide, round turns to skim the snow (see figure c). Practice the turn shape for success in back bowls. Too much edge spoils the effect and traps the ski in deep snow.

c

Skidding

Active skidding through leg steering is not just for beginners. It can be used to mellow the pace, to mute speed, or to lessen energy in the turn. However, too much skidding makes you stall out. You can also use active leg turns to mute built-up energy. As the energy builds, flatten the skis and pivot your feet progressively to produce a skid (see figure d). Aim for a smooth transition. Avoid shutting it all down at once with a heavy edge set.

d

Carving

When carving in deep snow, initiate turns by tipping the skis and applying pressure with proper body alignment, moving through an arc. The energy builds for a very dynamic, fast turn in powder (see figure e). In deep snow, narrow skis will dive, so use a dolphin action to start and end turns. The tips dive into the snow at the beginning of the turn, disappear in the middle, and reemerge at the end. This technique requires expert powder skills and good overall fitness.

e

> continued

> continued

Scarving

A blend of skidding and carving is the best way to handle steep slopes with variable snow (see figure *f*). Rocketing into a steep, variable slope while carving high-speed arcs is foolish. Most experts judge the snow consistency and terrain obstacles and sample a few types of turns before committing to action.

f

Slicing

Skiing over packed snow on steep terrain requires slicing actions (not buttering) in order for the ski to react along the length of the edges. Place the ski at the appropriate angle by steering or using a down stem and slice the ski edge across the slope (see figure *g*). Over-twisting or too much force of the downhill ski causes it to break away on firm snow.

g

Tactics Drills for Speed Management

Chapter 5 reveals the strengths and weaknesses of applying this tactic to different terrain. Look at your scores in the terrain assessments to see necessary areas for improvement in speed management. The following drills are prescribed for maintaining a score of 3 or improving scores of 2 or 1.

Pushing the Envelope of Speed and Tempo

SCORE OF 3

Skiing longer pitches at a sustained tempo and speed will become your most effective tool for practice. Don't be afraid to push the envelope on your personal speedometer. As you prepare for a series of turns, commit to finishing all the turns with your weight on the outside ski. A bobble or two doesn't matter; just keep your engine running. As your confidence builds, choose a longer pitch of 5 to 8 turns. When you're ready, try a 10- to 15-turn run. Before long, you will be skiing 1200 vertical feet without stopping.

Checking Your Speed

SCORE OF 2

Speed increases when you move from the rounder, slower lines to ones that are faster and more direct. This change takes commitment and confidence. Committing to a predetermined line without spots to rest or turn out requires a sustainable, short turn. Conserving rotational range of motion for the end of the turn and hitting your edges sideways can give you the final speed check you need. This last-minute bleed of speed brings the throttle back for a comfortable entrance into the next turn.

Choosing the Correct Tempo

SCORE OF 2

Fragmented and choppy rhythm is a routine error in skiing. The tempo you set for your turns has to match your desired outcome and the beat set by the terrain. Fast, precise turns need a quick, peppy rhythm. Wider, rounder turns need a progressive and gradual cadence because of their intensity and duration. Longer turns take more time and require progressive movements, and short turns take less time and require quick response.

Getting Into Gear

SCORE OF 1

Skiing on steep terrain requires a downward flow of synchronized movements. If this flow is interrupted, you will feel like you're stuck n neutral on the side of the hill. Never stop! If you feel the need to stop, just slow down until you reach a manageable tempo. If your legs are tired, stand taller, aligning your skeleton for more support. Once you are in a rhythm, you are winning the energy struggle between you and the slope. Your skis will work more effectively when they are engaged than when they are parked on the side of a run.

Maintaining Three Points of Contact

SCORE OF 1

Missing a pole plant causes temporary loss of control and induces unwanted speed. Avoid the runaway-train syndrome by maintaining three points of contact at all times to broaden your base of support. Think of your poles as a handrail for walking down the staircase of varied terrain. If you keep both skis in contact with the snow and plant your poles solidly, you will always have three points of contact.

Selecting Effective Entries for Narrow Terrain

Most mistakes are made in the first two turns, since skiers underestimate the pull of gravity as they move onto a slope. Enter in the spot where you feel most comfortable. Look for the entry point that matches the intensity level that is right for you. Check the hardness of the snow with your pole and slide in. Feeling the texture gives you more information to use in your overall plan. Once you have analyzed the snow, you can use one of three entries to set up a good first turn.

Air In

This tactic is for advanced skiers who understand the snow's consistency and want a thrilling start to the run. Skiers make three major mistakes when airing into a run. They typically take off out of balance because they have placed their hands back. In the air, their ski tips may rise up as they sit back. When coming down, they may forget to stretch their legs, landing with a thud. To air in correctly, take off from the lip with confidence, placing your hands forward and keeping them balanced. In the air, stay poised and position your skis to match the pitch of the slope. When landing, stretch your legs for suspension, spot the landing with your eyes, and land softly.

Side Hop

The side hop is a good option if you are testing the snow's consistency because it gives you a chance to feel the snow and to warm up your legs for your first turn. Entering with speed and air creates instant velocity. Be ready for a big slide. When entering with the side hop, slide your skis in sideways, hopping laterally or jumping in with your skis pointed downhill. Of course, jumping requires expert technique for speed control. When done right, this is very exhilarating. The side hop both controls speed and moves you down the slope until you feel comfortable making your first turn.

Slip In

The slip-in is the easiest way to enter a run because as you slide downhill, you can control your speed with your edges and position yourself for a comfortable first turn. If you are comfortable with the first turn, your subsequent turns will also feel balanced. The act of slipping deliberately onto a steep, narrow slope will give you valuable cues to the consistency and stability of the snow under your feet. To best develop a comfortable connection to the snow surface in a chute or gulley, caress it with a slip-in action and let the external cues guide you down the natural fall line.

Tactics Drills for Line Choice

Chapter 5 lists the strengths and weaknesses for applying the tactic of line choice when faced with different terrain. Look at your score in the terrain assessments to see your necessary areas for improvement. The following drills are prescribed for maintaining a score of 3 or improving scores of 2 or 1.

Managing Runnels

SCORE OF 3

In the spring, loose snow streams down the center of a chute or steep gully, creating a mini river of continuously cascading snow known as a *runnel*. Depending on the width and intensity of the flow, runnels might not be an issue. However, sometimes they can knock you off your feet and carry you several body lengths down the slope. To avoid getting caught in the flow of a runnel, turn on either side of it until your line narrows and crossing is your only option.

To cross a runnel, lighten your skis and retract your legs as you skim over it, landing on your edges on the opposite side to control your speed. If you end up in the runnel, don't slow your momentum. Keep your speed up and slice straight through it at an angle. Bogging out in the middle of the runnel can result in loss of control and a fall. Frozen runnels can also be hazardous. Avoid them by absorbing terrain with your legs or delicately navigating through them with engaged edges.

Getting Out of a Rut
SCORE OF 2

When skiing bumps, it is not uncommon to feel like you have been taken hostage by the trough line because it literally follows a predetermined rut. As your legs tire and your reflexes slow, you may need to hop out of the trough and into a softer, rounder line. You can free yourself from the rut without losing your rhythm in three steps. Spot your takeoff bump, launch and redirect in the air, and land softly in the shoulder line. If you can continue without losing a beat, you have mastered this tactic.

Avoiding Gridlock
SCORE OF 2

Committing to one line down a slope is often a good tactical approach. However, in trees, rocks, slope changes, or other obstacles, you can easily get boxed in by random barriers which can put you in gridlock. The best skiers have developed the ability to adapt their turn shape and widen or shorten the arc of their turns as needed to adapt to obstacles. When approaching an obstacle, skidding gives you a second to reset your turn shape and helps you maintain symmetry as you pass the barrier.

Facing the Line
SCORE OF 1

Turning your back to the fall line is a real deal breaker when skiing steeps. As you approach a particularly steep section, it is common to tense up and twist your torso back uphill. This releases the tails of the ski and sends you flying backward. Instead, keep both hands out in front of you as you approach the steep section and punch your uphill hand toward the tip of your downhill ski. This action keeps you facing downhill and directs your body movement toward the next turn, maintaining your flow and rhythm.

Using Pole Plants to Maintain Your Line
SCORE OF 1

Pole dexterity complements and aids upper-body movements in dynamic skiing. Missing pole plants or not using them at all creates holes in your all-mountain skill set. Diverse terrain requires attention to rhythm and strong core movements that are directed down the fall line. Swing your pole to direct your momentum down the fall line and plant it to stabilize your body between turns. Get into a rhythm that moves you down the hill before stabilizing your upper body.

Glossing over your skills package is like forgetting to put gas in your car for a long trip: it's hard to get very far! Skills are built on components that act as the framework for your performance. They cannot be replaced by a quick fix or a shortcut. The drills in this chapter provide the fundamentals to help you progress toward skiing proficiency without limits.

PART III

10 11 12 13 14

Programming for Ski Performance

Guidelines for Program Development

Having a skiing-specific plan based on your unique physical and technical needs makes your training purposeful. The best training plans are simple to follow, flexible enough to adapt to your progress and recovery, and specific to your sport and individual needs. Physiological and technical specificity is the key to real improvement and sustained success.

The programs that follow in part III address the sport's total needs (as opposed to merely technique or equipment) by customizing your training needs according to the four main types of skiers. By adopting solutions that are unique to your needs, you will be able to practice your skiing even when you are not on the slopes. The prescribed series of exercises address deficits in mobility, stability, and fitness and can be performed at home. It will deliver big paybacks in performance and will increase the fun factor on the slopes. Additionally, specific drills for technique and tactics increase your quality time on the hill, leading to improvement that is faster and more consistent.

Your customized training program will be as unique as your thumbprint. No one-size-fits-all solution exists when it comes to addressing your skiing profile. However, there are some general rules of thumb that anyone can take advantage of when laying out a personalized skiing program.

Your Training Schedule

Without doubt, your most productive ski days are probably when you are well rested, free of injury, and equipped with the skills to take on all-mountain challenges. Unless you have a realistic timetable that allows you to peak physically during your planned outings, getting to that point may be more difficult than you had expected.

The first step in developing a training schedule you can stick to is to honestly look at the time you can commit to your training program. According to Malcolm Gladwell, author of *Outliers*, you must put in at least 10,000 hours of practice to become a master of a pursuit. This comes out to about 3 hours of practice each day for 10 years, or a whopping 10 hours a day for 3 years. Many people would never consider committing this amount of time to a passion; others are challenged by this number to transcend the purgatory of mediocrity and go where few have been before. The athletes who are most successful hit the 10,000-hour mark without knowing it because they are consumed with the joy of the sport, not the drudgery of the long journey toward improvement. Most of us fall somewhere in between. If we look at the actual hours we spend on snow, the task of true mastery seems even bleaker. Most skiers respond at some level to the amount of training suggested; however, each person's physiology determines the response time and adaptations required by repeated activity.

In simple terms, the most time you can expect to spend improving your skiing skills is 100 to 150 hours per season. At that rate, it would take you either 100 seasons or 50 back-to-back seasons, spreading your time between the northern and southern hemispheres, to meet the 10,000-hour requirement for true mastery. In reality, committed skiers with full-time jobs can expect, at best, to spend 50 to 60 days on snow. About 10 percent of the time is lost to weather in which the lifts do not run, leaving 35 to 45 possible days of training per year.

Unless you live on the mountain and you can ski in and out, allow for about 6 hours of scheduled skiing per day. Even then, you must subtract about 1.5 hours for time on the lifts (assuming you do 15 runs with a 6-minute ride between each one). This leaves you with about 4.5 hours of skiing time, but once again you must subtract about 50 percent of the time for warming up, taking breaks, and waiting for partners. In total, the average skier has about 2.25 hours per day of actual training time for mastering important movement patterns and tactical skills. However, don't give up yet! You can continue to work on your skiing without actually being on the snow. The programs outlined in the following chapters provide the exercises, drills, equipment adjustments, technique, and tactics to streamline the path to your 10,000-hour goal.

You can accomplish the 10,000 hours by changing your current daily lifestyle into a skiing lifestyle. According to Neville Owen, speaker at the American College of Sports Medicine's annual meeting (Seattle, May 2009), most people sit an average of 9.3 hours per day. Even if you are physically fit, this amount of inactivity is bad for your health, not to mention your skiing. A few changes to your daily routine can get you off your butt and push you closer to the hours needed to reach your goal. Walk or ride a bike instead of driving to work, stand at your desk, balance on one leg when taking a phone call, write e-mails in a squatting position, stand or stretch during informal meetings, or walk your dog. You can make these changes now, but this program's real power comes from the results of the screens in the previous chapters. The assessments for functional movement, fitness, technique, and tactics help you streamline your approach and craft an efficient path toward your skiing goals, cutting down the time and energy you might otherwise waste on dead-end, quick fixes.

Once you have uncovered the faults in your makeup and have discovered the exercises you need to improve, you can begin customizing your training program. Designing your program allows you to form realistic goals in terms of your training schedule. Your skiing season is split into three parts—preseason, in-season, and postseason—and your training schedule should reflect this calendar.

Preseason

For competitive athletes, the preseason period should begin 4 to 6 months before the competitive season and should establish a strong foundation for all future training. Recreational skiers often attempt the quick-fix plan in 4 to 6 weeks. This is a good start, but it rarely delivers the results necessary for making big changes in your skiing. The best way to judge the length of preseason training is to examine your physical condition from the past season. Did you get beat up last season? How much recovery time did you have over the summer? Were you able to work out during that time? If you are rehabilitating an injury or resting a chronic ache, your process will be more specific than if you are coming out of a period of active rest and getting your total baseline back up to par. The average preseason training time recommended for a recreational skier is at least 8 to 12 weeks. This gives you time to assess your condition and work on potentially weak areas in your functional movement and fitness.

Preseason training can be challenging if you are starting from scratch. Work on tailoring a lifestyle that includes activity and maintains your baseline fitness throughout the year. Preseason training shouldn't feel like a life-changing transformation equivalent to moving a mountain. Focus on establishing skiing-specific body movements and building cardiorespiratory and muscular strength.

In-Season

During the ski season, your focus shifts to the snow as you prepare specifically for scheduled events, planning backcountry outings, races, free-skiing competitions, helicopter-skiing trips, snowcat trips, or family holidays. If your days on the snow are limited, mix in other activities to maintain the edge you established in the preseason. By scheduling specific dates for in-season events, you will be able to build up and taper before the event. Specific dates are an excellent motivator for difficult training.

Postseason

Postseason is a period of active rest needed to transition through changes in intensity and movement. Your body needs time to relax and recover from the rigors of the active ski season. Playing other sports is a good way to broaden your scope of movement and patterns of power output. This break also keeps you fresh and motivated to set new goals and to revisit your base fitness needs.

Your Training Time

The average athletic American works out in a gym or at home 5.3 hours per week. If you are a competitive skier, your training probably includes even more gym time, particularly in the pre- and postseason.

Whatever your level, you can add these hours to your total training time if you have identified your skier type and narrowed down your weaknesses. Use this information to determine the necessary focus for your training and to make the most of your training time. Your focus will alternate between dryland and on-snow training and will depend on the time of year and your individual needs according to your assessments and skiing profile. Table 10.1 shows the basic timeline for developing your program based on the time of year.

TABLE 10.1   Time Commitment in Program Development

	Preseason	In-season	Postseason
Functional movement	3-6 times per week	3-5 times per week	3-6 times per week
Cardiorespiratory fitness	3-5 times per week	2-4 times per week	2-4 times per week
Muscular fitness (strength) and power and agility fitness	2-4 times per week	1-3 times per week	1-2 times per week
Technique		Each snow session*	
Tactics		Each snow session*	

*The only time you must work on perfecting your technique and improving your tactics is in-season, so address your needs in these areas each time you hit the slopes.

During the preseason, your time is consumed with dryland training. You should train three to six times per week and take at least one day off. During in-season, do dryland training one or two times per week. One day of aerobic activity helps flush you out, especially after consecutive skiing days or a ski weekend. A combination workout in zones 2 and 3 helps maintain your levels after a day off. The following figures provide a sample week of preseason, in-season, and postseason workouts that focus on cardiorespiratory fitness.

FIGURE 10.1A   Preseason Cardio Workouts

Monday	Zone 2	Cardio
Tuesday	Zone 3	Cardio, strength, and power*
Wednesday	Zone 1	Cardio
Thursday	Zone 2	Cardio
Friday	Zone 3	Cardio, strength, and power*
Saturday	Zone 1	Cardio
Sunday	Day off	Day off

*You can either train strength and power on one day or split them into two days.

FIGURE 10.1B   In-Season Cardio Workouts

Monday	Zone 1	Cardio
Tuesday	Day off	Day off
Wednesday	Zones 2 and 3	Cardio and strength
Thursday		Power
Friday		Ski
Saturday		Ski
Sunday		Ski

FIGURE 10.1C   Postseason Cardio Workouts

Monday	Zone 1	Cardio
Tuesday	Day off	Day off
Wednesday	Zones 2 and 3	Cardio and strength
Thursday	Zones 1 and 2	Power and agility
Friday	Day off	Day off
Saturday	Zone 1	Cardio
Sunday	Day off	Day off

Planning Your Dryland Training

Dryland training can be done year-round. It should be utilized as much as possible to address any weakness in the first two blocks of the pyramid and to maintain movements and fitness specific to skiing throughout the year. Remember, this kind of training adds to your total hours of mastery! Training sessions should focus on functional movement, cardiorespiratory fitness, muscular fitness, power, and agility. The intensity and frequency of these sessions are determined by the season and your fitness level.

Functional-Movement Training

Since functional movement is the foundation of your program, it must be intact in order for the rest of the pyramid's blocks to balance correctly. It also plays a critical role in preparing your body for exercise and skiing-specific movements. Perform a warm-up routine that focuses on functional movement before every workout or skiing day, even when focusing on fitness for power and agility or the cardiorespiratory and muscular systems. Your goal is to prepare your body for activity by increasing blood flow and heart rate, going through the necessary range of motion, and priming your stability, mobility, and balance for the demands of your scheduled workout or on-snow training.

Based on your results from the functional-movement assessments in chapter 2 (use your summary sheet as a guide!), choose exercises for your workout that are recommended for your particular areas of weakness. If you only have time to focus on one segment, the functional-movement block is the best choice for long-lasting improvement, performance, and durability. If you miss a training day, go back to the functional-movement exercises and get at least one round in. On skiing days, you can use an adapted, on-snow version. See chapters 11 through 14 for more information.

The preworkout routine takes you through warm-up and dynamic preparation before moving into actual functional-movement training. The following section takes a closer look at the two phases of the preworkout routine.

Warm-Up   Your workout routine should begin with a 5- to 10-minute warm-up that brings your heart rate up and makes you sweat. Activities that relate to the movement in the actual workout are best (for example, walk or jog prior to a running workout), but anything that increases your heart rate and warms up the appropriate muscles will work. On skiing days, take a 5- to 10-minute hike around the lodge or do some light skating or poling across flat terrain to get your heart pumping. You will then be ready for the next phase of your preworkout routine, dynamic prep.

Dynamic Preparation   Once your heart rate is up and your muscles are warmed up, you are ready to work through the range of motion that follows either in your workout or your day of skiing. Figures 10.2 and 10.3 provide dynamic preparation routines for both dryland and on-snow days. Both routines incorporate full-body movement to further warm up the key muscles and to engage the nervous system.

The dynamic-prep routine for dryland days in figure 10.2 enhances functional-movement training. Although some of the exercises may be the same, this prep routine is not a substitute for actual functional-movement training. Everyone, regardless of score or level, can do this core routine before every workout. If you scored a 3 in your functional-movement assessments in chapter 2, only a few stretches are recommended for wrapping up your preworkout routine. However, you may want to include some functional-movement exercises in a customized dryland routine to help maintain your score. If you do choose to create your own dynamic-prep routines, make sure that the overall workout targets full-body movement.

The dynamic-prep routine for on-snow days in figure 10.3 is adapted from the dryland versions to accommodate skiing clothes and equipment. These routines specifically prepare you for the dynamic demands of skiing. They should not be substituted for the prescribed dryland training

FIGURE 10.2   Dynamic-Prep Routines for Dryland Days

	Routine 1 (10-15 min.)			Routine 2 (10-15 min.)	
1	Single-leg bridge for glutes (p. 102)	2 sets of 6-8 reps	1	Single-leg bridge for glutes (p. 102)	2 sets of 6-8 reps
2	Inchworm (p. 112)	2 sets of 5 reps	2	Backward lunge with arm raise (p. 109)	1 set of 5 reps to the left and 5 reps to the right
3	Miniband walking routine (p. 95)	1 set; Walk for 30 ft. (9 m) and return, moving sideways	3	Knee-and-ankle grab (p. 101)	1 set of 5 reps to the left and 5 reps to the right
4	Lateral lunge (p. 16)	1 set of 5 reps to the left and 5 reps to the right	4	Lateral lunge (p. 16)	1 set of 5 reps to the left and 5 reps to the right
5	Tuck jump (p. 134)	1 set of 5 reps (hold tuck for 30 sec.)	5	Leg drops (p. 103)	1 set of 5 reps to the left and 5 reps to the right
6	Jumping rope (p. 136)	2 sets of 1 min. each (classic jump rope)	6	Miniband walking routine (p. 95)	1 set; Walk for 30 ft. (9 m), return moving sideways

FIGURE 10.3   Dynamic-Prep Routines for On-Snow Days

	Routine 1 (10-15 min.)			Routine 2 (10-15 min.)	
1	Swing leg forward and backward without skis	4-6 reps in each direction	1	Run in place for 10 sec.	2 sets
2	Swing leg from side to side without skis	4-6 reps on each side	2	Lateral lunge	1 set of 5 reps to the left and 5 reps to the right
3	Twist core with poles on shoulders	6-8 reps in each direction	3	Twist core with poles on shoulders	6-8 reps in each direction
4	Swing arms forward and backward	6-8 reps on each side	4	Half squat with raised arm	1 set of 5 reps to the left and 5 reps to the right
5	Tuck jumps without skis	6-10 reps	5	Outdoor stork	1 set of 3 reps to the left and 3 reps to the right
6	Tuck turns with skis	20-25 reps	6	Inverted hamstring stretch	1 set of 3 reps to the left and 3 reps to the right
7	Uphill side step with skis	10-15 reps	7	Uphill duck walk with skis	10-15 reps
8	Single-leg jump from side to side with skis	6-12 reps on each side	8	Downhill side step with skis	10-15 reps
9	Two-leg jump from side to side with skis	6-8 reps	9	Jump in place with skis	10-15 reps

according to the assessment. Unlike the other routines, they do not lead into functional-movement training sessions indoors. Rather, once you complete the dynamic-prep routine on the snow, you can adapt some stretches from your functional-movement routines before taking the chairlift up for your first ski run!

Once you have completed your dynamic-prep routine for dryland days, you are ready to train for endurance and strength. For an on-snow day, do a few adapted stretches from chapter 7, such as stretches for the quads, hamstrings, and hip flexors. Be sure to complete the prescribed number of functional-movement sessions off the snow during the week. If you scored a 3 in the functional-movement assessments in chapter 2, no training is prescribed. Simply pick some stretches from chapter 7, making sure to hit each major muscle group.

You should do functional-movement training consistently throughout the year to maintain this block of the pyramid. Continue to assess your functional movement for changes in mobility and stability. The tests may show improvements in your areas of asymmetry, weakness, or stiffness as a result of your training. During the preseason, focus on quality of movement, making sure to fire the right muscles and avoiding compensations in order to prevent misalignment and overuse. Remember to retest, since the rigors of the season can cause muscle imbalances and overuse injuries. Keeping track of your progress helps you avoid setbacks like injuries or chronic pain. During the postseason, focus on recovering and reactivating the muscle groups you neglected over the season. Continually engaging one group of muscles can repress the opposing group, causing stiffness and imbalance. Essential movement exercises work all groups.

Cardiorespiratory Training

Since you can do cardiorespiratory training at three different intensities, plan some training time at each level for a primed engine. Refer to your test results from chapter 3 to determine your type of workout or level of training intensity. The time of year may also factor in. Keep track of your intensity by monitoring your heart rate throughout the workout. Each of the three workout intensities targets a specific heart rate zone (calculated as a percent of your maximum heart rate).

As chapter 3 mentions, the common formula for your maximum heart rate (HRmax) of subtracting your age from 220 is only correct for 50 percent of the population. HRmax can vary greatly depending on age, training level, and training history. A similar formula with one extra calculation will get you closer to your exact numbers. First, take your resting HR (RHR) when you wake up in the morning and determine how many times your heart beats in one minute. Next, put this number into the following calculation: ((220 - age) - RHR × 60 to 70 percent) + RHR = 60 to 70 percent training zone. For example, if you are a 40-year-old with an RHR of 60 bpm, the formula for 60 percent of HRmax would look like this: (((220 - 40) - 60) × .60) + 60 = 132 bpm. The number for 70 percent of HRmax would be 144. Therefore, your easy training zone would be 132 to 144 bpm.

Aerobic Training (Zone 1)   Use this zone for base training in the preseason and active-rest days once you have established a baseline of fitness. When working out aerobically, keep your heart rate at 50 to 70 percent of HRmax. Your activity should last for at least 30 minutes. Do something you enjoy, such as hiking, back-country skiing, swimming, biking, jogging, or skate skiing. If you struggle to dial it back on rest days, use a heart rate monitor with an alarm that can alert you when you go beyond your target zone.

Anaerobic-Threshold Training (Zone 2)   In this interval stage, your should be at 75 to 85 percent of HRmax. This training intensity develops the endurance needed for longer, steeper runs during preseason and in-season training. Intervals should last 3 to 10 minutes before dropping down to an easier intensity for 2 minutes to let your heart rate recover to zone 1.

Anaerobic-Power Training (Zone 3)   This zone is one beat closer to your HRmax than zone 2. You will need to push through the uncomfortable stage for at least 20 seconds and as long as 2 minutes. Rest for 2 minutes between intervals, letting your heart rate recover to zone 1. The duration of this stage depends on how fast your heart rate returns to zone 1, but usually lasts between 1 and 2 minutes.

Establish an aerobic base in zone 1 before training across intensity levels. To build your aerobic base, do three to six cardio workouts per week, increasing total time or mileage by no more than 5 to 20 percent, depending on your chosen activity (refer to table 3.1 in chapter 3 for guidelines). You should be able to score at least a 2 on your assessment (see page 30 in chapter 3) before adding any anaerobic-threshold workouts.

Once you have established your aerobic base, substitute or add anaerobic-threshold workouts from zone 2 to your cardiorespiratory routine as indicated by your test results. For anaerobic-threshold workouts to be most effective, you must maintain the same intensity over the entire interval (see chapter 8 for sample workouts and progressions). Perform the base workout for anaerobic threshold, which is the same as the assessment test in chapter 3, every two weeks to monitor your progress. Once you have reached the anaerobic threshold needed for a score of 2, you can add in anaerobic-power training in zone 3.

You can build anaerobic power as a workout on its own, at the end of an aerobic workout (zone 1), or as part of a mixed workout that combines the various phases with shorter, timed intervals. These intervals require you to go all out, leaving nothing in the tank. Although they are extremely grueling, they build confidence and mental toughness. As you transition from training in zone 1 and start adding training sessions of higher intensity in terms of anaerobic threshold and power, do not perform these workouts back to back. Many people alternate aerobic training with strength training, but high-intensity strength training can be just as draining as a high-intensity cardio workout. Listen to your body and build rest and active-recovery days into your training schedule. Ideally, you will have started anaerobic-threshold and anaerobic-power training (zones 2 and 3) six weeks into the start of the season. Of course, this timing is contingent on the progression you have established. Your amount of activity also depends on how much you are skiing.

During the season, do no more than two aerobic and two anaerobic sessions per week. If you are skiing several days per week, you could even reduce your training to one aerobic session and one anaerobic, combined-phase session. As the season wraps up, return to two to four aerobic workouts each week. Your body will tell you which schedule is right. If you feel tired and unmotivated, take a longer break. Once you recover fully, go back to two to four aerobic workouts (zone 1). As you begin to feel stronger, start adding the anaerobic-threshold and power workouts (zones 2 and 3) back in.

Training for Strength, Power, and Agility

When training for strength, power, and agility, the intensity of your workouts depends on the amount of stress placed on your muscles and connective tissues and the weight used for the exercises. Choose a weight that lets you accomplish the necessary reps with good technique. Progress from light to heavy intensity for steady improvement; for example, lifting light weights for more reps until you can use heavy weights for low reps helps you build strength. You should also focus on quality movement and form while performing the exercises. Do you remember how your aerobic workout ended when you were no longer able to recover in the prescribed time? The same is true with weight training. Once you fail to perform an exercise with good form, end the set and reduce the weight for the next one. If you continue with bad form, you may injure yourself or develop compensations.

As you begin to work the key muscles, progress from larger to smaller muscle groups to maximize your full energy potential. Since the bigger muscles require more fuel, it is difficult to push through the exercises that require more weight if you lack energy at the end of your workout. You can work the smaller muscles first if you want to mix up your practiced routine. If you need to rest during the workout, try coupling exercises, making sets of reciprocal and complementary components, such as a set of pull-ups, chest stretches (reach and roll on a stability ball), and the alternating dumbbell press. This practice balances intensity and rest while continuously working the needed components.

Building strength in the early stages of the preseason requires you to focus on low intensity and high duration (lighter weight and maximum reps), such as 2 or 3 sets of 8 to 12 reps per exercise. As you develop strength and get deeper into the preseason timeframe, increase intensity and lower your duration. For example, do 3 or 4 sets of 5 to 8 reps per exercise. During this time, you should always rest for at least one day between sessions and should do no more than two sessions a week.

As you move into the actual ski season, continue this schedule of rest and work days (you can reduce work sessions to one per week if necessary). During the season, lift close to 100 percent of your maximum weight with good form, keeping the intensity high and the volume low with three or four sets of three to six reps. As you progress, move up to four or five sets of four to six reps. Once the skiing season begins, you will be at maximum strength fitness, but you still may experience off days. Some days everything will click and you will be in the zone, and other days, you will feel like you are skiing with two left feet. Watch your progress and keep track of your sleep patterns, quality of food and quantity of water, and amount of mental breaks. Skiing will make you tired, so replace some of your strength days with days on the hill. As a rule of thumb, high-intensity strength days should taper off during the season and active-recovery days should take their place.

During the postseason, your workouts are less intense as you enter the recovery period needed to replenish and rest your body. However, continue to do at least one or two workouts per week to maintain your fitness level or two or three per week to improve it. Now you can relax and work out any aches or pains that nagged you during the season. Focus on regenerating your body, mind, and soul.

Planning Your On-Snow Training

When training on the snow, you must know what you need to work on before you hit the hill. Skiing goals are essential for motivation and effective progress. Without them, you can drift aimlessly from one popular ski move to the next. Each day, fix your sights on both your long-term goals and the specific technical or tactical drills for that session. You should also review your test results and repeat them regularly to track your progress and to pinpoint areas to work on during your sessions. Review daily notes before skiing to remember what you should be working on. As you monitor your training, you will see how your progress speeds or slows, depending on your motivation, recovery, preseason preparation, and susceptibility to injury.

The following training framework will guide your on-snow training and development from week to week. Remember to activate your muscles before all workouts by performing a warm-up and on-snow dynamic prep. The following sections break down the components of your on-snow sessions.

Active Free Ski

Active free skiing is an open time for you to contemplate your focus. What are your training cues? Where are your training runs? How much time do you take before active training? When you first get on the hill, cue in to your intuitive side and open yourself up to the sensations of snow and the skis and the environmental subtleties of the day. Spend between 30 and 40 minutes checking out the conditions, bringing your awareness to your energy and your ability to react and produce desired movements. Get used to the sliding sensations of the skis and key in to your balance cues.

Active Training

This is the time for actually practicing exercises and drills, focusing on proper execution, their results, and the cues that tell you if you are doing them correctly. Once you have practiced the exercises and drills, start applying these feelings to the terrain and conditions while skiing. Practice the exercises and drills for anywhere from 40 to 90 minutes, then spend the same amount of time applying the movements on the snow.

On-snow exercises and drills are best done in a progressive manner. Always start with a static drill so you can focus on its objective without the added complexity of sliding and speed. For example, if you are working on leg turning, you can lift your leg while standing at the top of the run and twist your ski by rotating your femur. You could then progress to a complementary drill that mimics and builds on this static drill. Perform it while moving across the slope, making half turns. Finally, you could finish with yet another drill that uses full turns in the fall line while moving.

The necessary time for this process of skill acquisition is different for everyone, but the process is always the same. It begins with basic understanding of a skill-development drill and how to perform it. Next, incorporate the key movements until they become consistent and synchronized in your skiing. These movements should become coordinated with your skiing and present in a natural sequence of flow and rhythm. Finally, refine these movements and apply them to challenging terrain and conditions. This process may take several runs, several weeks, or several years, depending on the complexity of the movements and the time you commit to the skill acquisition.

The outcome of this process helps you establish a style that is rooted in the fundamentals of good skiing. It also allows you to create your own approach based on your intuition and individual preferences. This process both shapes you and helps you develop into a role model that others can look up to. Once your skill execution is precise, see how the integrity of your skill set stands up to the extreme stresses of the mountain environment.

Exploring Terrain and Conditions

Applying your technique to the terrain and other skiing conditions helps ingrain the movements and gives you time for tactical practice. Spend anywhere from one to two hours on this and include drills that relate to the terrain you are skiing. For example, if you are headed toward steep terrain, practice turn-shape drills that control speed and encourage rhythm. If you are working on a specific technical focus like carving, pick a drill or two that highlights edging and pressure control. The following charts suggest suitable technique and tactics for various terrain and conditions. Table 10.2 lists techniques from chapter 4 and the terrain that corresponds for ideal practice. Table 10.3 lists ski tactics from chapter 5 and relates them to key tactical concepts and terrain.

Cool Down

When cooling down, ski slowly with proper form. Finish your day with some cruising runs to review the sensations you've established without the added stress of challenging terrain. Complete these runs on terrain that is conducive to low-intensity skiing (at a lower angle with fewer hazards). During this time, reduce your intensity and focus on the connection between your skis and the snow that you explored at the beginning of the session. Make sure your stance and posture are good and correct any compensations that may have developed with fatigue. Enjoy the snow!

TABLE 10.2 Ski Techniques and Related Terrain

Technique	Terrain
Basic stance	• Run with natural runout • Flat, consistent pitch • Groomed snow
Engaged stance	• Flat to moderate pitch • Open slope with low traffic • Groomed snow • Firm snow
Leg turn	• Flat to moderate pitch • Open slope with banked sides • Smart terrain • Groomed snow • Firm snow
Parallel turn	• Moderate pitch • Gently rolling terrain with progressive steeps • Groomed snow • Firm conditions • Hard pack
Carved turn	• Steep snow (both groomed and ungroomed) • Progressively steeper runs • Firm conditions • Icy snow with extreme hard pack

TABLE 10.3 Ski Tactics and Related Terrain

Terrain	KEY TACTICAL CONCEPTS			
	Reading terrain	Applying turn shape	Speed management	Line choice
Steeps	Read the pitch	C-, J-, S-, and Z-shaped turns	Slow, medium, or fast	Safety line and center punchline
Bumps	See the line	C-, J-, and S-shaped turns	Slow, medium, or fast	Basic, shoulder, trough, and zipper lines
Chutes and gullies	Know the parts	Z- to S-shaped turns	Slow to fast	Entries, middle line, and sequences
Back bowls	Be creative	Bigger turns, higher speeds	Medium to fast	Big turns, fall line
Trees	See the gaps using visual skills	Vary size and shape	Medium to fast	Make lane changes

At the start of every season, you should focus on free skiing and developmental exercises and drills. Free skiing helps reawaken your nervous system to the movement patterns you mastered last season. The developmental drills ground your movements in sound fundamentals. As the season progresses, spend more time on terrain-specific training and tactical practice. Of course, your schedule should be based on how well you have ingrained fundamental technique components. If the core skills of stance, balance, and the ability to turn the skis with your legs fall apart in new terrain, you must spend more time on these basic skills. As the season winds down, revisit functional-movement exercises to end the season cleanly.

Putting It All Together

Sequencing your workouts with high- and low-intensity days helps prevent burnout and keeps you fresh and eager to progress. Mixing up your workout types and including recovery days in your training schedule are recommended. A common training strategy is to alternate days of strength training and aerobic workouts. This gives you fresh legs for the different types of workouts. For example, if you work out hard, focusing on strength one day, add a recovery day before your next heavy workout. At most, you should only attempt two consecutive days of heavy work as your fitness level gets higher.

Things get a little more complicated when the focus turns to the snow, but you still need to balance your on-snow training with days for maintaining or improving functional movement and fitness. As before, it is best to separate days of aerobic or strength training and technical or tactical training. You can do light aerobic and light strength workouts on the same day as on-snow training, but you should perform them after your snow session or later in the day to prevent injury and skiing on tired legs, which can impair your ability to execute correct technique or tactics and can promote bad habits. The same holds true for strength training. Monitor your safety and technique when performing a strength-training workout after a skiing session.

The following chapters outline training guidelines for the different types of skiers. These suggestions will help you achieve maximum performance as efficiently as possible. You will be able to tailor the prescribed programs to your specific needs as identified in the assessments from Part I. This training plan will give you direction and purpose, leading to real and measurable results.

11

The Overpowered Skier

If you are an overpowered skier, you scored well (average of 3) in the assessments for technique, tactics, and fitness in chapters 3 through 5, but scored lower (score of 1 or 2) in the functional-movement test in chapter 2. Overpowered skiers commonly have the skills to complete the milestones of technique and tactics, but lack the stability and mobility to address varied terrain configurations without making compensations or risking injury. Although they may do well on lower-level maneuvers, they begin to make compensations in terrain that is more advanced. A program that focuses on fundamental movement and mobility will enhance overpowered skiers' durability and longevity.

The program for overpowered skiers combines developmental exercises and correctional exercises that address the weaknesses in their assessments. A progression of skills and exercises is used to identify weaknesses. The screens from chapters 2 through 5 also show areas for improvement. To avoid compensations due to inefficiencies, learn the following red flags and address the problems before they become bad habits:

- *Stiff outside leg.* Bracing with taut leg muscles due to poor mobility in the hips is a common symptom for overpowered skiers. The resulting movement pattern is inefficient.

- *Body follows skis around while turning.* Lack of separation of the lower and upper body due to stiff hip flexors and tight quads makes it difficult for overpowered skiers to turn their legs without moving the upper body.

- *Hopping skis around turns.* Excessive reliance on larger muscles creates ballistic, hurried movements that prevent precise turns.

- *Upper body rotates first when beginning a turn.* Overpowered skiers commonly have underdeveloped smaller muscles and overdeveloped larger muscles. As a result, they lead with the shoulders and the midsection.

- *Choppy and asymmetrical rhythm.* Lack of coordination and agility needed to synchronize movement disrupts the flow of efficient skiing.

- *Heavy pressure on the skis.* This is due to dominant but powerful leg movements. The lack of touch or finesse may be related to poor mobility and coordination.

- *Upper body is stiff.* Lack of mobility in the midsection can make these skiers look like statues.

Program Design for Overpowered Skiers

Since overpowered skiers have a solid base of muscular strength and endurance but lack mobility and agility, the main emphasis of their program is functional movement. The upside is that their biggest flaw can be targeted year-round with functional-movement training and supplemented with agility training as ski season approaches. The frequency of functional-movement training should pick up during the preseason and in-season to correct this weakness. Even with a natural base of muscular fitness, they should focus on fitness training, both in preseason and throughout the season, as identified by their performance screens.

If you're working through this program, start training 12 weeks before the start of the season. This is a good time to retest and make sure that you are still averaging a score of 3 in the fitness assessments in chapter 3. If not, you have time to address any weaknesses that might have cropped up during the off-season. Retest every 4 to 6 weeks to monitor your maintenance and to gauge your improvement.

Once the ski season starts, reduce fitness training. However, you can continue your functional-movement training on days when you're not skiing. On the snow, focus on retooling your technique, relying more on mobility than on raw strength and power. This chapter provides samples of on-snow training programs that enhance neutral and engaged stances, leg turning, parallel turns, carved turns, and tactics by terrain. Although overpowered skiers already have a solid grasp of these techniques, they should revisit fundamentals to improve their movement patterns. Postseason training is for maintaining functional movement and fitness until the preseason starts again. It is a great time to try new activities to keep things fresh.

Table 11.1 shows the overall training schedule for the classic overpowered skier. It assumes a maximum of six training days per week. At least five days of training, with attention to all of the pyramid blocks, are recommended. Sessions can also be combined for fewer overall training days (please review the guidelines in chapter 10).

TABLE 11.1   Training Schedule for Overpowered Skiers

	Preseason	In-Season	Postseason
Functional movement	5-6 times per week (with dryland training)	4-5 times per week (with dryland training)	3-6 times per week (with dryland training)
Cardiorespiratory fitness	3-4 times per week	2-3 times per week	2-4 times per week
Muscular fitness (strength) and power and agility fitness	2-3 times per week	1-2 times per week	1-2 times per week
Technique		Each snow session	
Tactics		Each snow session	

The following sections outline a sample year of training sessions.

Preseason (12 Weeks)

When preseason begins, perform all of the dryland assessments from part I to gauge your current levels and to determine any needs that may have developed. Use this information to progress through the following goals for the preseason. Figures 11.1 through 11.3 identify different workouts for each set of weeks, and figure 11.5 on page 198 outlines specific details.

Weeks 1 to 4 (Foundation)

Use the first four weeks of the preseason to resume a specific training focus that is geared to your needs and goals for the upcoming season. Work primarily on functional movement and aerobic (zone 1) training. Increase the time for at least one aerobic workout each week. Although overpowered skiers have high marks for strength, the assessments in chapter 2 may indicate a few gaps. See chapter 8 for related exercises. Introduce agility moves in these early weeks to specifically target any movement deficiencies. Figure 11.1 shows a sample preseason program for weeks 1 through 4.

Figure 11.1 Sample Preseason Program for Weeks 1 to 4

	Day 1	Day 2	Day 3	Day 4	Day 5	Day 6	Day 7
Functional-movement training (2 sets of 8-12 reps for stability; 2 sets of 10-20 sec. for mobility)	Dynamic-prep routine (p. 181), plus any mobility exercises from assessments in ch. 2	Dynamic-prep routine (p. 181), plus any stability and mobility exercises from tests for overhead-depth squat and single-leg squat (pp. 11 and 13)	Dynamic-prep routine (p. 181), plus any stability and mobility exercises for rotational-stability and lateral-lunge tests (pp. 15 and 16)	Dynamic-prep routine (p. 181), plus any stability and mobility exercises from tests for overhead-depth squat and single-leg squat (pp. 11 and 13)	Day off or dynamic-prep routine (p. 181), plus any mobility exercises from assessments in ch. 2	Dynamic-prep routine (p. 181), plus any stability and mobility exercises from rotational-stability and lateral-lunge tests (pp. 15 and 16)	Day off
Cardio-respiratory training	Long workout in zone 1 (as directed in ch. 3)	Day off	Medium workout in zone 1*	Day off	Day off or short to medium workout in zone 1*	Short workout in zone 1*	Day off
Strength and agility training (2-3 sets of 8-12 reps for strength)	Day off	Workouts A or B (p. 198), plus any exercises from assessments in ch. 3	Day off	Alternate workouts A and B (p. 198), plus any exercises from assessments in ch. 3	Day off	Day off or workout C (p. 198), plus any exercises from assessments in ch. 3	Day off

*The duration of medium and short cardiorespiratory sessions should be determined in relation to that of your long workout for the week. In general, a medium workout should be one-half to two-thirds of the length of the long workout. A short workout should be one-third to one-half of the length of the long workout.

Weeks 5 to 8 (Development)

Use weeks 5 to 8 of the preseason to add intensity to your cardiorespiratory work with anaerobic-threshold (zone 2) training. As before, increase the time of at least one aerobic workout each week. Continue to address any areas of weakness identified in strength testing. Focus primarily on functional-movement, agility, and power training. Figure 11.2 shows a sample of the preseason program during weeks 5 through 8.

Figure 11.2 Sample Preseason Program for Weeks 5 to 8

	Day 1	Day 2	Day 3	Day 4	Day 5	Day 6	Day 7
Functional-movement training (2-3 sets of 10-15 reps for stability; 2-3 sets of 15-25 sec. for mobility)	Dynamic-prep routine (p. 181), plus any mobility exercises from assessments in ch. 2	Dynamic-prep routine (p. 181), plus any stability and mobility exercises from tests for overhead-depth squat and single-leg squat (pp. 11 and 13)	Dynamic-prep routine (p. 181), plus any stability and mobility exercises from tests for rotational stability and lateral lunges (pp. 15 and 16)	Dynamic-prep routine (p. 181), plus any stability and mobility exercises from tests for overhead-depth squat and single-leg squat (pp. 11 and 13)	Dynamic-prep routine (p. 181), plus any stability and mobility exercises from tests for rotational stability and lateral lunges (pp. 15 and 16)	Day off or dynamic-prep routine (p. 181), plus any mobility exercises from assessments in ch. 2	Day off
Cardio-respiratory training	Long workout in zone 1 (as directed in ch. 3)	Day off	Zone 2 workout (see ch. 3 for test and ch. 8 for workout)	Day off	Mix zones 1 and 2 in short or medium workout* (see p. 121 in ch.8 for options)	Day off or short workout in zone 1*	Day off
Strength, power, and agility (2 sets of 8-12 reps for strength)	Day off	Workouts D or E (p. 198), plus any exercises from assessments in ch. 3	Day off	Alternate workout D and E (p. 198), plus any exercises from assessments in ch. 3	Day off	Day off or workout C (p. 198), plus any exercises from assessments in ch. 3	Day off

*The duration of medium and short cardiorespiratory training sessions is determined in relation to that of your long workout for the week. In general, medium workouts are one-half to two-thirds the length of the long workout. Short workouts are one-third to one-half the length of the long workout

Weeks 9 to 12 (Peak)

Use weeks 9 through 12 to finalize your ski preparation by adding anaerobic power (zone 3). Continue to focus on functional-movement and agility training. As before, increase the time of at least one aerobic workout per week. Finally, focus on movements that mimic the range of joint movement needed for dynamic ski turns and terrain management. Add power and agility work while continuing strength training. Figure 11.3 shows a sample preseason program for weeks 9 through 12.

Figure 11.3 Sample Preseason Program for Weeks 9 to 12

	Day 1	Day 2	Day 3	Day 4	Day 5	Day 6	Day 7
Functional-movement training (3 sets of 10-15 reps for stability; 3 sets of 15-30 sec. for mobility)	Dynamic-prep routine (p. 181), plus any mobility exercises from assessments in ch. 2	Dynamic-prep routine (p. 181) plus any stability and mobility exercises from tests for overhead-depth squat and single-leg squat (pp. 11 and 13)	Dynamic-prep routine (p. 181), plus any stability and mobility exercises for rotational-stability and lateral-lunge tests (pp. 15 and 16)	Dynamic-prep routine (p. 181), plus any stability and mobility exercises from tests for overhead-depth squat and single-leg squat (pp. 11 and 13)	Day off or dynamic-prep routine (p. 181), plus any mobility exercises from assessments in ch. 2	Dynamic-prep routine (p. 181), plus any stability and mobility exercises from rotational-stability and lateral-lunge tests (pp. 15 and 16)	Day off
Cardio-respiratory training	Long workout in zone 1 (as directed in ch. 3)	Day off	Workout in zone 3 (See p. 30 of ch. 3 for test and pp. 119-120 in ch. 8 for workout options)	Day off	Day off or medium workout in zone 1*	Mix zones 1 and 2 in short or medium workout* (see p. 121 in ch.8 for workout options)	Day off
Strength, power, and agility training (3-4 sets of 5-8 reps for strength)	Day off	Workouts D or E (p. 198), plus any exercises from assessments in ch. 3	Day off	Alternate workouts D and E (p.198), plus any exercises from assessments in ch. 3	Day off	Day off or workout F (p. 198), plus any exercises from assessments in ch. 3	Day off

*The duration of medium and short cardiorespiratory sessions should be determined in relation to that of your long workout for the week. In general, a medium workout is one-half to two-thirds the length of the long workout. A short workout is one-third to one-half the length of the long workout.

In-Season (16 Weeks)

During the season, functional-movement, cardiorespiratory, strength, power, and agility training remain the same, reflecting the goal of maintenance. However, the training program for technique and tactics changes each month as you progress toward mastery. Figure 11.4 provides a sample weekly program for the in-season. See figures 11.5 on page 198 and 11.6 on page 200 for more details.

Weeks 1 to 4 (Foundation)

Use the first four weeks of the season to get your body back to basic skiing skills and to build a strong foundation for your movement and performance. Perform on-snow assessments to pinpoint the areas that need the most work. Focus on mastering and progressing through the technical milestones in order, identifying and correcting faults in technique due to lack of mobility and compensations.

You can decrease fitness training to focus more on maintenance and recovery. Skiing all day taxes your muscles, especially your quads, so keep them balanced by working the lesser-used muscles (in this case, the hamstrings) to maintain equal strength throughout the body and to avoid injury. Continue to focus on functional-movement training, which is your main limiting factor. However, you can reduce the frequency slightly to give your legs at least one day's rest from the combination of functional-movement and skiing training.

Weeks 5 to 12 (Development)

Use weeks 5 through 12 of the in-season to retrain techniques while adding tactical exploration and training to the mix. Use races and competitions primarily as training tools to improve technique and tactics under pressure. In other words, build on previous performance while maintaining a training focus. Continue functional-movement and fitness training with the same focus on maintenance and recovery.

Weeks 12 to 16 (Peak)

Use weeks 12 to 16 of the in-season to maintain your progress in mastering technique while shifting the focus to tactics and racing (for those who are so inclined). This is a great time to try new terrain and conditions that require new tactics. Expanding your tactical toolbox in unfamiliar scenarios builds awareness that can improve decision making. Again, continue functional-movement and fitness training with a focus on maintenance and recovery.

Postseason

During the postseason, maintain a base-fitness level that allows you to start preseason training without missing a beat. Try other sports for a change of pace. Regardless of how you proceed with your fitness, include functional-movement training as often as possible to maintain mobility from the previous season. Test every six to eight weeks to check your levels. If you notice any losses during assessment, adjust your routine to include correctional exercises. Maintain cardiorespiratory fitness with aerobic (zone 1) training. If you feel burned out after the ski season, reduce your cardio. To prepare for preseason training, commit to doing cardiorespiratory training twice a week. Similarly, commit to muscular-fitness training at least once a week. Routine C is ideal for the off-season.

Figure 11.4 Sample Weekly In-Season Program

	Day 1	Day 2	Day 3	Day 4	Day 5	Day 6	Day 7
Functional-movement training (2 sets of 10-15 reps for stability; 2-3 sets of 15-30 sec. for mobility)	Dynamic-prep routine (p. 181), plus any mobility exercises from assessments in ch. 2	Dynamic-prep routine (p. 181), plus any stability and mobility exercises from tests for overhead-depth squat and single-leg squat (pp. 11 and 13)	Dynamic-prep routine (p. 181), plus any mobility exercises from assessments in ch. 2	Dynamic-prep routine (p. 181), plus any stability and mobility exercises from rotational-stability and lateral-lunge tests (pp. 15 and 16)	Day off or dynamic-prep routine (p. 181), plus any mobility exercises from assessments in ch. 2	Dynamic-prep routine (p. 181); This is an on-snow warm-up, not a functional-movement session.	Dynamic-prep routine (p. 181); This is an on-snow warm-up, not a functional-movement session.
Cardio-respiratory training	Long workout in zone 1 (as directed in ch. 3)	Day off	Mixed workout of zones 2 and 3 (see p. 122 in ch. 8 for workout options)	Day off	Day off or short or medium workout in zone 1*	Day off	Day off
Strength, power, agility training (3-5 sets of 4-6 reps for strength)	Day off	Alternate workouts D and E (p. 198), plus any exercises from assessments in ch. 3	Day off	Alternate workouts D and E (p. 198), plus any exercises from assessments in ch. 3	Day off	Day off	Day off
TECHNIQUE AND TACTICS							
Weeks 1-4	Day off	Day off	Day off	Day off	Day off or skill-practice session C (p. 200)	Skill-practice session A (p. 200)	Skill-practice session B (p. 200)
Weeks 5-8	Day off	Day off	Day off	Day off	Day off or skill-practice session A or B (p. 200)	Skill-practice session C (p. 200)	Skill-practice session D (p. 200)
Weeks 9-12	Day off	Day off	Day off	Day off	Day off or skill-practice session A, B, or C (p. 200)	Skill-practice session D (p. 200)	Skill-practice session E (p. 200)
Weeks 13-16	Day off	Day off	Day off	Day off	Day off or skill-practice session A, B, C, or D (p. 200)	Skill-practice session E (p. 200)	Design your own tactical exploration

*The duration of medium and short cardiorespiratory sessions should be determined in relation to that of your long workout for the week. In general, a medium workout is one-half to two-thirds the length of the long workout. A short workout is one-third to one-half the length of the long workout.

**If performing one workout for strength, power, and agility per week, do either C or F (p. 198), plus any solution exercises for your scores from chapter 3.

Workouts for Overpowered Skiers

Although the previous programs provide a general overview for your training, the following program outlines the actual instruction and exercises for your seasonal workouts. Simply locate the appropriate workouts in figures 11.5 and 11.6 in order to assemble your training plan for the day.

Functional-Movement Training

As previously mentioned in the outlines for seasonal programs, see pages 181 to 183 of chapter 10 for dynamic-prep routines. Add any correctional exercises as needed based on your functional-movement score from the assessment in chapter 2.

Cardiorespiratory Training

Train by using or tweaking the sample workouts and progression guidelines in chapter 8 (see pages 116-122).

Strength, Power, and Agility Training

See figure 11.5 for the designated workout for strength, power, and agility training. Workouts A and B are meant to be performed in the same week, creating a comprehensive, full-body training program that is specific to the strength needs of skiers. These workouts also introduce agility work to focus on the movement deficiencies of the overpowered skier. Workout C is a condensed, full-body strength workout that can be used on its own or combined with a short cardiorespiratory workout. Workouts D and E add power work. Workout F is a condensed strength, power, and agility workout.

See chapter 8 for descriptions and variations of the following exercises (exercises with variations are marked with an asterisk). Earlier in the season, you can start with the easier variation, but you should work to progress to the harder variation by the end of the season. Although distinct exercises exist for the different scores for the upper-body and core screens, the leg screens require the same solution exercises regardless of the score. In this case, the easier variation should be performed by those scoring a 1 and the harder variation should be performed once the score progresses to a 3.

Technique and Tactics

Start your on-snow sessions with a warm-up and one of the on-snow, dynamic-prep routines (see pages 181 to 183 in chapter 10). Next, progress through your training session in three phases as outlined in chapter 10. As an overpowered skier, you must address functional movement in addition to agility to get the most from the technical and tactical information in this section. Efficient skiing is attained through ingraining the correct movement sequences. Technical and tactical improvement also requires functional-mobility and stability training.

Active-Free Ski

Take approximately 30 to 40 minutes to check out the conditions of the day and to tap into your energy and your ability to react and produce the movements you desire. Become aware of sliding sensations and your focus cues. Figure 11.6 provides the key cues for each workout. Overpowered skiers can explore the ranges of movement needed for effective skills application in the active-free ski simply by exaggerating the amount of movement.

Figure 11.5 Training Workouts for Strength, Power, and Agility

	Workout A	Workout B	Workout C	Workout D	Workout E	Workout F
Upper-body strength	• Push-up (with or without stability ball), p. 124* • Lat pull-down, p. 127	• Supine row with feet elevated, p. 125* • Horizontal row, p. 127	• Bench press with dumbbells, p. 125* • Kneeling single-arm row, p. 126*	• Push-up (with or without stability ball), p. 124* • Kneeling single-arm row, p. 126*	• Bench press with dumbbells, p. 125* • Supine row with feet elevated, p. 125*	• Bench press with dumbbells, p. 125*
Core strength	• Supine leg-up, p.129 • Medicine-ball toss with sit-ups, p. 128*	• Hanging-leg hip raise, p. 129 • Medicine-ball side toss, p. 128*	• Sit-up, p. 130*	• Supine leg-up, p. 129* • Medicine-ball toss with sit-ups, p. 128*	• Hanging-leg hip raise, p. 129* • Medicine-ball side toss, p. 128*	• Sit-up, p. 130*
Lower-body strength	• Split squat, p. 131* • Lateral lunge, p. 131*	• Romanian deadlift, p. 132* • Bridge on stability ball, p. 132*	• Split squat, p. 131* • Romanian deadlift, p. 132*	• Romanian deadlift, p. 132* • Bridge on stability ball, p. 132*	• Split squat, p. 131* • Lateral lunge, p. 131*	• Split squat, p. 131*
Power**	--	--	--	• Lateral box blast, p. 133, for 2-3 sets of 6-10 jumps on each foot* • Reactive step-up, p. 133, for 2-3 sets of 6-10 jumps on each foot*	• Tuck jump, p. 134, for 2-3 sets of 6-10 jumps* • Lateral hurdle jump, p. 134, for 2-3 sets of 6-10 jumps on each foot*	• Lateral box blast, p. 133, for 2-3 sets of 5-10 jumps on each foot* • Tuck jump, p. 134, for 2-3 sets of 5-10 jumps* • Reactive step-up, p. 133, for 2-3 sets of 5-10 jumps on each foot* • Lateral hurdle jump, p. 134, for 2-3 sets of 5-10 jumps on each foot*
Agility	• Jumping rope (slalom, p. 136); follow progression guidelines in ch. 8	• In-in-out-out agility ladder, p. 135, 2 times through a 30 ft. (9 m) ladder	• Agility ladder (Ickey shuffle, p. 136, and crossover zigzag, p. 136) 2 times each through a 30 ft. (9 m) ladder	• Jumping rope (slalom, p. 136); follow progression guidelines in ch. 8	• Agility ladder (in-in-out-out, p. 135; Ickey shuffle, p. 136; crossover zigzag, p. 136) 2-4 times each through a 30 ft. (9 m) ladder	• Agility ladder (in-in-out-out, p. 135; Ickey shuffle, p. 136; crossover zigzag, p. 136) 2-4 times each through a 30 ft. (9 m) ladder

**The ranges of sets and reps given for the power exercises allow for progression during the preseason and a subsequent reduction in volume during the in-season. Do the lower amount of total jumps at the start of the preseason and progress throughout the 12 weeks, first by increasing the reps (staying at two sets), and then moving to three sets with fewer reps. Taper down to the lower end of the range during the in-season.

Active Training (Technique)

Figure 11.6 provides five skill workouts (A through E) for use in your practice sessions that progress from easy to difficult. The easier workouts emphasize basic skiing essentials and focus on drills that establish a base of support and balance on the outside ski. Overpowered skiers lose the finesse that comes from balance and allows for precision movements with the outside ski. With this in mind, practice drills that focus on base of support, outside-leg balance, leg turning, and precision-edging movements. The workouts that are more difficult focus on skill sequences that combine these components together. Workouts A and B address the starting points for the milestones of the neutral stance, the engaged stance, and leg turning. Workout C acts as a bridge between essentials and the sequential movements needed to complete dynamic drills and turns, with an emphasis on parallel and carved turns. Workouts D and E help refine the movements necessary to complete the skills package, again emphasizing parallel and carved turns.

Figure 11.6 assigns a practice time to each session that is recommended for ingraining technique and working toward mastery. Obviously, the amount of time you practice depends on your personal schedule or situation. To determine how much time to spend on each drill, simply divide the total time of each session by the number of recommended drills. For example, four drills over 40 minutes translates to 10 minutes of work on each drill. If you need more practice on a particular drill, you can add more time to the overall workout or decrease the time you spend on one drill in order to add time to another. Overpowered athletes tend to muscle out their training sessions. The key to improvement is to rein in the power moves and spend more time building finesse and touch.

Finally, be advised that these practice sessions are based on an average progression. It is up to you to monitor your progress and to work in a session until you are ready to move on. The results from your assessment in part I should be the driving force in terms of the drills you perform. Don't blindly follow the drills listed in the table. The following workouts are ideal for overpowered skiers, but you need to personalize them by substituting or adding drills according to your test results in chapter 4.

Exploring Terrain and Conditions (Tactics)

Figure 11.6 also identifies the tactical concepts you should practice in a specific progression for each terrain. The terrain and conditions are listed in order from most common to most challenging. Each skier brings a slightly different frame of reference to the practice, so look carefully at the prescribed drills and concepts and begin with the practice that best fits your starting point. For example, most overpowered skiers have a strong skill set of technique and tactics, so they naturally move toward challenging terrain early in the session. Pull back on the throttle of intensity and speed to let your body adapt to the terrain gradually and build slowly toward the higher-end challenges. When mastering new sensations, don't overstress your body with the compound challenges of aggressive terrain, new skills, and challenging conditions all at once. Overpowered skiers should start slowly and build up to terrain and conditions that are more challenging. Refer to the results of your tactical assessment in chapter 5 to identify the areas that need the most work. Remember to assess, drill, practice, explore, and then assess again.

Carve out at least one hour, preferably two, for practicing terrain exploration. It takes some time to find the terrain listed in the practice session in addition to the practice time. By the time you ride the lift, find terrain, practice the drill, and return to the lift, you might lose 20 to 30 minutes for a single drill or run. Therefore, you will not be able to practice every terrain in each practice session. However, if you progress quickly, you can follow the suggested drills for the next terrain listed. Realistically, you will only get through two or three types of terrain in one session. Pick your terrains and spend several runs practicing the recommended tactics.

Regardless of the terrain where you are working, the listed drills progress you through the tactical milestones outlined in chapter 9. Practices A, B, and C emphasize basic tactics, such as making terrain transitions, reading terrain, and applying turn shape, which are necessary for the advanced tactics of speed and line management that appear in practices D and E. Again, remember that the sample seasonal programs from earlier in the chapter represent the average time for mastering these concepts. Individualize your program and move at the pace that is best for you, retesting every four weeks.

Figure 11.6 Sample Technical and Tactical Practice Sessions

ACTIVE-FREE SKI (30-40 MIN.)

	Practice A	Practice B	Practice C	Practice D	Practice E
Focus cues	Establishing precision balance on the outside ski	Developing awareness of edge versus flat skis	Focusing on turning with your legs	Ingraining outside-leg dominance	Experiencing the efficiency of a ski that is edged and tracking

ACTIVE TRAINING (40-90 MIN.)

Practice each drill for at least 2 runs. Take time to practice quality movements 30 to 60 times, or for a total of 4,500 vertical feet (1372 m). The total vertical feet skied may vary, depending on the length of run at your resort, the drill, and conditions of the day. 3,000 to 6,000 total vertical feet (914-1829 m) is a good target. If you do more than 6,000 vertical feet, focus on quality execution of movements.

Tech-nique	Practice				
	Practice A (40-60 min.)	Practice B (40-60 min.)	Practice C (40-60 min.)	Practice D (60-90 min.)	Practice E (60-90 min.)
Neutral stance	• High-low drill, p. 142 • Hop drill, p. 141	• Shuffle drill, p. 141 • Lateral-step drill, p. 140	• Shuffle drill, p. 141 • Hop drill, p. 141	--	--
Engaged stance	• Traverse and reverse traverse drill, p. 145	• Traverse drill, p. 145	• Traverse drill on steeper terrain, p. 144	• Engaged stance at higher speeds, p. 144	• Engaged stance at higher speeds, p. 144
Leg turn	• Hands-on-hips drill, p. 149	• Leg turn on one ski, p. 147	• Clock-face drill, p. 148	• Leg turn on one ski, p. 147	--
Parallel turn	• Pole plant and release, p. 152	• One-leg pivot, p. 152	• Hand on hip and hand in the air, p. 156	• Stepping through the turn, p. 151	• Two skis to one ski, p. 153
Carved turn	--	--	• Long leg, short leg, p. 158	• Carved turn with hands on knees, p. 158	• Short-turn pole touch, p. 157

> continued

EXPLORING TERRAIN AND CONDITIONS (60-120 MIN.)

Practice each drill for 2-6 runs, totaling at least 4,500 (1372 m) vertical feet. Take time to practice quality movements. The total vertical feet skied may vary, depending on the length of the runs at your resort, the drill, and conditions of the day, but 3,000 to 6,000 (914-1829 m) total vertical feet is a good target. If you do more than 6,000 vertical feet, focus on quality execution of movements.

Terrain	Practice				
	Practice A (60-90 min.)	Practice B (60-120 min.)	Practice C (60-120 min.)	Practice D (90-120 min.)	Practice E (90-120 min.)
Steeps	• Basic terrain transitions (Gentle to steep slopes, p. 163) • Reading complex terrain (Unlocking freeze frame, p. 164)	• Basic terrain transitions (Groomed to ungroomed snow, p. 163) • Reading complex terrain (Redirecting focus, p. 164)	• Basic terrain transitions (Firm to soft snow, p. 163) • Reading complex terrain (Unlocking freeze frame, p. 164) • Turn management (Maintaining a strong finishing turn, p. 166)	• Turn management (Regulating pressure and edge on turns, p. 166) • Speed management (Checking your speed, p. 171)	• Speed management (Checking your speed, p. 171) • Line management (Scrubbing, p. 168)
Bumps	• Basic terrain transitions (Gentle to steep slopes, p. 163) • Reading complex terrain (Redirecting focus, p. 164)	• Basic terrain transitions (Groomed to ungroomed snow, p. 163) • Reading complex terrain (Unlocking freeze frame, p. 164)	• Basic terrain transitions (Wet to dry snow, p. 163) • Reading complex terrain (Unlocking freeze frame, p. 164) • Turn management (Establishing turn shape with ski placement, p. 166)	• Turn management (Fishhook ending in a J-shape, p. 165) • Speed management (Choosing the correct tempo, p. 171)	• Speed management (Choosing the correct tempo, p. 171) • Line management (Getting out of a rut, p. 173)

> *continued*

> continued

Terrain	Practice				
	Practice A (60-90 min.)	Practice B (60-120 min.)	Practice C (60-120 min.)	Practice D (90-120 min.)	Practice E (90-120 min.)
Chutes and gullies	• Basic terrain transitions (Gentle to steep slopes, p. 163) • Reading complex terrain (Unlocking freeze frame, p. 164)	• Reading complex terrain (Unlocking freeze frame, p. 164) • Turn management (Skidding, p. 169)	• Reading complex terrain (Redirecting focus, p. 164) • Turn management (Buttering, p. 169) • Line management (Creating symmetrical patterns in turns, p. 165)	• Speed management (Choosing the correct tempo, p. 171) • Line management (Avoiding gridlock, p. 173)	• Speed management (Pushing the envelope of speed and tempo, p. 171) • Line management (Managing runnels, p. 172)
Trees	• Reading complex terrain (Unlocking freeze frame, p. 164)	• Reading complex terrain (Redirecting focus, p. 164) • Turn management (Carving, p. 169)	• Reading complex terrain (Redirecting focus, p. 164) • Turn management (Scarving, p. 170) • Line management (Creating symmetrical patterns in turns, p. 165)	• Speed management (Choosing the correct tempo, p. 171) • Line management (Avoiding gridlock, p. 173)	• Speed management (Pushing the envelope of speed and tempo, p. 171) • Line management (Getting out of a rut, p. 173)
Back bowls	• Basic terrain transitions (Groomed to ungroomed snow, p. 163) • Reading complex terrain (Redirecting focus, p. 164)	• Reading complex terrain (Unlocking freeze frame, p. 164) • Turn management (Skidding, p. 169)	• Turn management (Carving, p. 169) • Speed management (Pushing the envelope of speed and tempo, p. 171) • Line management (Slashing, p. 168)	• Turn management (Buttering, p. 169) • Speed management (Pushing the envelope of speed and tempo, p. 171) • Line management (Scrubbing, p. 168)	• Speed management (Pushing the envelope of speed and tempo, p. 171) • Line management (Slashing, p. 168)

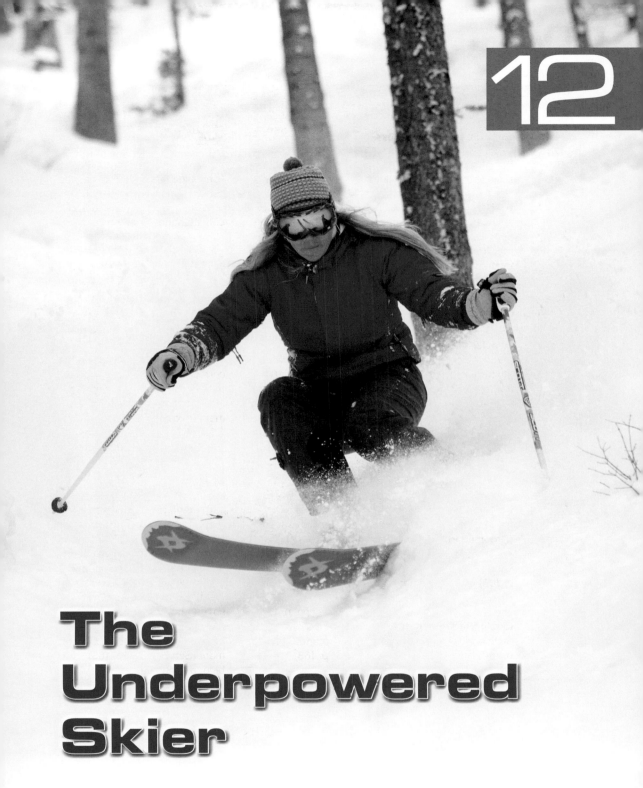

The Underpowered Skier

If you are an underpowered skier, you scored an average of 3 for the technique and tactics assessments in chapters 4 and 5, but a 1 or 2 in functional movement and fitness. The underpowered skier is different than the overpowered skier who primarily has weakness in mobility, with some holes in fitness. The underpowered skier is simply not strong enough, showing some weaknesses in fitness and stability, yet indicates good technique and tactical skills. Underpowered skiers can consistently perform most tasks and maneuvers. However, after a certain point, lack of strength and endurance cause movement patterns to deteriorate. This program focuses on endurance and strength to give you staying power and help you effectively apply skills.

The program for underpowered skiers focuses on a combination of correctional and developmental exercises based on the compensations seen in part I. It also incorporates technical movement cues. To avoid compensations due to inefficiencies, learn the following cues and address them before they become bad habits:

- *Lack of balance*. Underpowered skiers feel balanced for the first half of a run, but quickly tire and lean on the uphill ski and pole.
- *Lack of proactive movements*. Since they lack the ability to anticipate and move into a turn with the leg muscles, they wait for the turn to come to them. This habit results in late edging and uncontrolled skids.
- *Inability to link short turns straight down the fall line*. Skiers take a wide path, turning across the hill.
- *Muscles get overworked easily*. Quick-twitch muscles are muted by fatigue and lack of agility.

Program Design for Underpowered Skiers

Underpowered skiers have a solid base of functional-movement mobility, core-specific stability, and natural agility. However, they lack overall functional-movement stability, endurance, strength, and power. The main emphasis of their program design is fitness and stability training. The frequency of training should pick up during the preseason and in-season to target this weakness, but year-round training leads to lasting improvement. Even a natural mobility base must be maintained with functional-movement training in the dryland workouts.

For variety, you can use different conditioning approaches throughout the off-season. However, leading up to and throughout the ski season, you should focus fitness training with the methods, exercises, and drills identified by the results of your assessments in part I. Start adding this focus into your athletic program 12 weeks before the ski season starts. This is also a good time to retest to make sure that you're still scoring 3 in the functional-movement assessments. If not, you have time to address any weaknesses that might have cropped up during the off-season. After this time, you should retest every 4 to 6 weeks to monitor your maintenance and to gauge your improvement.

Once ski season starts, reduce the frequency of your dryland training. However, it is still useful in order to maintain the gains you have made. On the snow, focus on revisiting basic techniques and exploring tactics, applying your newly-gained fitness to more complex terrain or longer runs. Postseason training is for maintaining functional movement and fitness until the preseason starts again. It is a great time to try new activities to keep things fresh.

Table 12.1 shows the overall training schedule for the classic underpowered skier. It assumes a maximum of six training days per week. At least five days of training, with attention to all of the pyramid blocks, are recommended. Sessions can also be combined for fewer overall training days (please review the guidelines in chapter 10).

TABLE 12.1   Training Schedule for Underpowered Skiers

	Preseason	In-Season	Postseason
Functional movement	5-6 times per week (with dryland training)	4-5 times per week (with dryland training)	3-6 times per week (with dryland training)
Cardiorespiratory fitness	3-5 times per week	2-4 times per week	2-4 times per week
Muscular fitness (strength) and power and agility fitness	2-4 times per week	2-3 times per week	2 times per week
Technique		Each snow session	
Tactics		Each snow session	

The following sections outline a sample year of training sessions.

Preseason (12 weeks)

When preseason begins, perform all of the dryland assessments from part I to gauge your current levels and to determine any needs that may have developed. Use this information to progress through the following goals for the preseason. Figures 12.1 through 12.3 identify different workouts for each set of weeks, and figure 12.5 on page 212 outlines specific details.

Weeks 1 to 4 (Foundation)

Use the first four weeks of the preseason to resume a specific training focus, to ramp up your fitness training, and to gear your program for your specific needs and goals. Your cardiorespiratory focus should be on building endurance through aerobic (zone 1) training. Increase the time of at least one aerobic workout each week. During strength training, specifically address any areas of weakness identified through testing, using the solution exercises from the screens in chapter 8. Work on creating a balanced workout across all parts of your body so you can add power training in the next four weeks. Perform functional-movement training before cardiorespiratory and strength workouts in order to specifically prepare for the in-season. Although you average high marks for the functional-movement screens overall, you may still need to perform a handful of solution exercises as indicated in chapter 2. Figure 12.1 shows a sample preseason program for weeks 1 through 4.

Figure 12.1 Sample Preseason Program for Weeks 1 to 4

	Day 1	Day 2	Day 3	Day 4	Day 5	Day 6	Day 7
Functional-movement training (2 sets of 8-12 reps for stability; 2 sets of 10-20 sec. for mobility)	Dynamic-prep routine (p. 181), plus any mobility exercises from assessments in ch. 2	Dynamic-prep routine (p. 181), plus any stability and mobility exercises from assessments in ch. 2	Dynamic-prep routine (p. 181), plus any mobility exercises from assessments in ch. 2	Dynamic-prep routine (p. 181), plus any stability and mobility exercises from assessments in ch. 2	Dynamic-prep routine (p. 181), plus any mobility exercises from assessments in ch. 2	Day off or dynamic-prep routine (p. 181), plus any mobility exercises from assessments in ch. 2	Day off
Cardio-respiratory training	Long workout in zone 1 (as directed in ch. 3)	Day off	Medium workout in zone 1*	Day off	Short or medium workout in zone 1*	Day off or short workout in zone 1*	Day off
Strength and power training (2 sets of 8-12 reps for strength)	Day off	Alternate workouts A and B (p. 212), plus any exercises from assessments in ch. 3	Day off	Alternate workouts A and B (p. 212), plus any exercises from assessments in ch. 3	Day off	Day off or workout D (p. 212), plus any exercises from assessments in ch. 3	Day off

*The duration of medium and short cardiorespiratory sessions should be determined in relation to that of your long workout for the week. In general, a medium workout is one-half to two-thirds of the length of the long workout. A short workout is one-third to one-half of the length of the long workout.

Weeks 5 to 8 (Development)

Use weeks 5 through 8 of the preseason to improve your cardiorespiratory endurance, strength, and power with extra fitness sessions. Increase both the frequency and intensity of your cardio work by adding anaerobic-threshold (zone 2) training. As before, increase the length of at least one aerobic workout each week. The weekly program includes one more session of strength training and two sessions for power and agility. Continue functional-movement training to further ingrain good movement patterns. Figure 12.2 shows a sample preseason program for underpowered skiers during weeks 5 through 8.

Figure 12.2 Sample Preseason Program for Weeks 5 to 8

	Day 1	Day 2	Day 3	Day 4	Day 5	Day 6	Day 7
Functional-movement training (2-3 sets of 10-15 reps for stability; 2-3 sets of 15-25 sec. for mobility)	Dynamic-prep routine (p. 181), plus any mobility exercises from assessments in ch. 2	Dynamic-prep routine (p. 181), plus any stability and mobility exercises from assessments in ch. 2	Dynamic-prep routine (p. 181), plus any mobility exercises from assessments in ch. 2	Dynamic-prep routine (p. 181), plus any stability and mobility exercises from assessments in ch. 2	Dynamic-prep routine (p. 181), plus any mobility exercises from assessments in ch. 2	Dynamic-prep routine (p. 181), plus any stability and mobility exercises from assessments in ch. 2	Day off
Cardio-respiratory training	Mix zones 1 and 2 in medium workout* (see p. 121 in ch. 8 for options)	Day off	Long workout in zone 1 (as directed in ch. 3)	Short workout in zone 1*	Zone-2 workout (see p. 33 in ch. 3 for test and pp. 117-118 in ch. 8 for workout options)	Short workout in zone 1*	Day off
Strength, power, and agility training (2-3 sets of 8-12 reps for strength)	Workout C (p. 212), plus any exercises from assessments in ch. 3	Workout D (p. 212), plus any exercises from assessments in ch. 3	Day off	Workout E (p. 212), plus any exercises from assessments in ch. 3	Day off	Workout F (p. 212), plus any exercises from assessments in ch. 3	Day off

*The duration of medium and short cardiorespiratory sessions should be determined in relation to that of your long workout for the week. In general, a medium workout is one-half to two-thirds the length of the long workout. A short workout is one-third to one-half the length of the long workout.

**Ideally, underpowered skiers should work out six days a week. If you don't have time, take day 4 off and alternate workouts E and F (p. 212) on day 6.

Weeks 9 to 12 (Peak)

Use weeks 9-12 to finalize your preparation for the ski season by adding anaerobic power (zone 3). As before, increase the time of at least one aerobic workout each week. Continue strength training as in weeks 5 through 8, but focus more on increasing strength and power by lifting heavier weights for fewer reps. Perform more sets with greater speed. You will improve your power training in terms of number of contacts and speed of execution. Finally, continue agility and functional-movement training to target movements that mimic the range of joint movement needed for dynamic ski turns and terrain management. Figure 12.3 shows a sample preseason program for underpowered skiers during weeks 9 through 12.

Figure 12.3 Sample Preseason Program for Weeks 9 to 12

	Day 1	Day 2	Day 3	Day 4	Day 5	Day 6	Day 7
Functional-movement training (3 sets of 10-15 reps for stability; 3 sets of 15-30 sec. for mobility)	Dynamic-prep routine (p. 181), plus any mobility exercises from assessments in ch. 2	Dynamic-prep routine (p. 181), plus any mobility exercises from assessments in ch. 2	Dynamic-prep routine (p. 181), plus any mobility exercises from assessments in ch. 2	Dynamic-prep routine (p. 181), plus any stability and mobility exercises from assessments in ch. 2	Dynamic-prep routine (p. 181), plus any mobility exercises from assessments in ch. 2	Dynamic-prep routine (p. 181), plus any stability and mobility exercises from assessments in ch. 2	Day off
Cardio-respiratory training	Mix zones 1 and 2 in short or medium workout* (see p. 121 in ch. 8 for workout options)	Long workout in zone 1 (as directed on p. 31 in ch. 3)	Zone-2 workout (see pp. 117-118 in ch. 8 for options)	Day off	Zone-3 workout (see p. 33 in ch. 3 for test and pp. 118-120 in ch. 8 for workout options)	Short workout in zone 1*	Day off
Strength, power, and agility training (3-4 sets of 5-8 reps for strength)	Workout E (p. 212), plus any exercises from assessments in ch. 3	Day off	Workout C (p. 212), plus any exercises from assessments in ch. 3	Workout D (p. 212), plus any exercises from assessments in ch. 3	Day off	Workout F (p. 212), plus any exercises from assessments in ch. 3	Day off

*The duration of medium, short, and mixed cardiorespiratory sessions should be determined in relation to that of your long workout for the week. In general, a medium workout is one-half to two-thirds the length of the long workout. A short workout is one-third to one-half the length of the long workout.

**Ideally, underpowered skiers should work out six days each week. If you don't have time for this, take day 1 off and alternate workouts E and F (p.212) on day 6. On day 6, choose between a short workout in zone 1 or a short or medium workout that mixes zones 1 and 2.

In-Season (16 Weeks)

During the season, the functional-movement, cardiorespiratory, strength, power, and agility training remain the same, reflecting the goal of maintenance. However, the program for technique and tactics changes each month as you progress toward mastery. See figure 12.4 for a sample weekly program for the in-season. See figures 12.5 on page 212 and 12.6 on page 214 for more details.

Weeks 1 to 4 (Foundation)

Use weeks 1 through 4 of the in-season to get back to skill basics and to build a strong foundation for movement and performance. At this time, perform the on-snow assessments from part I to pinpoint the areas that need the most work. During this month, focus on retraining, progressing through the technical milestones in order, and maintaining good technique over longer runs.

You can reduce fitness training to focus on maintenance and recovery. Skiing all day taxes your muscles, especially your quads, so keep them balanced by working out the lesser-used muscles (in this case, the hamstrings) to maintain strength throughout the body and to avoid injury. Continue functional-movement training as you did in the preseason.

Weeks 5 to 12 (Development)

Use weeks 5 through 12 of the in-season to progress technique to a higher level, performing longer, more-frequent runs over more-taxing terrain and conditions. Use races and competitions primarily as training tools for improving technique and tactics under pressure. In other words, build on previous performance while maintaining a training focus. Continue functional-movement and fitness training with the same focus on maintenance and recovery.

Weeks 12 to 16 (Peak)

Use weeks 12 through 16 of the in-season to maintain your progress in mastering technique while shifting the focus to all-mountain tactics and racing (for those who are so inclined). This is a great time to seriously train in terrain and conditions that require new tactics. Expanding your tactical toolbox in unfamiliar scenarios will improve your decision making. Again, continue functional-movement and fitness training with the same focus on maintenance and recovery.

Postseason

During the off-season, maintain a base-fitness level that will allow you to start preseason training without missing a beat. Try other sports for a change of pace. Regardless of how you proceed with your fitness, maintain your gains by training at an aerobic level at least twice a week and mixing strength workouts A and B into your weekly regimen. Test every six to eight weeks to watch for any significant losses. If you notice any dips, add correctional exercises to your postseason routine.

Figure 12.4 Sample Weekly In-Season Program

	Day 1	Day 2	Day 3	Day 4	Day 5	Day 6	Day 7
Functional-movement training (2 sets of 10-15 reps for stability; 2 sets of 15-30 sec. for mobility)	Dynamic-prep routine (p. 181), plus any stability and mobility exercises from assessments in ch. 2	Dynamic-prep routine (p. 181), plus any mobility exercises from assessments in ch. 2	Dynamic-prep routine (p. 181), plus any stability and mobility exercises from assessments in ch. 2	Dynamic-prep routine (p. 181), plus any mobility exercises from assessments in ch. 2	Day off or dynamic-prep routine (p. 181), plus any mobility exercises from assessments in ch. 2	Dynamic-prep routine (p. 181); This is an on-snow warm-up, not a functional-movement training session.	Dynamic-prep routine (p. 181); This is an on-snow warm-up, not a functional-movement training session.
Cardio-respiratory training	Day off or mix of zones 1 and 2 in short or medium workout*	Long workout in zone 1 (should be within 10 min. of longest preseason workout)	Day off	Zone-3 workout (see pp. 118-120 in ch. 8) or mix of zones 2 and 3 in short or medium workout*	Day off or short workout in zone 1*	Day off	Day off
Strength, power, and agility training (3-5 sets of 4-6 reps for strength)	Workout C (p. 212), plus any exercises from assessments in ch. 3	Day off	Workout D (p. 212), plus any exercises from assessments in ch. 3	Day off	Day off or alternate workouts E and F (p. 212), plus any exercises from assessments in ch. 3	Day off	Day off

TECHNIQUE AND TACTICS TRAINING

	Day 1	Day 2	Day 3	Day 4	Day 5	Day 6	Day 7
Weeks 1-4	Day off	Day off	Day off	Day off	Day off or skill-practice session C (p. 214)	Skill-practice session A (p. 214)	Skill-practice session B (p. 214)
Weeks 5-8	Day off	Day off	Day off	Day off	Day off or skill-practice session A or B (p. 214)	Skill-practice session C (p. 214)	Skill-practice session D (p. 214)
Weeks 9-12	Day off	Day off	Day off	Day off	Day off or skill-practice session A, B, or C (p. 214)	Skill-practice session D (p. 214)	Skill-practice session E (p. 214)
Weeks 13-16	Day off	Day off	Day off	Day off	Day off or skill-practice session A, B, C, or D (p. 214)	Skill-practice session E (p. 214)	Design your own tactical exploration

*The duration of medium, short, and mixed cardiorespiratory sessions should be determined in relation to that of your long workout for the week. In general, a medium workout is one-half to two-thirds the length of the long workout. A short workout is one-third to one-half the length of the long workout.

**If you can't perform three routines for strength, power, and agility per week, do workouts E and F (p. 212).

Workouts for Underpowered Skiers

Although the previous programs provide a general overview for your training, the following program outlines the actual instruction and exercises for your seasonal workouts. Simply locate the appropriate workouts in figures 12.5 and 12.6 in order to assemble your training plan for the day.

Functional-Movement Training

As previously mentioned in the outlines for seasonal programs, see pages 181-182 of chapter 10 for dynamic-prep routines. Add any correctional exercises as needed based on your functional-movement score from the assessment in chapter 2.

Cardiorespiratory Training

To maintain your preseason cardiorespiratory levels, train by using or tweaking the sample workouts and progression guidelines in chapter 8 (see pages 116-122).

Strength, Power, and Agility Training

See figure 12.5 to find the designated workout for strength, power, and agility training. Workouts A and B are meant to be performed in the same week, resulting in a balanced, full-body training program that is specific to building muscular strength and endurance for underpowered skiers. They also introduce power moves. Workout C is an upper-body, core-focused workout that is meant to be performed with workout D, a lower-body, core-focused workout, for a comprehensive, full-body, strength and power workout. Workouts E and F combine strength, power, and agility work.

See chapter 8 for descriptions and variations of the following exercises (exercises with variations are marked with an asterisk). Earlier in the season, you can start with the easier variation, but you should work to progress to the harder variation by the end of the season. Although distinct exercises exist for the different scores for the upper-body and core screens, the leg screens require the same solution exercises regardless of the score. In this case, the easier variation should be performed by those scoring a 1 and the harder variation should be performed once the score progresses to a 3.

Technique and Tactics

Start your on-snow sessions with a warm-up and one of the on-snow, dynamic-prep routines (see pages 181-183 in chapter 10). Next, progress through your training session in three phases as outlined in chapter 10. As an underpowered skier, you should make adjustments in your reps, sets, and vertical to build slowly, avoiding fatigue and compensating movements.

Active-Free Ski

Take approximately 30 to 40 minutes to check out the conditions of the day and to tap into your energy and your ability to react and produce the movements you desire. Become aware of sliding sensations and your focus cues. Figure 12.6 provides key cues for each workout. Waking up your neuromuscular system with skiing sensations is a key component to active-free ski.

Figure 12.5 Training Workouts for Strength, Power, and Agility

	Workout A	Workout B	Workout C	Workout D	Workout E	Workout F
Upper-body strength	• Push-up, p. 124* • Horizontal row, p. 127	• Chest press, p. 126 • Lat pull-down, p. 127	• Push-up (with or without stability ball), p. 124* • Horizontal row, p. 127 • Lat pull-down, p. 127 • Chest press, p. 126	--	• Supine row with feet elevated, p. 125* • Bench press with dumbbells, p. 125*	• Push-up on stability ball, p. 124* • Kneeling single-arm row, p. 126*
Core strength	• Sit-up, p. 130* • Supine leg-up, p. 129*	• Sit-up, p. 130* • Supine leg up, p. 129*	• Medicine-ball toss with sit-ups, p. 128* • Medicine-ball side toss, p. 128	• Supine leg-up, p. 129* • Sit-up, p. 130*	• Medicine-ball toss with sit-ups, p. 128* • Supine leg-up, p. 129*	• Medicine-ball side toss, p. 128 • Hanging-leg hip raise, p. 129
Lower-body strength	• Split squat, p. 131* • Bridge on stability ball, p. 132*	• Romanian deadlift, p. 132* • Lateral lunge, p. 131*	--	• Split squat, p. 131* • Lateral lunge, p. 131* • Bridge on stability ball, p. 132* • Romanian deadlift, p. 132*	• Split squat, p. 131* • Bridge on stability ball, p. 132*	• Romanian deadlift, p. 132* • Lateral lunge, p. 131*
Power**	• Jumping rope (classic swing, p. 136); follow progression guidelines in ch. 8.	• Jumping rope (classic swing, p. 136); follow progression guidelines in ch. 8.	--	• Lateral box blast, p. 133, for 2-3 sets of 4-8 jumps on each foot* • Reactive step-up, p. 133, 2-3 sets of 4-8 jumps on each foot*	• Tuck jump, p. 134 for 2-3 sets of 5-15 jumps* • Lateral hurdle jump, p. 134, for 2-3 sets of 5-15 jumps on each foot*	• Lateral box blast, p. 133, for 2-3 sets of 6-10 jumps on each foot* • Reactive step-up, p. 133, for 2-3 sets of 6-10 jumps on each foot*
Agility	--	--	--	--	• Agility ladder (in-in-out-out, p. 135, and Ickey shuffle, p. 136), and 2-3 times each through a 30 ft. (9 m) ladder	• Jumping rope (slalom, p. 136); follow progression guidelines in ch. 8. • Crossover zigzag agility ladder, p. 136, 2-3 times through a 30 ft. (9 m) ladder

**The ranges of sets and reps given for the power exercises allow for progression during the preseason and a subsequent reduction in volume during the in-season. Do the lower amount of total jumps at the start of the preseason and progress throughout the 12 weeks, first by increasing the reps (staying at two sets), and then moving to three sets with fewer reps. Taper down to the lower end of the range during the in-season.

Active Training (Technique)

Figure 12.6 provides five skill workouts (A through E) for use in your practice sessions that progress from easy to difficult. The easier workouts emphasize basic skiing essentials and the workouts that are more difficult focus on skill sequences that combine these components. Workouts A and B address the starting points for the milestones of the neutral stance, the engaged stance, and leg turning. Workout C acts as a bridge from essentials to the sequential movements needed to complete the dynamic drills and turns, with an emphasis on parallel and carved turns. Workouts D and E help refine the movements necessary to complete the skills package, again emphasizing parallel and carved turns. Milestones may come in relation to your progress in strength and endurance. Feeling tired or washed out is a sign from your body that you need to back off and focus on recovery or easier milestones. Underpowered skiers often start out feeling strong enough to do the drills prescribed for a score-3 skier, but soon find out that drills for scores of 1 or 2 are more appropriate.

Figure 12.6 assigns a practice time to each session that is recommended for ingraining technique and working toward mastery. Obviously, the amount of time you will practice depends on your personal schedule or situation. To determine how much time to spend on each drill, simply divide the total time of each session by the number of recommended drills. For example, four drills over 40 minutes translates to 10 minutes of work on each drill. You can adapt the time frames to meet your energy level for the day. Take 40 minutes for two drills if that is what your body needs. The time recommendations are guidelines. Feel free to modify the program to fit your specific needs.

Finally, be advised that these practice sessions are based on an average progression. It is up to you to monitor your progress and to work in a session until you are ready to move on. The results from your assessment in part I should be the driving force in terms of the drills you perform. Don't blindly follow the drills listed in the table. The following workouts are ideal for underpowered skiers, but you need to personalize them by substituting or adding drills according to your test results in chapter 4.

Exploring Terrain and Conditions (Tactics)

Figure 12.6 also identifies the tactical concepts you should practice in specific progression for each terrain. The terrain and conditions themselves are listed in order from most common to most challenging. Each skier brings a slightly different frame of reference to the practice session, so look carefully at the prescribed drills and concepts and begin with the practice that best fits your starting point. For example, most underpowered skiers visit terrain that is steep and slightly bumpy before they tire out later in the day. This is a good judgment call, given their profile. Refer to the results of your tactical assessment in chapter 5 to identify the areas that need the most work. Remember to assess, drill, practice, explore, and then assess again.

Carve out at least one hour, preferably two, for practicing terrain exploration. It takes some time to find the terrain listed in the practice session in addition to the practice time. By the time you ride the lift, find terrain, practice the drill, and return to the lift, you might lose 20 to 30 minutes for a single drill or run. Therefore, you will not be able to practice every terrain in each practice session. Underpowered skiers may want to stay on the conservative side with a practice session of one hour. If you are energetic and able to repeat quality movements, you can extend your training session and follow the suggested drills for the next terrain listed. Realistically, you will only get through two or three types of terrain in one session. Pick your terrains and spend several runs practicing the recommended tactics.

Regardless of the terrain where you are working, the listed drills progress you through the tactical milestones outlined in chapter 9. Practices A, B, and C emphasize basic tactics, such as making terrain transitions, reading terrain, and applying turn shape, which are necessary for the advanced tactics of speed and line management that appear in practices D and E. Again, remember that the sample seasonal programs from earlier in the chapter represent the average time for mastering these concepts. Individualize your program and move at the pace that is best for you, retesting every four weeks.

Figure 12.6 Sample Technical and Tactical Practice Sessions

ACTIVE-FREE SKI (30-40 MIN.)

	Practice A	Practice B	Practice C	Practice D	Practice E
Focus cues	Establishing a centered position over skis	Developing edge engagement and edge release with quick, ballistic movements	Focusing on precise, active foot and leg turning while keeping the upper body stable	Ingraining parallel turns with quick, dynamic edging and pivot movements	Experiencing dynamic carved turns with increased speed and downhill intensity

ACTIVE TRAINING (40-90 MIN.)

Practice each drill for at least 2 runs. Take time to practice quality movements 20 to 30 times, or for an average of 1,000 vertical feet (300 m) each run. The total vertical feet skied may vary, depending on your resort, the drill, and conditions, but 2,500 to 6,000 total vertical feet (762-1829 m) is a good target. If you do more than 6,000 vertical feet, focus is on quality execution of movements.

Technique	Practice				
	Practice A (40-60 min.)	Practice B (40-60 min.)	Practice C (40-60 min.)	Practice D (60-90 min.)	Practice E (60-90 min.)
Neutral stance	• High-low drill, p. 142	• Pole-spin drill, p. 143	• Marching drill, p. 142	• Lateral-step drill, p. 140	• Shuffle drill, p. 141
Engaged stance	• Engaged stance with low-edge angle, p. 146	• Engaged stance with low-edge angle, p. 146	• Engaged stance on one ski, p. 146	• Traverse drill on steeper terrain, p. 144	• Traverse drill on steeper terrain, p. 144
Leg turn	• Leg turn with feet on bindings, p. 148	• Wedge leg turn, p. 149 • Leg turn with feet on bindings, p. 148	• Hands-on-hips drill, p. 149	• Leg turn on one ski, p. 147 • Hands-on-hips drill, p. 149	• Clock-face drill, p. 148
Parallel turn	--	--	Pick 1: • Simultaneous edge change, p. 154 • Parallel-turn garland, p. 155	Pick 1: • Two skis to one ski, p. 153 • One-leg pivot, p. 152	• Hand on hip and hand in the air, p. 156 • One-leg pivot, p. 152
Carved turn	--	--	• Traverse edge change, p. 160	• Tuck turn, p. 162	• Long leg, short leg, p. 158 • Tuck turn, p. 162

Practice each drill for at least 2 runs. Take time to practice quality movements. The total vertical feet skied may vary depending on your resort, the drill, and conditions, but 2,500 to 6,000 (762-1829 m) total vertical feet is a good target. If you do more than 6,000 vertical feet, focus on quality execution of movements.

Terrain	Practice				
	Practice A (60-90 min.)	Practice B (60-120 min.)	Practice C (60-120 min.)	Practice D (90-120 min.)	Practice E (90-120 min.)
Steeps	• Basic terrain transitions (Gentle to steep slopes, p. 163) • Reading complex terrain (Unlocking freeze frame, p. 164)	• Basic terrain transitions (Groomed to ungroomed snow, p. 163) • Reading complex terrain (Unlocking freeze frame, p. 164)	• Basic terrain transitions (Firm to soft snow. p. 163) • Reading complex terrain (Redirecting focus, p. 164) • Turn management (Maintaining a strong finishing turn, p. 166)	• Turn management (Creating symmetrical patterns in turns, p. 165) • Speed management (Pushing the envelope of speed and tempo, p. 171)	• Speed management (Checking your speed, p. 171) • Line management (Carving, p. 169)
Bumps	• Basic terrain transitions (Gentle to steep slopes, p. 163) • Reading complex terrain (Unlocking freeze frame, p. 164)	• Basic terrain transitions (Groomed to ungroomed snow, p. 163) • Reading complex terrain (Unlocking freeze frame, p. 164)	• Basic terrain transitions (Wet to dry snow, p. 163) • Reading complex terrain (Redirecting focus, p. 164) • Turn management (Establishing turn shape with ski placement, p. 166)	• Turn management (Fishhook ending in a J-shape, p. 165) • Speed management (Checking your speed, p. 171)	• Speed management (Pushing the envelope of speed and tempo, p. 171) • Line management (Scrubbing, p. 168)
Chutes and gullies	• Basic terrain transitions (Gentle to steep slopes, p. 163) • Reading complex terrain (Redirecting focus, p. 164)	• Reading complex terrain (Unlocking freeze frame, p. 164) • Turn management (Skidding, p. 169)	• Reading complex terrain (Redirecting focus, p. 164) • Turn management (Buttering, p. 169) • Line management (Using pole plants to maintain your line, p. 173)	• Speed management (Choosing the correct tempo, p. 171) • Line management (Avoiding gridlock, p. 173)	• Speed management (Checking your speed, p. 171) • Line management (Buttering, p. 169)
Trees	• Basic terrain transitions (Gentle to steep slopes, p. 163) • Reading complex terrain (Unlocking freeze frame, p. 164)	• Reading complex terrain (Redirecting focus, p. 164) • Turn management (Skidding, p. 169)	• Reading complex terrain (Unlocking freeze frame, p. 164) • Turn management (Carving, p. 169)	• Speed management (Choosing the correct tempo, p. 171) • Line management (Avoiding gridlock, p. 173)	• Speed management (Choosing the correct tempo, p. 171) • Line management (Scarving, p. 170)
Back bowls	• Basic terrain transitions (Groomed to ungroomed snow, p. 163) • Reading complex terrain (Unlocking freeze frame, p. 164)	• Reading complex terrain (Redirecting focus, p. 164) • Turn management (Skidding, p. 169)	• Turn management (Carving, p. 169) • Speed management (Pushing the envelope of speed and tempo, p. 171) • Line management (Slicing, p. 170)	• Turn management (Buttering, p. 169) • Speed management (Pushing the envelope of speed and tempo, p. 171) • Line management (Scrubbing, p. 168)	• Speed management (Pushing the envelope of speed and tempo, p. 171) • Line management (Slashing, p. 168)

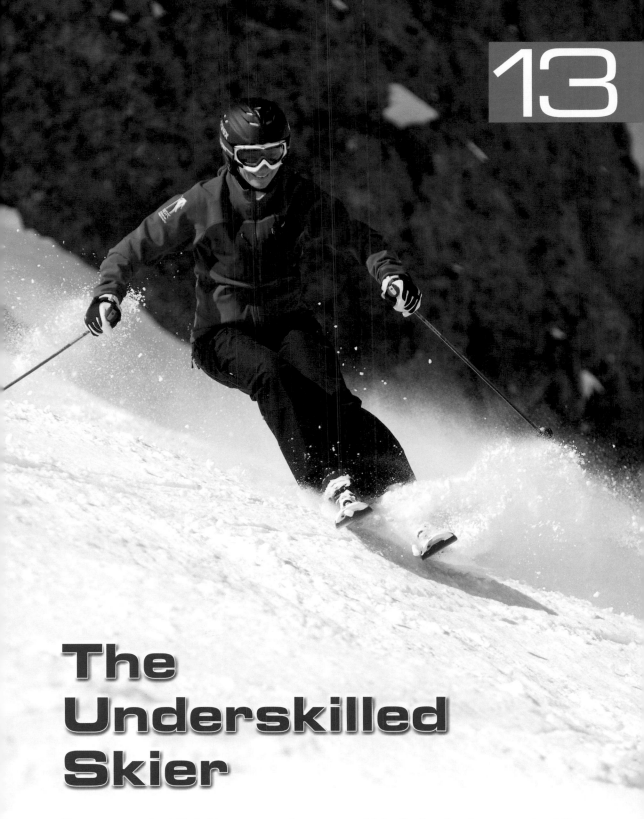

The Underskilled Skier

If you are an underskilled skier, you scored an average of 3 for the functional-movement and fitness assessments in chapters 2 and 3, but an average of 1 or 2 for the technique and tactics assessments in chapters 4 and 5. You have a good base of fitness and functional performance, but you lack the on-snow skills for meeting technical and tactical terrain challenges and for skiing efficiently.

You may lack miles on the snow or you may have learned fundamental skills incorrectly. If you lack miles, use a progression of fundamental movements that will help you improve with time on the snow. If you have ingrained ineffective movements, develop a program of correctional movements to reestablish a foundation of solid skills.

The program for underskilled skiers focuses on developmental drills. Skiing fundamentals include stance, leg turning, parallel turns, carving, terrain use, and tactics. A solid fitness base and properly fitted equipment will help you move through these levels effectively. As you progress through skills, inefficiencies can pop up, sidetracking your progress. Underskilled skiers easily ingrain bad habits, since their high level of fitness allows them to repeat incorrect moves. To avoid compensations due to inefficiencies, learn the following red flags and address the problems before they become ingrained:

- *Fear of falling.* This can cause skiers to quickly push skis across the hill without control.
- *Defensiveness in the fall line.* When defensive, skiers often miss pole plants or use them ineffectively. Without the stabilizing effects of the pole plant, timing is lost, causing skiers to lose balance and make gross recovery actions.
- *Choppy movements.* Fragmented movements stem from a lack of skill, causing poor coordination and the inability to smoothly link movement sequences. Movements are often forceful and ballistic, causing snow to come off the skis all at once.
- *Compromised balance.* A smaller base of support, such as when trying to balance over skis that are tipped up, causes skiers to lose control and the ability to stand upright.

Program Design for Underskilled Skiers

Underskilled skiers already have a solid base of functional movement and fitness, which is likely due to an established fitness program or participation in other sports. However, as the ski season approaches, training should be specific to skiing.

Start adding this focus to your athletic program 12 weeks before the skiing season begins. Remember, functional-movement training can help you log the hours needed for mastering technique, even when there is no snow in sight! This is a good time to retest to make sure that you have maintained a score of 3 in the functional-movement and fitness assessments. If not, you have time before the season starts to address any weaknesses that might have cropped up during the off-season. From this point on, you should retest every 4 to 6 weeks to monitor your maintenance and to gauge your improvement.

Once the ski season starts, reduce your dryland training and focus on mastering fundamental techniques, exploring tactics, and applying skills. This chapter provides sample on-snow training programs to help you progress through neutral and engaged stances, leg turns, parallel turns, and carved turns. You'll also learn to apply tactics to various terrains. Postseason training is for maintaining functional movement and fitness until the preseason starts again. It is a great time to try new activities to keep things fresh.

Table 13.1 shows the overall training schedule for the classic underskilled skier. It assumes a maximum of six training days per week. At least five days of training, with attention to all of the pyramid blocks, are recommended. Sessions can also be combined for fewer overall training days (please review the guidelines in chapter 10).

TABLE 13.1 Training Schedule for Underskilled Skiers

	Preseason	In-Season	Postseason
Functional movement	5-6 times per week (with dryland training)	4-5 times per week (with dryland training)	3-5 times per week (with dryland training)
Cardiorespiratory fitness	3-4 times per week	2-3 times per week	2-4 times per week
Muscular fitness (strength) and power and agility fitness	2-3 times per week	1-2 times per week	1-2 times per week
Technique		Each snow session	
Tactics		Each snow session	

The following sections outline a sample year of training sessions.

Preseason (12 weeks)

When preseason begins, perform all of the dryland assessments from part I to gauge your current levels and to determine any needs that may have developed. Use this information to progress through the following goals for the preseason. Figures 13.1 through 13.3 identify different workouts for each set of weeks, and figure 13.5 on page 226 outlines specific details.

Weeks 1 to 4 (Foundation)

Use the first four weeks of the preseason to resume a specific training focus that is geared to your needs and goals for the upcoming skiing season. Focus on functional-movement training and aerobic (zone 1) training. Although you average high marks for the functional-movement assessments overall, you may still need to perform a handful of solution exercises as indicated in chapter 2. Increase the time of at least one aerobic workout each week. During strength training, address any areas of weakness identified by the screens or supplement your workouts with exercises from chapter 8 for maintenance. Figure 13.1 shows a sample preseason program for weeks 1 through 4.

Figure 13.1   Sample Preseason Program for Weeks 1 to 4

	Day 1	Day 2	Day 3	Day 4	Day 5	Day 6	Day 7
Functional-movement training (2 sets of 8-12 reps for stability; 2 sets of 10-20 sec. for mobility)	Dynamic-prep routine (p. 181), plus any mobility exercises from assessments in ch. 2	Dynamic-prep routine (p. 181), plus any stability and mobility exercises from assessments in ch. 2	Dynamic-prep routine (p. 181), plus any mobility exercises from assessments in ch. 2	Dynamic-prep routine (p. 181), plus any stability and mobility exercises from assessments in ch. 2	Day off or dynamic-prep routine (p. 181), plus any mobility exercises from assessments in ch. 2	Dynamic-prep routine (p. 181), plus any mobility exercises from assessments in ch. 2	Day off
Cardio-respiratory training	Long workout in zone 1 (see ch. 3)	Day off	Medium workout in zone 1*	Day off	Day off or short or medium workout in zone 1*	Short or medium workout in zone 1*	Day off
Strength training (2 sets of 8-12 reps)	Day off	Alternate workouts A and B (p. 226), plus any exercises from assessments in ch. 3	Day off	Alternate workouts A and B (p. 226), plus any exercises from assessments in ch. 3	Day off	Day off or workout C (p. 226), plus any exercises from assessments in ch. 3	Day off

*The duration of medium and short cardiorespiratory training sessions should be determined in relation to that of your long workout for the week. In general, a medium workout is one-half to two-thirds of the length of the long workout. A short workout is one-third to one-half of the length of the long workout.

Weeks 5 to 8 (Development)

Use weeks 5 through 8 of the preseason to further prepare for the in-season by adding power and agility training one day a week and by increasing the intensity of your cardiorespiratory work with anaerobic-threshold (zone 2) training. As before, increase the length of at least one aerobic workout each week. During strength training, continue to address any areas of weakness identified in the assessments or supplement your routines with ski-specific exercises. Figure 13.2 shows a sample preseason program for underskilled skiers for weeks 5 to 8.

Figure 13.2 Sample Preseason Program for Weeks 5 to 8

	Day 1	Day 2	Day 3	Day 4	Day 5	Day 6	Day 7
Functional-movement training (2-3 sets of 10-15 reps for stability; 2-3 sets of 15-25 sec. for mobility)	Dynamic-prep routine (p. 181), plus any mobility exercises from assessments in ch. 2	Dynamic-prep routine (p. 181), plus any stability and mobility exercises from assessments in ch. 2	Dynamic-prep routine (p. 181), plus any mobility exercises from assessments in ch. 2	Dynamic-prep routine (p. 181), plus any stability and mobility exercises from assessments in ch. 2	Day off or dynamic-prep routine (p. 181), plus any mobility exercises from assessments in ch. 2	Dynamic-prep routine (p. 181), plus any stability and mobility exercises from assessments in ch. 2	Day off
Cardio-respiratory training	Long workout in zone 1 (see ch. 3)	Day off	Zone-2 workout (see p. 33 in ch. 3 for test and pp. 117-118 in ch. 8 for workout options)	Day off	Choose from day off, medium workout in zone 1,* or short workout with mix of zones 1 and 2* (see p. 121 in ch.8 for workout options)	Short workout in zone 1*	Day off
Strength, power, and agility training (2-3 sets of 8-12 reps for strength)	Day off	Alternate workouts A and B (p. 226), plus any exercises from assessments in ch. 3	Day off	Alternate workouts A and B (p. 226), plus any exercises from assessments in ch. 3	Day off	Workout F (p. 226), plus any exercises from assessments in ch. 3	Day off

*The duration of medium and short cardiorespiratory sessions should be determined in relation to the length of your long workout for the week. In general, a medium workout is one-half to two-thirds the length of the long workout. A short workout is one-third to one-half the length of the long workout.

**If you don't have time for three workouts that focus on strength, power, and agility each week, do workouts C and F (p. 226).

Weeks 9 to 12 (Peak)

Use weeks 9 to 12 of the preseason to finalize your preparation for the skiing season by adding anaerobic power (zone 3). As before, increase the time of at least one aerobic workout each week. Continue strength training as you did for weeks 5 through 8, but focus more on increasing strength and power by lifting heavier weights for fewer reps. Perform more sets with greater speed. You will improve your power training in terms of number of contacts and speed of execution. Finally, focus on movements that mimic the range of joint movement needed for dynamic ski turns and terrain management. This program adds one training session for power and agility each week. Figure 13.3 shows a sample preseason program for underskilled skiers for weeks 9 through 12.

Figure 13.3 Sample Preseason Program for Weeks 9 to 12

	Day 1	Day 2	Day 3	Day 4	Day 5	Day 6	Day 7
Functional-movement training (3 sets of 10-15 reps for stability; 3 sets of 15-30 sec. for mobility)	Dynamic-prep routine (p. 181), plus any mobility exercises from assess-ments in ch. 2	Dynamic-prep routine (p. 181), plus any stability and mobility exercises from assess-ments in ch. 2	Dynamic-prep routine (p. 181), plus any mobility exercises from assess-ments in ch. 2	Dynamic-prep routine (p. 181), plus any stability and mobility exercises from assess-ments in ch. 2	Day off or dynamic-prep routine (p. 181), plus any mobility exercises from assess-ments in ch. 2	Dynamic-prep routine (p. 181), plus any mobility exercises from assess-ments in ch. 2	Day off
Cardio-respiratory training	Long work-out in zone 1 (as directed in ch. 3)	Day off	Zone-3 work-out (see p. 33 in ch. 3 for test and pp. 118-120 in ch. 8 for workout options)	Day off	Day off or short or medium workout in zone 1*	Short or medium workout, mixing zones 1 and 2 * (see p. 121 in ch. 8 for workout options)	Day off
Strength, power, and agility train-ing (3-4 sets of 5-8 reps for strength)	Day off	Workouts D or E (p. 226), plus any exer-cises from assessments in ch. 3	Day off	Alternate workouts D and E (p. 226), plus any exer-cises from assessments in ch. 3	Day off	Day off or workout F (p. 226), plus any exer-cises from assessments in ch. 3	Day off

*The duration of medium, short, and mixed cardiorespiratory sessions should be determined in relation to that of your long workout for the week. In general, a medium workout is one-half to two-thirds the length of the long workout. A short workout is one-third to one-half the length of the long workout.

In-Season (16 Weeks)

During the season, the functional-movement, cardiorespiratory, strength, power, and agility training remain the same, reflecting the goal of maintenance. However, the training program for technique and tactics changes each month as you progress toward mastery. Figure 13.4 provides a sample weekly program during the in-season. See figures 13.5 on page 226 and 13.6 on page 228 for more details.

Weeks 1 to 4 (Foundation)

Use weeks 1 through 4 of the in-season to get back to skill basics and to build a strong foundation for movement and performance. At this time, perform the on-snow assessments from part I to pinpoint the areas that need the most work. During this month, focus on mastering and progressing through the technical milestones in order. This training and progression will likely extend beyond the initial month of training.

You can reduce fitness training to focus on maintenance and recovery. Skiing all day taxes your muscles, especially your quads, so keep them balanced by working the lesser-used muscles (in this case, the hamstrings) to maintain equal strength throughout the body and to avoid injury. Continue functional-movement training as you did in the preseason.

Weeks 5 to 12 (Development)

Use weeks 5 through 12 of the in-season to master the milestone techniques, adding tactical exploration and training to the mix. Races should primarily use competitions as a training tool for improving technique and tactics under pressure. In other words, build on the previous performance while maintaining a training focus. Continue functional-movement and fitness training with the same focus on maintenance and recovery.

Weeks 12 to 16 (Peak)

Use weeks 12 through 16 of the in-season to maintain your progress in mastering technique while shifting the focus to tactics and racing (for those who are so inclined). This is a great time to try terrain and conditions that require new tactics. Expanding your tactical toolbox in unfamiliar scenarios builds awareness that improves your decision making. Again, continue functional-movement and fitness training with the same focus on maintenance and recovery.

Postseason

During the off-season, maintain a base-fitness level that will allow you to start preseason training without missing a beat. Try other sports for a change of pace. Regardless of how you proceed with your fitness, maintain your functional-movement score by performing one of the dynamic-prep routines prior to your workout. Test every six to eight weeks to maintain your levels. If you notice any losses during assessment, add correctional exercises to your postseason routine.

You can maintain cardiorespiratory fitness with aerobic (zone 1) training. If you feel burned out after the skiing season, reduce your cardio work. However, to prepare for preseason training, you must commit to doing cardio twice a week. Similarly, you should commit to muscular-fitness training at least once a week. Routine C is ideal for maintenance in the off-season.

Figure 13.4 Sample Weekly In-Season Program

	Day 1	Day 2	Day 3	Day 4	Day 5	Day 6	Day 7
Functional-movement training (3 sets of 10-15 reps for stability; 3 sets of 15-30 sec. for mobility)	Dynamic-prep routine (p. 181), plus any mobility exercises from assessments in ch. 2	Dynamic-prep routine (p. 181), plus any stability and mobility exercises from assessments in ch. 2	Dynamic-prep routine (p. 181), plus any mobility exercises from assessments in ch. 2	Dynamic-prep routine (p. 181), plus any stability and mobility exercises from assessments in ch. 2	Day off or dynamic-prep routine (p. 181), plus any mobility exercises from assessments in ch. 2	Dynamic-prep routine (p. 181); This is an on-snow warm-up, not a functional-movement training session.	Dynamic-prep routine (p. 181); This is an on-snow warm-up, not a functional-movement training session.
Cardio-respiratory training	Long workout in zone 1 (should be within 10 min. of longest preseason workout)	Day off	Short workout mixing zones 2 and 3* (see p. 122 in ch.8 for workout options)	Day off	Day off or short or medium workout in zone 1*	Day off	Day off
Strength, power, and agility training (3-5 sets of 4-6 reps for strength)	Day off	Alternate workouts D and E (p. 226), plus any exercises from assessments in ch. 3	Day off	Alternate workouts D and E (p. 226), plus any exercises from assessments in ch. 3	Day off	Day off	Day off

TECHNIQUE AND TACTICS

	Day 1	Day 2	Day 3	Day 4	Day 5	Day 6	Day 7
Weeks 1-4	Day off	Day off	Day off	Day off	Day off or skill-practice session C (p. 228)	Skill-practice session A (p. 228)	Skill-practice session B (p. 228)
Weeks 5-8	Day off	Day off	Day off	Day off	Day off or skill-practice session A or B (p. 228)	Skill-practice session C (p. 228)	Skill-practice session D (p. 228)
Weeks 9-12	Day off	Day off	Day off	Day off	Day off or skill-practice session A, B, or C (p. 228)	Skill-practice session D (p. 228)	Skill-practice session E (p. 228)
Weeks 13-16	Day off	Day off	Day off	Day off	Day off or skill-practice session A, B, C, or D (p. 228)	Skill-practice session E (p. 228)	Design your own tactical exploration

*The duration of medium, short, and mixed cardiorespiratory sessions should be determined in relation to that of your long workout for the week. In general, a medium workout is one-half to two-thirds the length of the long workout. A short workout is one-third to one-half the length of the long workout.

**If performing one workout for strength, power, and agility each week, do workout F (p. 226), plus any exercises for your scores from chapter 3.

Workouts for Underskilled Skiers

Although the previous programs provide a general overview for your training, the following program outlines the actual instruction and exercises for your seasonal workouts. Simply locate the appropriate workouts in figures 13.5 and 13.6 in order to assemble your training plan for the day.

Functional-Movement Training

As previously mentioned in the outlines for seasonal programs, see pages 181 to 183 of chapter 10 for dynamic-prep routines. Add any correctional exercises as needed based on your functional-movement score from the assessment in chapter 2.

Cardiorespiratory Training

To maintain your preseason cardiorespiratory levels, train by using or tweaking the sample workouts and progression guidelines in chapter 8 (see pages 116-122).

Strength, Power, and Agility Training

See figure 13.5 to find the designated workout for strength, power, and agility training. Workouts A and B are meant to be performed in the same week, resulting in a comprehensive, full-body training program that is specific to the strength needs of skiers. Workout C provides the option of another strength session each week, repeating the best two exercises for the upper body, core, and lower body. Workouts D and E add power and agility work. Workout F is a condensed strength, power, and agility workout.

See chapter 8 for descriptions and variations of the following exercises (exercises with variations are marked with an asterisk). Earlier in the season, you can start with the easier variation, but you should work to progress to the harder variation by the end of the season. Although distinct exercises exist for the different scores for the upper-body and core screens, the leg screens require the same solution exercises regardless of the score. In this case, the easier variation should be performed by those scoring a 1 and the harder variation should be performed once the score progresses to a 3.

Techniques and Tactics

Start your on-snow sessions with a warm-up and one of the on-snow, dynamic-prep routines (see pages 181-183 in chapter 10). Next, progress through your training session in three phases as outlined in chapter 10. As an underskilled skier, you should make your movements precise and symmetrical. Ingraining faulty movements will derail any future development.

Active-Free Ski

Take approximately 30 to 40 minutes to check out the conditions of the day and to tap into your energy and your ability to react and produce the movements you desire. Become aware of sliding sensations and your focus cues. Figure 13.6 provides the key cues for each workout. Waking up your neuromuscular system with skiing sensations is a key component to active-free ski.

Active Training (Technique)

Figure 13.6 provides five skill workouts (A through E) for use in your practice sessions that progress from easy to difficult. The easier workouts emphasize basic skiing essentials and the workouts that are more difficult focus on skill sequences that combine these skill components. Workouts A and B address the starting points for the milestones of neutral stance, engaged stance, and leg turning. Workout C acts as a bridge from essentials to the sequential movements needed to complete dynamic drills and turns, with an emphasis on parallel and carved turn. Workouts D and E help

Figure 13.5 Training Workouts for Strength, Power, and Agility

	Workout A	Workout B	Workout C	Workout D	Workout E	Workout F
Upper-body strength	• Push-up, p. 124* • Lat pull-down, p. 127)	• Chest press, p. 126 • Horizontal row, p. 127	• Bench press with dumb-bells, p. 125* • Kneeling single-arm row, p. 126*	• Push-up (with or without stability ball), p. 124* • Lat pull-down, p. 127 • Kneeling single-arm row, p. 126*	• Supine row with feet elevated, p. 125* • Bench press with dumb-bells, p. 125*	• Bench press with dumbbells, p. 125*
Core strength	• Supine leg-up, p. 129* • Sit-up, p. 130*	• Medicine-ball toss with sit-ups, p. 128* • Medicine ball side toss, p. 128*	• Supine leg-up, p. 129* • Sit-up, p. 130*	• Hanging-leg hip raise, p. 129 • Supine leg-up, p. 129*	• Medicine-ball toss with sit-ups, p. 128* • Medicine ball side toss, p. 128*	• Sit-up, p. 130*
Lower-body strength	• Split squat, p. 131* • Lateral lunge, p. 131* • Romanian deadlift, p. 132* • Bridge on stability ball, p. 132*	• Split squat, p. 131* • Lateral lunge, p. 131* • Romanian deadlift, p. 132* • Bridge on stability ball, p. 132*	• Split squat, p. 131* • Romanian deadlift, p. 132*	• Bridge on stability ball, p. 132* • Romanian deadlift, p. 132*	• Split squat, p. 131* • Lateral lunge, p. 131*	• Split squat, p. 131*
Power**	--	--	--	• Lateral box blast, p. 133, for 2-3 sets of 4-8 jumps on each foot* • Tuck jump, p. 134 for 2-3 sets of 4-8 jumps* • Reactive step-up, p. 133, for 2-3 sets of 4-8 jumps on each foot* • Lateral hurdle jump, p. 134, for 2-3 sets of 6-10 jumps on each foot	• Jumping rope (classic swing, p. 136); follow progression guidelines in ch. 8.	• Lateral box blast, p. 133, for 2-3 sets of 6-10 jumps on each foot* • Tuck jump, p. 134, for 2-3 sets of 4-10 jumps* • Reactive step-up, p. 133, for 2-3 sets of 6-10 jumps on each foot* • Lateral hurdle jump, p. 134, for 2-3 sets of 6-10 jumps on each foot
Agility	--	--	--	• Jumping rope (slalom, p. 136); follow progression guidelines in ch. 8.	• Agility ladder (in-in-out-out, p. 135; Ickey shuffle, p. 136; crossover zigzag, p. 136), 2-3 times each through a 30 ft. (9 m) ladder	• Agility ladder (in-in-out-out, p. 135; Ickey shuffle, p. 136; crossover zigzag, p. 136), 2-3 times each through a 30 ft. (9 m) ladder

**The ranges of sets and reps given for the power exercises allow for progression during the preseason and a subsequent reduction in volume during the in-season. Do the lower amount of total jumps at the start of the preseason and progress throughout the 12 weeks, first by increasing the reps (staying at two sets), and then moving to three sets with fewer reps. Taper down to the lower end of the range during the in-season.

refine the movements necessary to complete the skills package, again emphasizing parallel and carved turns. Milestones for underskilled skiers may not be linear, as indicated in this chapter. It is not uncommon for skiers to hop around from one maneuver or drill to the other, skipping one to spend more time on another in order to best improve in the shortest amount of time. If you feel you have mastered a milestone or drill, move to the next one that is recommended.

Figure 13.6 assigns a practice time to each session that is recommended for ingraining technique and working toward mastery. Obviously, the amount of time you will practice depends on your personal schedule or situation. To determine how much time to spend on each drill, simply divide the total time of each session by the number of recommended drills. For example, four drills over 40 minutes translates to 10 minutes of work on each drill. If you need more practice on a particular drill, you can add more time to the overall workout or decrease the time you spend on one drill in order to add time to another.

Finally, be advised that these practice sessions are based on an average progression. It is up to you to monitor your progress and to work in a session until you are ready to move on. The results from your assessment in part I should be the driving force in terms of the drills you perform. Don't blindly follow the drills listed in the table. The following workouts are ideal for underskilled skiers, but you need to personalize them by substituting or adding drills according to your test results in chapter 4.

Exploring Terrain and Conditions (Tactics)

Figure 13.6 also identifies the tactical concepts you should practice in a specific progression for each terrain. The terrain and conditions themselves are listed in order from most common to most challenging. Each skier brings a slightly different frame of reference to the practice session, so look carefully at the prescribed drills and concepts and begin with the practice that best fits your starting point. For example, most underskilled skiers visit terrain that is steep and slightly bumpy before they venture into tighter skiing situations or into back bowls. With that said, even skiers who are more experienced (but still underskilled) will benefit from working on basic tactics for the first two types of terrain listed. Refer to the results of your tactical assessment in chapter 5 to identify the areas that need the most work. Remember to assess, drill, practice, explore, and then assess again.

Carve out at least one hour, preferably two, for practicing terrain exploration. It takes some time to find the terrain listed in the practice session in addition to the practice time. By the time you ride the lift, find terrain, practice the drill, and return to the lift, you might lose 20 to 30 minutes for a single drill or run. Therefore, you will not be able to practice every terrain in each practice session. However, if you progress quickly, you can follow the suggested drills for the next terrain listed. Realistically, you will only get through two or three types of terrain in one session. Pick your terrain and spend several runs practicing the recommended tactics.

Regardless of the terrain where you are working, the listed drills progress you through the tactical milestones outlined in chapter 9. Practices A, B, and C emphasize basic tactics, such as making terrain transitions, reading terrain, and applying turn shape, which are necessary for the advanced tactics of speed and line management that appear in practices D and E. Again, remember that the sample seasonal programs from earlier in the chapter represent the average time for mastering these concepts. Individualize your program and move at the pace that is best for you, retesting every four weeks.

Figure 13.6 Sample Technical and Tactical Practice Sessions

	ACTIVE-FREE SKI (30-40 MIN.)				
	Practice A	**Practice B**	**Practice C**	**Practice D**	**Practice E**
Focus cues	Establishing a centered position over skis	Developing edge awareness and leg turning	Focusing on precise, active foot and leg turning	Ingraining parallel turns and applying edge and pivot	Experiencing dynamic carved turns with increased speed

ACTIVE TRAINING (40-90 MIN.)

Practice each drill for at least 2 runs. Take time to practice quality movements 20 to 30 times, or for 1,000 vertical feet (300 m) each run. The total vertical feet skied may vary, depending on your resort, the drill, and conditions, but 2,000 to 5,000 total vertical feet (610-1524 m) is a good target. If you do more than 5,000 vertical feet, focus on quality execution of movements.

	Practice				
Technique	**Practice A (40-60 min.)**	**Practice B (40-60 min.)**	**Practice C (40-60 min.)**	**Practice D (60-90 min.)**	**Practice E (60-90 min.)**
Neutral stance	• High-low drill, p. 142 • Marching drill, p. 142	• Shuffle drill, p. 141 • Pole-spin drill, p. 143	• Shuffle drill, p. 141 • Marching drill, p. 142	--	--
Engaged stance	• Engaged stance with low-edge angle, p. 146	• Engaged stance with low-edge angle, p. 146	• Engaged stance on one ski, p. 146	• Traverse drill on steeper terrain, p.144	• Traverse drill on steeper terrain, p. 144
Leg turn	• Leg turn with feet on bindings, p. 148	• Wedge leg turn, p. 149 • Leg turn with feet on bindings, p. 148	• Hands-on-hips drill, p. 149	• Leg turn on one ski, p. 147 • Hands-on-hips drill, p. 149	• Clock-face drill, p. 148
Parallel turn	--	--	• Simultaneous edge change, p. 154 • Parallel-turn garland, p. 155	• Two skis to one ski, p. 153 • One-leg pivot, p. 152	• Hand on hip and hand in the air, p. 156 • One-leg pivot, p. 152
Carved turn	--	--	• Traverse edge change, p. 160	• Carved turn with hands on knees, p. 158 • Advanced railroad track, p. 159	• Long leg, short leg, p. 158 • Tuck turn, p. 162

EXPLORING TERRAIN AND CONDITIONS (60-120 MIN.)

Practice each drill for at least 2 runs. Take time to practice quality movements. The total vertical feet skied may vary, depending on your resort, the drill, and conditions, but 2,000 to 5,000 (610-1524 m) total vertical feet is a good target. If you do more than 5,000 vertical feet, focus on quality execution of movements.

Terrain	Practice				
	Practice A (60-90 min.)	Practice B (60-120 min.)	Practice C (60-120 min.)	Practice D (90-120 min.)	Practice E (90-120 min.)
Steeps	• Basic terrain transitions (Gentle to steep slopes, p. 163) • Reading complex terrain (Having a plan B, p. 165)	• Basic terrain transitions (Groomed to ungroomed snow, p. 163) • Reading complex terrain (Unlocking freeze frame, p. 164)	• Basic terrain transitions (Firm to soft snow, p. 163) • Reading complex terrain (Having a plan B, p. 165) • Turn management (Maintaining a strong finishing turn, p. 166)	• Turn management (Ingraining the C-curve, p. 167) • Speed management (Getting into gear, p. 171)	• Speed management (Checking your speed, p. 171) • Line management (Using pole plants to maintain your line, p. 173)
Bumps	• Basic terrain transitions (Gentle to steep slopes, p. 163) • Reading complex terrain (Anticipating terrain changes, p. 164)	• Basic terrain transitions (Groomed to ungroomed snow, p. 163) • Reading complex terrain (Unlocking freeze frame, p. 164)	• Basic terrain transitions (Wet to dry snow, p. 163) • Reading complex terrain (Having a plan B, p. 165) • Turn management (Establishing turn shape with ski placement, p. 166)	• Turn management (Fishhook ending in a J-shape, p. 165) • Speed management (Maintaining three points of contact, p. 171)	• Speed management (Choosing the correct tempo, p. 171) • Line management (Using pole plants to maintain your line, p. 173)
Chutes and gullies	• Basic terrain transitions (Gentle to steep slopes, p. 163) • Reading complex terrain (Having a plan B, p. 165)	• Reading complex terrain (Unlocking freeze frame, p. 164) • Turn management (Skidding, p. 169)	• Reading complex terrain (Anticipating terrain changes, p. 164) • Turn management (Buttering, p. 169) • Line management (Using pole plants to maintain Your line, p. 173)	• Speed management (Choosing the correct tempo, p. 171) • Line management (Avoiding gridlock, p. 173)	• Speed management (Getting into gear, p. 171) • Line management (Facing the line, p. 173)

> continued

> continued

Terrain	Practice				
	Practice A (60-90 min.)	**Practice B (60-120 min.)**	**Practice C (60-120 min.)**	**Practice D (90-120 min.)**	**Practice E (90-120 min.)**
Trees	• Basic terrain transitions (Gentle to steep slopes, p. 163) • Reading complex terrain (Unlocking freeze frame, p. 164)	• Reading complex terrain (Redirecting focus, p. 164) • Turn management (Skidding, p. 169)	• Reading complex terrain (Having a plan B, p. 165) • Turn management (Carving, p. 169)	• Speed management (Choosing the correct tempo, p. 171) • Line management (Avoiding gridlock, p. 173)	• Speed management (Choosing the correct tempo, p. 171) • Line management (Facing the line, p. 173)
Back bowls	• Basic terrain transitions (Groomed to ungroomed snow, p. 163) • Reading complex terrain (Anticipating terrain changes, p. 164)	• Reading complex terrain (Facing the line, p. 173) • Turn management (Skidding, p. 169)	• Turn management (Carving, p. 169) • Speed management (Getting into gear, p. 171) • Line management (Facing the line, p. 173)	• Turn management (Buttering, p. 169) • Speed management (Getting into gear, p. 171) • Line management (Scrubbing, p. 169)	• Speed management (Pushing the envelope of speed and tempo, p. 171) • Line management (Slashing, p. 168)

The Combination Skier

The three types of combination skiers blend profiles from chapters 11 through 13. The first is a combination of overpowered and underskilled traits. The second mixes underpowered and under-skilled types. The mixed-combination skier blends all three profiles from chapters 11 through 13.

Many skiers can relate to the mixed-combination profile because it represents a diverse mix of flaws in skills, tactics, fitness, mobility, and stability. A program for this skier takes advantage of the full array of solutions in this book. However, isolating your weakness and thoroughly addressing the most pressing needs as illustrated in the other profiles can often be the most efficient solution toward improvement. It is only when you are a true combination skier does it make sense to follow the combination program. The mixed-combination skier exhibits deficiencies from all three profiles, experiencing a wide range of strengths and weaknesses and random scores in functional movement, fitness, technique, and tactics. A corrective program draws from several exercise levels to meet specific needs. The programs for the other two types of combination skiers include exercises from three blocks of the performance pyramid.

Overpowered-underskilled skiers are challenged by a lack of mobility and a lack of mileage on snow. They have not skied for very long, but are keen to try anything because they are athletic and have experienced success in other sports. Their learning curve is steep, and they often make huge strides in their progress. Their lack of mobility, especially in the hips, torso, and back, gets in their way. Since they excel in the fitness component, they should focus on developing mobility, technique, and tactics.

Underpowered-underskilled skiers have great mobility, which is important in skiing, but lack the strength to deal with difficult terrain. They become challenged by the rigors of the downhill environment and by the process of skill development. Fitness, technique, and tactics drills make up the bulk of their program.

To review, overpowered-underskilled skiers should focus on functional movement, technique, and tactics. Underpowered-underskilled skiers should focus on fitness, technique, and tactics. These two types of combination skiers should combine the dryland programs for their respective profiles from chapters 11 and 12 with the snow sessions from chapter 13.

The rest of this chapter focuses on the needs of the mixed-combination skier, providing a base program of the drills and exercises needed to progress through the season. This program (workouts A through E) is appropriate for every mixed-combination skier, regardless of individual flaws. Skiers may supplement the program with specific exercises as indicated by the screens in chapters 2 through 5.

To avoid compensations due to inefficiencies, mixed-combination skiers should learn the following red flags and address the problems before they become bad habits:

- *Uneven turns from side to side.* This habit leads to asymmetries between left and right turns.
- *Wobbly legs when balancing on the outside ski.* This creates lack of finesse when executing a balance maneuver, such as skiing on one leg.
- *Misalignment of body parts.* Combination skiers exhibit poor stance, leaning too far back, forward, or to the side.
- *Fragmented movements.* Timing of movements may be impaired. For example, pole plants may be out of sync with leg movements.

Program Design for Mixed-Combination Skiers

Since mixed-combination skiers have a blend of deficiencies, their program design balances functional movement with the phases of fitness, technique, and tactics. The good news is that mixed-combination skiers can train year-round to minimize the effects of any low scores in the functional-movement and fitness blocks of the performance pyramid. By addressing these flaws during preseason and postseason, they might only have to deal with deficiencies in the technique and tactics blocks when the ski season hits. Since everyone progresses at different rates, they should retest often and maintain dryland training throughout the season as needed.

You should start training specifically for the ski season 12 weeks before it starts. This is a good time to assess your current levels and to ensure that you are using the exercises and drills most suited to your particular needs. From this point on, retest every 4 to 6 weeks to monitor your maintenance and to gauge your improvement.

Once the ski season starts, reduce your fitness training, but continue functional-movement training on days when you don't ski. On the snow, focus on progressing through the milestones of technique and tactics, sharpening the skills that are already strong and retooling others that are weaker. This chapter provides sample on-snow training programs to help you master neutral and engaged stances, leg turning, parallel turns, carved turns, and tactics by terrain. Postseason training is for maintaining functional movement and fitness until the preseason starts again. It is a great time to try new activities to keep things fresh.

Table 14.1 shows a sample training schedule for mixed-combination skiers. The ranges vary widely, since the number of days for each training block is determined by the assessments in chapters 2 through 5. The schedule assumes a maximum of six training days per week. At least five days of training, with attention to all of the pyramid blocks, are recommended. Sessions can also be combined for fewer overall training days (please review the guidelines in chapter 10).

TABLE 14.1   Training Schedule for Mixed-Combination Skiers

	Preseason	In-Season	Postseason
Functional movement	3-5 times per week	3-5 times per week	3-5 times per week
Cardiorespiratory fitness	3-6 times per week	2-3 times per week	2-4 times per week
Muscular fitness (strength) and power and agility fitness	2-4 times per week	1-2 times per week	1-2 times per week
Technique		Each snow session	
Tactics		Each snow session	

The following sections outline a sample year of training sessions.

Preseason (12 Weeks)

When preseason begins, perform all of the dryland assessments from part I to gauge your current levels and to determine any needs that may have developed. Use this information to progress through the following goals for the preseason. Figures 14.1 through 14.3 identify different workouts for each set of weeks, and figure 14.5 on page 240 outlines specific details.

Weeks 1 to 4 (Foundation)

Use the first four weeks of the preseason to resume a specific training focus that is geared to your needs and goals for the upcoming skiing season. Focus on functional-movement training and aerobic (zone 1) training. Increase the time of at least one aerobic workout each week. During strength training, build a base of endurance so that you can easily add power and agility training later in the preseason. You should also seriously work on the solution exercises identified by the functional-movement, cardiorespiratory, and strength assessments in chapters 2 and 3. Figure 14.1 shows a sample preseason program for weeks 1 through 4.

Figure 14.1 Sample Preseason Program for Weeks 1 to 4

	Day 1	Day 2	Day 3	Day 4	Day 5	Day 6	Day 7
Functional-movement training (2 sets of 8-12 reps for stability; 2 sets of 10-20 sec. for mobility)	Dynamic-prep routine (p. 181), plus any mobility exercises from assessments in ch. 2	Dynamic-prep routine (p. 181), plus any stability and mobility exercises from tests for overhead-depth squat and single-leg squat (pp. 11 and 13)	Dynamic-prep routine (p. 181), plus any stability and mobility exercises from rotational-stability and lateral-lunge tests (pp. 15 and 16)	Dynamic-prep routine (p. 181), plus any stability and mobility exercises from tests for overhead-depth squat and single-leg squat (pp. 11 and 13)	Dynamic-prep routine (p. 181), plus any stability and mobility exercises from rotational-stability and lateral-lunge tests (pp. 15 and 16)	Day off or dynamic-prep routine (p. 181), plus 1 stability exercise and 1 mobility exercise from assessments in ch. 2	Day off
Cardio-respiratory training	Long workout in zone 1 (as directed in ch. 3)	Day off	Medium workout in zone 1*	Day off	Short or medium workout in zone 1*	Day off or short workout in zone 1*	Day off
Strength training (2 sets of 8-12 reps)	Day off	Workout A or B (p. 240), plus any exercises from assessments in ch. 3	Day off	Alternate workouts A and B (p. 240), plus any exercises from assessments in ch. 3	Day off	Day off or exercises from assessments in ch. 3	Day off

*The duration of medium and short cardiorespiratory sessions should be determined in relation to that of your long workout for the week. In general, a medium workout is one-half to two-thirds the length of the long workout. A short workout is one-third to one-half the length of the long workout.

Weeks 5 to 8 (Development)

Use weeks 5 through 8 of the preseason to further prepare for the in-season by adding intensity to your cardiorespiratory work with anaerobic-threshold (zone 2) training. As before, increase the time of at least one aerobic workout each week. During strength training, continue to address the areas of weakness identified by the assessments and perform balanced, full-body workouts for increasing strength. This program introduces power and agility training to provide the stimulus needed for on-snow moves. Continue to focus on functional-movement training as well. Figure 14.2 shows a sample preseason program for mixed-combination skiers for weeks 5 through 8.

Figure 14.2 Sample Preseason Program for Weeks 5 to 8

	Day 1	Day 2	Day 3	Day 4	Day 5	Day 6	Day 7
Functional-movement training (2-3 sets of 10-15 reps for stability; 2-3 sets of 15-25 sec. for mobility)	Dynamic-prep routine (p. 181), plus any mobility exercises from assessments in ch. 2	Dynamic-prep routine (p. 181), plus any stability and mobility exercises from tests for overhead-depth squat and single-leg squat (pp. 11 and 13)	Dynamic-prep routine (p. 181) plus any stability and mobility exercises from rotational-stability and lateral-lunge tests (pp. 15 and 16)	Dynamic-prep routine (p. 181), plus any stability and mobility exercises from tests for overhead-depth squat and single-leg squat (pp. 11 and 13)	Dynamic-prep routine (p. 181), plus any stability and mobility exercises from rotational-stability and lateral-lunge tests (pp. 15 and 16)	Day off or dynamic-prep routine (p. 181), plus 1 stability exercise and 1 mobility exercise from assessments in ch. 2	Day off
Cardio-respiratory training	Long workout in zone 1 (as directed in ch. 3)	Day off	Zone-2 workout (see p. 33 of ch. 3 for test and pp. 117-118 in ch. 8 for workout options)	Day off	Mix zones 1 and 2 in short or medium workout* (see p. 121 in ch. 8 for workout options)	Day off or short workout in zone 1*	Day off
Strength, power, and agility training (2 sets of 8-12 reps for strength exercises)	Day off	Workout C or D (p. 240), plus any exercises from assessments in ch. 3	Day off	Alternate workouts C and D (p. 240), plus any exercises from assessments in ch. 3	Day off	Day off or any exercises from assessments in ch. 3	Day off

*The duration of medium and short cardiorespiratory sessions should be determined in relation to that of your long workout for the week. In general, a medium workout is one-half to two-thirds the length of the long workout. A short workout is one-third to one-half the length of the long workout.

Weeks 9 to 12 (Peak)

Use weeks 9 through 12 of the preseason to finalize your preparation for the skiing season by adding anaerobic power (zone 3) and continuing to focus on functional movement and strength. As before, increase the time of at least one aerobic workout each week. Finally, focus on movements that mimic the range of joint movement and power needed for dynamic ski turns and terrain management. This program adds power and agility work. Figure 14.3 shows a sample preseason program for mixed-combination skiers during weeks 9 through 12.

Figure 14.3 Sample Preseason Program for Weeks 9 to 12

	Day 1	Day 2	Day 3	Day 4	Day 5	Day 6	Day 7
Functional-movement training (3 sets of 10-15 reps for stability; 3 sets of 15-30 sec. for mobility)	Dynamic-prep routine (p. 181), plus any mobility exercises from assessments in ch. 2	Dynamic-prep routine (p. 181), plus any mobility exercises from tests for overhead-depth squat and single-leg squat (pp. 11 and 13)	Dynamic-prep routine (p. 181), plus any stability and mobility exercises from rotational-stability and lateral-lunge tests (pp. 15 and 16)	Dynamic-prep routine (p. 181), plus any stability and mobility exercises from tests for overhead-depth squat and single-leg squat (pp. 11 and 13)	Dynamic-prep routine (p. 181), plus any stability and mobility exercises from rotational-stability and lateral-lunge tests (pp. 15 and 16)	Day off or dynamic-prep routine (p. 181), plus 1 stability exercise and 1 mobility exercise from assessments in ch. 2	Day off
Cardio-respiratory training	Long workout in zone 1 (as directed in ch. 3)	Day off	Zone-3 workout (see p. 33 in ch. 3 for test and pp. 118-120 in ch. 8 for workout options)	Day off	Mix of zones 1 and 2 in short or medium workout* (see p. 121 in ch. 8 for workout options)	Day off or short workout in zone 1*	Day off
Strength, power, and agility training (3-4 sets of 5-8 reps for strength exercises)	Day off	Workout E or F (p. 240), plus any exercises from assessments in ch. 3	Day off	Alternate workouts E and F (p. 240), plus any exercises from assessments in ch. 3	Day off	Day off or any exercises from assessments in ch. 3	Day off

*The duration of medium and short cardiorespiratory sessions should be determined in relation to that of your long workout for the week. In general, a medium workout is one-half to two-thirds the length of the long workout. A short workout is one-third to one-half the length of the long workout.

In-Season (16 Weeks)

During the season, the functional-movement, cardiorespiratory, strength, power, and agility training remain the same, reflecting the goal of maintenance. However, the training program for technique and tactics changes each month as you progress toward mastery. Figure 14.4 provides a sample weekly program for the in-season. See figures 14.5 on page 240 and 14.6 on page 242 for more details.

Weeks 1 to 4 (Foundation)

Use weeks 1 through 4 of the in-season to get back to skill basics and to build a strong foundation for movement and performance. At this time, perform the on-snow assessments from part I to pinpoint the areas that need the most work. During this month, focus on mastering and progressing through the technical milestones in order. For mixed-combination skiers, this means identifying and correcting faults in technique due to a previous lack of functional movement or fitness.

You can either maintain or reduce fitness training as you focus on balance and recovery. Skiing all day taxes your muscles, especially your quads, so keep them balanced by working the lesser-used muscles (in this case, the hamstrings) to maintain equal strength throughout the body and to avoid injury. Continue to focus on functional-movement training, which is the major limiting factor for many mixed-combination skiers.

Weeks 5 to 12 (Development)

Use weeks 5 through 12 of the in-season to retrain any imperfect techniques, adding tactical exploration and training to the mix. Racers should primarily use competitions as a training tool for improving technique and tactics under pressure. In other words, build on the previous performance while maintaining a training focus. Continue functional-movement and fitness training with the same focus on maintenance and recovery.

Weeks 12 to 16 (Peak)

Use weeks 12 through 16 of the in-season to maintain your progress in mastering technique while shifting the focus to tactics and racing (for those who are so inclined). This is a great time to try terrain and conditions that require new tactics. Expanding your tactical toolbox in unfamiliar scenarios builds awareness that improves your decision making. Again, continue functional-movement and fitness training with a focus on maintenance and recovery.

Postseason

During the off-season, maintain a base-fitness level that will allow you to start preseason training without missing a beat. Try other sports for a change of pace. Regardless of how you proceed with your fitness, include functional-movement training as often as possible to maintain levels of mobility and stability. Test every six to eight weeks to check your levels. If you notice any losses during assessment, add correctional exercises to your postseason routine. You can maintain cardiorespiratory fitness with aerobic (zone 1) training. If you feel burned out after the skiing season, reduce your time or distance. However, in order to prepare for preseason training, you must commit to doing cardio twice a week. Similarly you should commit to muscular-fitness training at least once a week. You can alternate strength routines A and B for maintenance during the off-season.

Figure 14.4 Sample Weekly In-Season Program

	Day 1	Day 2	Day 3	Day 4	Day 5	Day 6	Day 7
Functional-movement training (2 sets of 10-15 reps for stability; 2 sets of 15-30 sec. for mobility)	Dynamic-prep routine (p. 181), plus any mobility exercises from assessments in ch. 2	Dynamic-prep routine (p. 181), plus any mobility exercises from assessments in ch. 2	Dynamic-prep routine (p. 181), plus any mobility exercises from tests for overhead-depth squat and single-leg squat (pp. 11 and 13)	Dynamic-prep routine (p. 181), plus any stability and mobility exercises from rotational-stability and lateral-lunge tests (pp. 15 and 16)	Day off or dynamic-prep routine (p. 181), plus 1 stability exercise and 1 mobility exercise from assessments in ch. 2	Dynamic-prep routine (p. 181); This is an on-snow warm-up, not a functional-movement training session.	Dynamic-prep routine (p. 181); This is an on-snow warm-up, not a functional-movement training session.
Cardio-respiratory training	Day off	Long workout in zone 1 (as directed in ch. 3)	Day off	Day off or mix of zones 2 and 3 in short-to-medium workout in zone 1* (see p. 122 in ch.8 for workout options)	Day off or short-to-medium workout in zone 1*	Day off	Day off
Strength, power, and agility training (3-5 sets of 4-6 reps for strength)	Alternate workouts E and F (p.240), plus any exercises from assessments in ch.3	Day off	Alternate workouts E and F (p. 240), plus any exercises from assessments in ch.3	Day off	Day off or any exercises from assessments in ch. 3	Day off	Day off
TECHNIQUE AND TACTICS							
Weeks 1-4	Day off	Day off	Day off	Day off	Day off or skill-practice session C (p. 242)	Skill-practice session A (p. 242)	Skill-practice session B (p. 242)
Weeks 5-8	Day off	Day off	Day off	Day off	Day off or skill-practice session A or B (p. 242)	Skill-practice session C (p. 242)	Skill-practice session D (p. 242)
Weeks 9-12	Day off	Day off	Day off	Day off	Day off or skill-practice session A, B, or C (p. 242)	Skill-practice session D (p. 242)	Skill-practice session E (p. 242)
Weeks 13-16	Day off	Day off	Day off	Day off	Day off or skill-practice session A, B, C, or D (p.242)	Skill-practice session E (p. 242)	Design your own tactical exploration

*The duration of medium and short cardiorespiratory sessions should be determined in relation to that of your long workout for the week. In general, a medium workout is one-half to two-thirds the length of the long workout. A short workout is one-third to one-half the length of the long workout.

**If performing one workout for strength, power, and agility each week, do workout F (p. 240), plus any exercises for your scores from chapter 3.

Workouts for Mixed-Combination Skiers

Although the previous programs provide a general overview for your training, the following program outlines the actual instruction and exercises for your seasonal workouts. Simply locate the appropriate workouts in figures 14.5 and 14.6 in order to assemble your training plan for the day.

Functional-Movement Training

As previously mentioned in the outlines for seasonal programs, see pages 181 to 183 of chapter 10 for dynamic-prep routines. Add any correctional exercises as needed based on your functional-movement score from the assessment in chapter 2.

Cardiorespiratory Training

Train by using or tweaking the sample workouts and progression guidelines in chapter 8 (see pages 116-122).

Strength, Power, and Agility Training

See figure 14.5 to find the designated workout for strength, power, and agility training. Supplement these short, base workouts with specific correctional exercises identified through the screens in chapter 3. Workouts A and B are meant to be performed in the same week, resulting in a balanced, full-body training program specific to the strength needs of skiers. Workouts C and D introduce training for both power and agility. Workouts E and F provide additional power and agility work and complete the base program for strength, power, and agility.

See chapter 8 for descriptions and variations of the following exercises (exercises with variations are marked with an asterisk). Earlier in the season, you can start with the easier variation, but you should work to progress to the harder variation by the end of the season. Although distinct exercises exist for the different scores for the upper-body and core screens, the leg screens require the same solution exercises regardless of the score. In this case, the easier variation should be performed by those scoring a 1 and the harder variation should be performed once the score progresses to a 3.

Technique and Tactics

Start your on-snow sessions with a warm-up and one of the on-snow, dynamic-prep workouts (see pages 181 to 183 in chapter 10). Next, progress through your training session in three phases as outlined in chapter 10. Follow the guidelines and programs for mixed-combination skiers. Regardless of your type, ingraining proper movements while working on functional movement and fitness is a powerful combination for improvement.

Active-Free Ski

Take approximately 30 to 40 minutes to check out the conditions of the day and to tap into your energy and your ability to react and produce the movements you desire. Become aware of sliding sensations and your focus cues. Waking up your neuromuscular system with skiing sensations is a key component to active-free ski. Before each session, focus on building essential movements.

Figure 14.6 provides the key cues for each workout for mixed-combination skiers. Two cue options are provided for each workout, progressing from basic to advanced. Depending on your level, you may opt to focus on one or the other, or even to focus on the first cue for the first half of your active-free skiing session and the second cue for the second half.

Figure 14.5 Training Workouts for Strength, Power, and Agility

	Workout A	Workout B	Workout C	Workout D	Workout E	Workout F
Upper-body strength	Pick 2: • Chest press, p. 126, or bench press with dumbbells, p. 125* • Horizontal row, p. 127, or kneeling single-arm row, p. 126*	Pick 2: • Push-up, p. 124,* or push-up on stability ball, p. 124* • Horizontal row, p. 127, or kneeling single-arm row, p. 126*	Pick 2: • Chest press, p. 126, or bench press with dumbbells, p. 125* • Horizontal row, p. 127, or kneeling single-arm row, p. 126,* or supine row with feet elevated, p. 125*	Pick 2: • Push-up, p. 126,* or push-up on stability ball, p. 124* • Horizontal row, p. 127, kneeling single-arm row, p. 126,* or supine row with feet elevated, p. 125*	Pick 1: • Chest press, p. 126, or bench press with dumbbells, p. 125*	Pick 1: • Horizontal row, p. 127, kneeling single-arm row, p. 126,* or supine row with feet elevated, p. 125*
Core strength	Pick 2: • Sit-ups, p. 130* or medicine-ball toss with sit-ups, p. 128* • Supine leg-up, p. 129*	Pick 2: • Sit-up, p. 130,* or medicine-ball side toss, p. 128 • Supine leg-up, p. 129*	Pick 2: • Sit-up, p. 130,* or medicine-ball toss with sit-ups, p. 128* • Supine leg-up, p. 129,* or hanging-leg hip raise, p. 129	Pick 2: • Sit-up, p. 130,* or medicine-ball side toss, p. 128 • Supine leg-up, p. 129,* or hanging-leg hip raise, p. 129	Pick 1: • Medicine-ball toss with sit-ups, p. 128,* or medicine-ball side toss, p. 128 (alternate each week)	Pick 1: • Supine leg-up, p. 129,* or hanging-leg hip raise, p. 129
Lower-body strength	• Split squat, p. 131* • Bridge on stability ball, p. 132*	• Romanian deadlift, p. 132* • Lateral lunge, p. 131*	• Split squat, p. 131* • Bridge on stability ball, p. 132*	• Romanian deadlift, p. 132* • Lateral lunge, p. 131*	• Split squat, p. 131*	• Romanian deadlift, p. 132*
Power**	--	--	--	• Tuck jump, p. 134, for 2-3 sets of 4-8 jumps* • Lateral hurdle jump, p. 134, for 2-3 sets of 5-10 jumps on each foot*	• Lateral box blast, p. 133, for 2-3 sets of 4-10 jumps on each foot* • Reactive step-up, p. 133, for 2-3 sets of 4-10 jumps on each foot*	• Tuck jump, p. 134, for 2-3 sets of 6-10 jumps* • Lateral hurdle jump, p. 134, for 2-3 sets of 10-15 jumps on each foot*

> continued

	Workout A	Workout B	Workout C	Workout D	Workout E	Workout F
Agility			• In-in-out-out agility ladder, p. 135) 2-4 times through a 30 ft. (9 m) ladder • Jumping rope (slalom, p. 136); follow progression guidelines in ch. 8.	--	• Agility ladder (Ickey shuffle, p. 136, and crossover zigzag, p. 136), 2-4 times each through a 30 ft. ladder	• Agility ladder (in-in-out-out, p. 135) 2-4 times through a 30 ft. (9 m) ladder • Jumping rope (slalom, p. 136); follow progression guidelines in ch. 8.

**The ranges of sets and reps given for the power exercises allow for progression during the preseason and a subsequent reduction in volume during the in-season. Do the lower amount of total jumps at the start of the preseason and progress throughout the 12 weeks, first by increasing the reps (staying at two sets), and then moving to three sets with fewer reps. Taper down to the lower end of the range during the in-season.

Active Training (Technique)

Figure 14.6 provides five skill workouts (A through E) for use in your practice sessions that progress from easy to difficult. The easier workouts emphasize basic skiing essentials and the workouts that are more difficult focus on skill sequences that combine these components. Workouts A and B address the starting points for the milestones of neutral stance, the engaged stance, and leg turning. Workout C acts as a bridge between essentials and the sequential movements needed to complete dynamic drills and turns, with an emphasis on parallel and carved turns. Workouts D and E help refine the movements necessary to complete the skills package, again emphasizing parallel and carved turns. The mixed combination skier will benefit from a wide spectrum of exercises that address the skill gaps identified earlier. These exercises can be taken from the parallel and carved turn sections or may even draw from the stance and leg turning sections. As the profile indicates a pattern of faults, a solution will be apparent that may be very diverse.

Figure 14.6 assigns a practice time to each session that is recommended for ingraining technique and working toward mastery. Obviously, the amount of time you practice depends on your personal schedule or situation. To determine how much time to spend on each drill, simply divide the total time of each session by the number of recommended drills. For example, four drills over 40 minutes translates to 10 minutes of work on each drill. If you need more practice on a particular drill, you can add more time to the overall workout or decrease the time you spend on one drill in order to add time to another.

Finally, be advised that these practice sessions are based on an average progression. It is up to you to monitor your progress and to work in a session until you are ready to move on. The results from your assessment in part I should be the driving force in terms of the drills you perform. Don't blindly follow the drills listed in the table. These routines are a progression of base workouts for mixed combination skiers that can be personalized by substituting and supplementing drills according to your test results in chapter 4.

Exploring Terrain and Conditions (Tactics)

Figure 14.6 also identifies the tactical concepts you should practice in a specific progression for each terrain. The terrain and conditions themselves are listed in order from most common to most challenging. Each skier brings a slightly different frame of reference to the practice session, so look carefully at the prescribed drills and concepts and begin with the practice that best fits your starting point. For example, some mixed skiers with overpowered tendencies attempt tighter situations or the back bowls before they have the skills to get there. Mixed skiers with underpowered tendencies hang back and underestimate their ability to ski tough terrain. Following the set progression gives mixed skiers the chance to progress at their own rate. Remember to assess, drill, practice, explore, and then assess again.

Carve out at least one hour, preferably two, for practicing terrain exploration. It takes some time to find the terrain listed in the practice session in addition to the practice time. By the time you ride the lift, find terrain, practice the drill, and return to the lift, you might lose 20 to 30 minutes for a single drill or run. Therefore, you will not be able to practice every terrain in each practice session. However, if you progress quickly, you can follow the suggested drills for the next terrain listed. Realistically, you will only get through two or three types of terrain in one session. Pick your terrains and spend several runs practicing the recommended tactics.

Regardless of the terrain where you are working, the listed drills progress you through the tactical milestones outlined in chapter 9. Practices A, B, and C emphasize basic tactics, such as making terrain transitions, reading terrain, and applying turn shape, which are necessary for the advanced tactics of speed and line management that appear in practices D and E. Again, remember that the sample seasonal programs from earlier in the chapter represent the average time for mastering these concepts. Individualize your program and move at the pace that is best for you, retesting every four weeks.

Figure 14.6 Sample Technical and Tactical Practice Sessions

ACTIVE-FREE SKI (30-40 MIN.)					
	Practice A	**Practice B**	**Practice C**	**Practice D**	**Practice E**
Focus cues	Establishing a centered position over skis or a centered stance balanced on one ski	Developing edge awareness and leg turning or edge engagement and release	Focusing on precise, active foot and leg turning or on quick, ballistic leg turning	Ingraining parallel turns and applying edge and pivot or making parallel turns with emphasis on a pole plant	Experiencing dynamic carved turns with increased speed and long radius or high-speed carving for short-radius turns

ACTIVE TRAINING (40-90 MIN.)

Practice each drill for at least 2 runs. Take time to practice quality movements 20 to 30 times, or for a total of 1,200 vertical feet (365 m) each run. The total vertical feet skied may vary, depending on your resort, the drill, and conditions, but 2,400 to 6,000 total vertical feet (731-1829 m) is a good target. If you do more than 6000 vertical feet, focus on quality execution of movements.

Technique	Practice				
	Practice A (40-60 min.)	**Practice B** (40-60 min.)	**Practice C** (40-60 min.)	**Practice D** (60-90 min.)	**Practice E** (60-90 min.)
Neutral stance	Pick 1: • Marching drill, p. 142 • High-low drill, p. 142 • Hop drill, p. 141	Pick 1: • Pole-spin drill, p. 143 • Shuffle drill, p. 141 • Lateral-step drill, p. 140	Pick 2: • Shuffle drill, p. 141, or high-low drill, p. 142 • Lateral-step drill, p. 140, or hop drill, p. 141	--	--
Engaged stance	Pick 1: • Engaged stance with low-edge angle, p. 146, or engaged stance on one ski, p. 146	Pick 1: • Engaged stance with low-edge angle, p. 146, or engaged stance on one ski, p. 146	Pick 1: • Engaged stance on one ski, p. 146, or traverse and reverse traverse drill, p. 145	Pick 1: • Traverse and reverse traverse drill, p. 145, or traverse drill on steeper terrain, p. 144	Pick 1 or 2: • Traverse drill on steeper terrain, p. 144, or engaged stance at higher speeds, p. 144
Leg turn	Pick 1: • Leg turn with feet on bindings, p. 148 • Hands-on-hips drill, p. 149	Pick 1: • Wedge leg turn, p. 149 • Leg turn with feet on bindings, p. 148	Pick 1: • Cross-hill leg turn, p. 150 • Hands-on-hips drill, p. 149	Pick 1: • Leg turn with feet on bindings, p. 148 • Leg turn on one ski, p. 147	Pick 1: • Hands-on-hips drill, p. 149 • Clock-face drill, p. 148
Parallel turn	--	--	Pick 1 or 2: • Simultaneous edge change, p. 154 • Parallel-turn garland, p. 155	Pick 1 or 2: • Hand on hip and hand in the air, p. 156 • Two skis to one ski, p. 153	Pick 1 or 2: • One-leg pivot, p. 152 • Stepping through the turn, p. 151 • Pole plant and release, p. 152
Carved turn	--	—	Pick 1 or 2: • Traverse edge change, p. 160 • Outside pole drag, p. 161	Pick 1 or 2: • Tuck turn, p. 162 • Advanced railroad track, p. 159	Pick 1 or 2: • Long leg, short leg, p. 158 • Short-turn pole touch, p. 157

> continued

> continued

EXPLORING TERRAIN AND CONDITIONS (60-120 MIN.)

Practice each drill for at least 2 runs. Take time to practice quality movements. The total vertical feet skied may vary, depending on your resort, the drill, and conditions, but 3,000 to 6,000 total vertical feet (914-1829 m) is a good target. If you do more than 6,000 vertical feet, focus on quality execution of movements.

Terrain	Practice				
	Practice A (60-90 min.)	Practice B (60-120 min.)	Practice C (60-120 min.)	Practice D (90-120 min.)	Practice E (90-120 min.)
Steeps	• Basic terrain transitions (Gentle to steep slopes, p. 163, or firm to soft snow, p. 163) • Reading complex terrain (Having a plan B, p. 165)	• Basic terrain transitions (Groomed to ungroomed snow, p. 163, or gentle to steep slopes, p. 163) • Reading complex terrain (Having a plan B, p. 165 or anticipating terrain changes, p. 164)	• Basic terrain transitions (Firm to soft snow, p. 163, or groomed to ungroomed snow, p. 163) • Reading complex terrain (Having a plan B, p. 165, or unlocking freeze frame, p. 164) • Turn management (Maintaining a strong finishing turn, p. 166, or regulating pressure and edge on turns, p. 166)	• Turn management (Ingraining the C-curve, p. 167) • Speed management (Getting into gear, p. 171, or maintaining three points of contact, p. 171)	• Speed management (Checking your speed, p. 171, or maintaining three points of contact, p. 171) • Line management (Using pole plants to maintain your line, p. 173)
Bumps	• Basic terrain transitions (Gentle to steep slopes, p. 163, or wet to dry snow, p. 163) • Reading complex terrain (Anticipating terrain changes, p. 164, or having a plan B, p. 165)	• Basic terrain transitions (Groomed to ungroomed snow, p. 163 or wet to dry snow, p. 163) • Reading complex terrain (Anticipating terrain changes, p. 164)	• Basic terrain transitions (Wet to dry snow, p. 163) • Reading complex terrain (Unlocking freeze frame, p. 164, or redirecting focus, p. 164) • Turn management (Establishing turn shape with ski placement, p. 166, or matching turn shape with conditions, p. 165)	• Turn management (Fishhook ending in a J-shape, p. 165, or establishing turn shape with ski placement, p. 166) • Speed management (Maintaining three points of contact, p. 171)	• Speed management (Choosing the correct tempo, p. 171) • Line management (Using Pole plants to maintain your line, p. 173)

Terrain	Practice				
	Practice A (60-90 min.)	Practice B (60-120 min.)	Practice C (60-120 min.)	Practice D (90-120 min.)	Practice E (90-120 min.)
Chutes and gullies	• Basic terrain transitions (Gentle to steep slopes, p. 163 • Reading complex terrain (Having a plan B, p. 165, or redirecting focus, p. 164)	• Reading complex terrain (Anticipating terrain changes, p. 164, or having a plan B, p. 165) • Turn management (Skidding, p. 169, or creating symmetrical patterns in turns, p. 165)	• Reading complex terrain (Redirecting focus, p. 164) • Turn management (Unlocking freeze frame, p. 164, or redirecting focus, p. 164) • Turn management (Buttering, p. 169) • Line management (Using pole plants to maintain your line, p. 173)	• Speed management (Choosing the correct tempo, p. 171, or pushing the envelope of speed and tempo, p. 171) • Line management (Avoiding gridlock, p. 173)	• Speed management (Pushing the envelope of speed and tempo, p. 171, or checking your speed, p. 171) • Line management (Facing the line, p. 173)
Trees	• Basic terrain transitions (Gentle to steep slopes, p. 163) • Reading complex terrain (Having a plan B, p. 165, or anticipating terrain changes, p. 164)	• Reading complex terrain (Redirecting focus, p. 164) • Turn management (Skidding, p. 169, or creating symmetrical patterns in turns, p. 165)	• Reading complex terrain (Having a plan B, p. 165) • Turn management (Carving, p. 169, or creating symmetrical patterns in turns, p. 165)	• Speed management (Choosing the correct tempo, p. 171, or pushing the envelope of speed and tempo, p. 171) • Line management (Avoiding gridlock, p. 173, or facing the line, p. 173)	• Speed management (Choosing the correct tempo, p. 171, or pushing the envelope of speed and tempo, p. 171) • Line management (Facing the line, p. 173)
Back bowls	• Basic terrain transitions (Groomed to ungroomed snow, p. 163) • Reading complex terrain (Anticipating terrain changes, p. 164, or redirecting focus, p. 164)	• Reading complex terrain (Anticipating terrain changes, p. 164, or redirecting focus, p. 164) • Line management (Facing the line, p. 173) • Turn management (Skidding, p. 169, or slashing, p. 168) • Speed management (Getting into gear, p. 171)	• Turn management (Carving, p. 169, or getting the right amount of edge angle, p. 166) • Speed management (Getting into gear, p. 171, or checking your speed, p. 171) • Line management (Facing the line, p. 173)	• Turn management (Buttering, p. 169, or slashing, p. 168) • Speed management (Getting into gear, p. 171, or pushing the envelope of speed and tempo, p. 171) • Line management (Scrubbing, p. 168)	• Speed management (Pushing the envelope of speed and tempo, p. 171, or checking your speed, p. 171) • Line management (Slashing, p. 168)

Bibliography

Skiing Tactics, Technique, and Training

Canadian Ski Instructors Alliance (CSIA). 2000. *Skiing and teaching methods.* Quebec: Canadian Ski Instructors Alliance.

———. 2006. *Skiing and teaching methods.* Quebec: Canadian Ski Instructors Alliance.

Chappaz, Gilles. 2004. *Les pulls rouges [The Red Sweater].* Grenoble, France: Editions Glenat.

DesLauriers, E., and R. DesLauriers. 2002. *Ski the whole mountain.* Boulder, CO: Mountain Sports Press.

Elling, R. M. 1998. *The all-mountain skier.* Camden, MI: Ragged Mountain Press.

Evrard, D., and W. Witherell. 1993. *The athletic skier.* Boulder, CO: Johnson Books.

Fellows, Chris. 2006. *Tactics for all-mountain skiing.* Lakewood, CO: The American Snowsports Education Foundation.

FISI. 1991. *Sci Italiano [Ski Italiano].* Milan, Italy: Federazione Italiana Sport Invernali.

Fry, John. 2006. *The story of modern skiing.* Lebanon, NH: University Press of New England.

Harb, H. 2001. *Anyone can be an expert skier 2.* Long Island City, NY: Hatherleigh Press.

———. 2006. *Harald Harb's essentials of skiing.* Long Island City, NY: Hatherleigh Press.

Hoppichler, F. 1983. *Schwingen : die osterreichische Schischule.* [*Schwingen, the official Austrian ski method.*] Laporte, CO: Poudre Press.

———. 1989. *Ski with us: The teaching method of the Austrian ski school.* London: Pelham Books.

———. 1990. *Die Osterreichische Skischule [The Austrian Ski School].* Austria: HERANT-Verlag Sportmagazin.

Jonas, B., and S. Masia. 1987. *Ski Magazine's Total skiing.* New York: Putnam.

Joubert, G. 1978. *Skiing: An art, a technique.* Laporte, CO: Poudre Publishing.

Joubert, G., and J. Vuarnet. 1967. *How to ski the French way.* New York: The Dial Press.

Larson, O., and J. Major. 1979. *World Cup ski technique: Learn and improve.* Laporte, CO: Poudre Publishing.

LeMaster, R. 1999. *The skier's edge.* Champaign, IL: Human Kinetics.

———. 2010. *Ultimate skiing.* Champaign, IL: Human Kinetics.

Lund, M., B. Gillen, and M. Bartlett. 1982. *The ski book.* New York: Arbor House.

Mahre, P., and S. Mahre (with J. Fry). 1985. *No hill too fast.* New York: Simon and Schuster.

Masia, S. 1992. *Terrain skiing.* New York: Simon and Schuster.

Owen, N. May 28, 2009. The science of sedentary behavior: Too much sitting and too little exercise. Lecture at the 56th Annual Meeting of the American College of Sports Medicine, Seattle, WA. Featuring studies by Genevieve Healy and David Dunstan, with Australia's Baker IDI Heart and Diabetes Institute. www.acsm.org/AM/Template.cfm?Section=Home_Page&TEMPLATE=/CM/ContentDisplay.cfm&CONTENTID=12889.

Peterson, Carl. 2004. *Fit to ski.* Vancouver, BC: Fit to Play.

Petrovic, K., I. Belehar, and R. Petrovic. 1987. *New developments of ski techniques and methodology*. Switzerland.

Post Foster, E. 1994. *Race skills for Alpine skiing*. South Hero, VT: Turning Point Ski Foundation.

———. 1995. *Conditioning skills*. South Hero, VT: Turning Point Ski Foundation.

———. 1995. *Technical skills for Alpine skiing*. South Hero, VT: Turning Point Ski Foundation.

———. 1996. *Skiing and the art of carving*. South Hero, VT: Turning Point Ski Foundation.

Professional Ski Instructors of America (PSIA). 1969. *The official American ski technique*. Salt Lake City: PSIA.

———. 2001. *Core concepts*. Lakewood, CO: PSIA Education Foundation.

———. 2002. *Alpine technical manual*. Lakewood, CO: PSIA Education Foundation.

Schaller, L. 1984. *Skiing techniques and training*. Innsbruck, Austria: Steiger Verlags Gessellschaft mbH.

Scharff, R. 1974. *Ski Magazine's encyclopedia of skiing*. New York: Harper and Row.

Tejada-Flores, R. 2001. *Breakthrough on the new skis*. Boulder, CO: Mountain Sports Press.

Twardokens, G. 1992. *Universal ski techniques, principles, and practices*. Reno, NV: University of Nevada.

Wallner, H. 2002. *Carven skilauf perfekt* [*Ski Perfect*]. Vienna, Austria: BAFL.

Witherell, W. 1972. *How the racers ski*. New York: Norton and Company.

Sports Performance Books

Chu, Donald. 1998. *Jumping into plyometrics*. Champaign, IL: Human Kinetics.

Cook, Gray. 2003. *Athletic body in balance*. Champaign, IL: Human Kinetics.

Dinubile, Nicholas. *Frame work*. New York: Rodale.

Farentinos, Robert, and James Radcliffe. 1999. *High powered plyometrics*. Champaign, IL: Human Kinetics.

Gladwell, Malcolm. 2008. *Outliers: The story of success*. New York: Little and Brown.

Hooge, Andrew. 2003. *Fitskiing*. Crested Butte, CO: Active Media.

Lopes, Brian, and Lee McCormack. 2005. *Mastering mountain bike skills*. Champaign, IL: Human Kinetics.

Roberts, Katherine. 2009. *Swing flaws and fitness fixes*. New York: Penguin.

Schurman, Courteny, and Doug Schurman. 2009. *The outdoor athlete*. Champaign, IL: Human Kinetics.

Sokolove, Michael. 2008. *Warrior girls*. New York: Simon and Schuster.

U.S. Ski Team. 1977. *Alpine training manual*. Park City, UT: U.S. Ski Team.

Verstegen, Mark. 2004. *Core performance*. New York: Rodale.

———. 2004. *Core performance endurance*. New York: Rodale.

Index